CAMBRIDGE STUDIES
IN
MEDIEVAL LIFE AND THOUGHT

Edited by G. G. COULTON, Litt.D., Hon. D.Litt., F.B.A.

*Fellow of St John's College, Cambridge, Honorary Fellow of
St Catharine's College, University Lecturer in English*

THE EARLY DOMINICANS

LONDON
Cambridge University Press
FETTER LANE

NEW YORK · TORONTO
BOMBAY · CALCUTTA · MADRAS
Macmillan

TOKYO
Maruzen Company Ltd

THE EARLY DOMINICANS

STUDIES
IN THIRTEENTH-CENTURY
DOMINICAN HISTORY

BY

R. F. BENNETT, M.A.

Hulsean Prizeman, 1934
late Donaldson Bye-Fellow, Magdalene College
Cambridge

CAMBRIDGE
AT THE UNIVERSITY PRESS
1937

PRINTED IN GREAT BRITAIN

To

MY MOTHER

GENERAL PREFACE

THERE is only too much truth in the frequent complaint that history, as compared with the physical sciences, is neglected by the modern public. But historians have the remedy in their own hands; choosing problems of equal importance to those of the scientist, and treating them with equal accuracy, they will command equal attention. Those who insist that the proportion of accurately ascertainable facts is smaller in history, and therefore the room for speculation wider, do not thereby establish any essential distinction between truth-seeking in history and truth-seeking in chemistry. The historian, whatever be his subject, is as definitely bound as the chemist "to proclaim certainties as certain, falsehoods as false, and uncertainties as dubious". Those are the words, not of a modern scientist, but of the seventeenth-century monk, Jean Mabillon; they sum up his literary profession of faith. Men will follow us in history as implicitly as they follow the chemist, if only we will form the chemist's habit of marking clearly where our facts end and our inferences begin. Then the public, so far from discouraging our speculations, will most heartily encourage them; for the most positive man of science is always grateful to anyone who, by putting forward a working theory, stimulates further discussion.

The present series, therefore, appeals directly to that craving for clearer facts which has been bred in these times of storm and stress. No care can save us altogether from error; but, for our own sake and the public's, we have elected to adopt a safeguard dictated by ordinary business commonsense. Whatever errors of fact are pointed out by reviewers or correspondents shall be publicly corrected with the least possible delay. After a year of publication, all copies shall be provided with such an erratum-slip without waiting for the chance of a second edition; and each fresh volume in this series shall contain a full list of the errata noted in its immediate predecessor. After the lapse of a year from the first publication of any volume, and at any time during the ensuing twelve months, any possessor of that volume who will send a stamped and addressed envelope to the Cambridge University Press, Fetter Lane, Fleet Street, London, E.C. 4, shall receive, in due course, a free copy of the *errata* in that volume. Thus, with the help of our critics, we may reasonably hope to put forward these monographs as roughly representing the most accurate information obtainable under present conditions. Our facts being thus secured, the reader will judge our inferences on their own merits; and something will have been done to dissipate that cloud of suspicion which hangs over too many important chapters in the social and religious history of the Middle Ages.

G. G. C.

July 1930

AUTHOR'S PREFACE

THE present work owes its origin to an essay with which I was successful in winning the Hulsean Prize for 1934. The subject set for that competition was "The Early Dominicans and their Times", and I have used a shortened form of this title for purposes of publication. In this connexion, however, I should like to draw attention to the word "Studies" in the sub-heading: the following pages make no wider claims than are here suggested, and have no pretension to be a complete history of the Order of Preachers in the thirteenth century. My object throughout has been simply to investigate certain important aspects of the Order's history at the time, and to present my results side by side under various headings—indicated by the chapter-titles—without attempting to combine all together into a full narrative, or to work out a final judgment.

The expansion and partial re-writing of the original essay was largely done during the past academic year in Munich, where I was given a much-appreciated opportunity of study through the generosity of the Master and Fellows of Magdalene College in electing me to the Donaldson Bye-Fellowship for 1935–6. I should like to express here my deep sense of indebtedness to the College for their kindness. The additions and alterations have been made at the suggestion and under the general direc-tion of Dr Coulton, to whom I also owe a very great debt of gratitude for help and advice during the past five years. I do not wish, however, to imply that either Dr Coulton or any other here mentioned is in any way responsible for errors and inaccuracies of which I may have been guilty.

I can scarcely hope that I have altogether avoided leaving traces of the two stages in which the work has been written, but must content myself with hoping that they are not too obvious and that repetitions are not too frequent. A word may be added in defence of my method of citing the *Acta Capitulorum Gene-ralium* by dates rather than by page-references. Dr Berthold Altaner has already complained (*Theologische Revue*, 1927, p. 382) that the latter method, which is customary, leaves much to be desired in that it obscures development by omitting chronological information, and suggests using both date *and* page. I have rejected this on account of its cumbrousness, which would lead to an unnecessary enlargement of the footnotes, and have decided to use dates alone because so much often depends upon them in the establishing of an argument. Since it is only at the end of the thirteenth century that the *Acta*, in Reichert's edition, occupy more than three or four pages each year, no great difficulty should be experienced by anyone who may wish to check my references.

In conclusion, it is my pleasant duty to thank the following, in addition to those already mentioned: the Electors to the Hulsean Prize, for permission to publish my work in an altered form; Professor Paul Lehmann and Professor Rudolf von Heckel, of the University of Munich, for their assistance and kindness in many ways during my stay in Germany; Herr J. Gabler, also of Munich, who put his wide knowledge of Dominican sources at my disposal; the Prior and Brothers of St Dominic's Priory, N.W. 5, for allowing me to use their library on many occasions, and for their kind hospitality; Mr Geoffrey Barraclough, of St John's College, for letters of introduction in Germany and for invaluable help with the proof-reading; and finally my parents, Mr F. R. Salter of Magdalene College, and others in Cambridge and elsewhere, for the constant encouragement they have given me.

R. F. BENNETT

MAGDALENE COLLEGE
CAMBRIDGE

April 1937

CONTENTS

CHAPTER I

INTRODUCTORY—EUROPE IN 1200

THE early Christian belief in the imminence of the Second Coming, a belief which profoundly influenced the medieval Church, is no isolated phenomenon, but merely the most widely-held of many similar prophetic ideas which have arisen at various periods. In an earlier age the Jews already had their Messianic teaching, and Zephaniah had foretold the Day of Doom in language that was later to inspire Thomas of Celano to that most impressive of religious poems, the Dies Irae. Even to-day, the idea is not dead; within the present century, the end of the world has been more than once confidently expected, and if we are to believe certain interpretations of the "Message of the Great Pyramid", our present economic and political difficulties are but signs of the coming of Armageddon and the catastrophic events which shall usher in the reign of peace. In the centuries with which we shall here be concerned, prophecies of an Apocalyptic or similar nature were common. The year A.D. 1000 was awaited with terror and foreboding by a great part of the population of Western Europe, and signs were easily found which seemed to indicate that the wrath of Heaven was about to overwhelm the world. Less dreadful in its implications was Merlin's supposed prediction of the fate of the devil-descended House of Anjou ("Lynx penetrans omnia exitio propriae gentis imminebit"), for which a fulfilment was even found in the rebellions of his sons against Henry II. The same idea is present in the German legend of the sleeping Barbarossa, who should some day awake and free the land from the tyranny of Rome. More influential than any of these, because more widely believed, were the prophecies of Joachim of Fiore, the twelfth-century Calabrian mystic. He preached the Eternal Gospel,[1] whose reign should commence in or about A.D. 1260; and, though he himself died in 1202, his doctrines convulsed

---

[1] Not a book, but a new and more spiritual interpretation of the existing Scriptures. The date 1260 is derived from Revelation xi. 3.

the Franciscan Order and the University of Paris before Frederick II unkindly upset the chronology and cast doubt upon the whole thing by dying ten years too early.

But there seems to have been no particular feeling connected with the approach of the year 1200; perhaps fortunately, or it would long ago have been seized on to mark an "epoch" with as disastrous results as that of the capture of Constantinople by the Turks in 1453—still to be found in many of our school text-books as "the beginning of the Renaissance". Yet 1200 has as good claims as any other year to be placed upon the select list of critical dates. In almost every sphere of life there was, as we can see now, a sense of the near approach of a climax at about this time. In politics, though the medieval theory of limitation and of the Divine Law is in its full glory—indeed Magna Carta is still to come and so are the early Parliaments, except in Spain—yet 1200 marks the middle of the reign of Philip Augustus and the first taste of what was long afterwards to be called royal absolutism. No theory of sovereignty had as yet been put forward, and was not to be for more than three centuries, so that half the force of *Quod principi placuit* was lost, despite its frequent quotation by the new school of lawyers which had been in existence at Bologna for fifty years; yet Henry VI, who probably came nearer in thought to complete triumph over his hereditary enemy at St Peter's than any Emperor before him, had just had his grandiose but practicable schemes cut short by death, and Frederick II, "the first of modern monarchs", was shortly to begin his tempestuous career.

At Rome Innocent III had been Pope for two years. In him the Hildebrandine Papacy reaches its highest point. John's surrender of his kingdom to Pandulf is an event of some importance in English history; to Innocent it was but an example of the position of feudal supremacy which he had managed to secure over almost the whole of Europe by the time of the Fourth Lateran Council (1215). Gregory IX, Innocent IV and Boniface VIII could only add unwise emphasis to his claims and attempt to translate a possible feudal control into an impossible absolute domination. Furthermore, as will appear in more detail later, Innocent III's tenure of the Papacy marks the real beginning of a new attempt on the part of the Roman Church to carry out the mission it had received from Constantine. Hitherto it had perhaps been more Roman than Catholic: the political results of Canossa are a more striking memorial to Hildebrand than the religious results of his enforcement of the Cluniac reform. The Lateran Council and the beginnings of the two orders of friars are indications of a concern with doctrine rather than domination which, more than hitherto, is to be the business of the Papacy until the age of Loyola and the Council of Trent.

In economics the position is similar. Medieval society was mainly agricultural until the twelfth century; the manor was generally the unit of life, and, partly in consequence, a purely static conception of society held sway. This had not really begun to give place to newer ideas in 1200, but the growth of the communes of Northern France and of Italy was already pointing to new developments. Twenty-four years earlier the Italian cities had shown their strength by defeating the Emperor at Legnano, and throughout the thirteenth century the Lombard League is a diplomatic factor of the first importance.

The development of commerce and the replacement in certain districts of a purely agricultural economy by a town economy brought into being a new class, till now unknown within the narrow limits of medieval life. The interests of their trades caused the members of this class to indulge in travel to a much greater extent than had been customary in earlier times, and the town populations were in consequence gradually becoming emancipated from an entirely parochial outlook. A cosmopolitan civilisation of the modern type had been unknown since the fall of Rome; the first signs of its return are visible towards the end of the twelfth century in Lombardy and Southern France. The holding of the Councils of 1245 and 1274 at Lyons may perhaps be construed as a recognition that the importance of this latter district was now rivalling that of Rome itself; the results upon the life of St Francis of Pietro Bernadone's periodical visits to the same town are well known; while finally it was Peter Waldo, a merchant of Lyons, who was the founder of a heresy second only to Catharism in magnitude.

Here we meet a third way in which the world of 1200 was, as

it were, expectant of something new. The previous century had seen the return of learning to Western Europe. Not that the Dark Ages were as unrelieved in their darkness as has been supposed; but the scholarship of those times had been far more restricted in its contacts with general life. The influence of the Irish emigrants had died even in the monasteries they founded; St Gall had continued their tradition, but was unable to perpetuate it beyond its own brief period of greatness in the tenth century; solitary figures like Fulbert of Chartres or Gerbert of Aurillac preserved what they received without diffusing it among great numbers of the succeeding generations. But the age of Abelard and Accursius had succeeded in re-discovering something of the past and in inducing contemporaries to follow them into new speculations and new tracts of knowledge. Yet in 1200 the problem set by the appearance of the new learning was unresolved; schools of Roman law had been set up, scholastic philosophy was started on its long career, but the outer world had not yet shown what its reaction was to be to the shock it had received.

It is in the communes, where these diverse elements are seen working together, that results now begin to follow. Politically the towns always tended to be turbulent; they fitted in very ill with feudalism, whether of Church or State. Frederick Barbarossa's difficulties in Lombardy can be paralleled many times over by conflicts between bishops and their cathedral towns. The commune of Laon, which sacked its bishop's palace, dragged him out of an empty wine-cask in which he had attempted to hide and murdered him in the open street (1112),[1] is by no means alone in its infamy. But the rise of a more educated and more educable race of citizens, with a wide range of interests, together with the new learning which appeared at the same time, intensified the problem. Not only did the citizens rebel against their lord, temporal or spiritual, in order to gain political independence, but they took it upon themselves to quarrel with the accepted doctrines of the Church.[2] Once Waldo had been

[1] H. W. C. Davis, *Medieval Europe*, p. 231.
[2] Balme and Lelaidier (*Cart.* i. 106) state that few peasants were found among the Albigenses, but without quoting their authority. More recently Grundmann (*Relig. Bewegungen*, pp. 29 sq., 157 sq.) has attacked the thesis of Zanoni (*Gli Umiliati*...Milan, 1911) that the heretics were drawn mainly

led to an interest in more than the externals of religion by
hearing a *jongleur* reciting the life of St Alexis, and had followed
this up by getting portions of the Bible translated into the
vernacular, a vital blow had been struck at the existing domination of Christendom by the hierarchy. For Waldo found, as
Luther was to find later, that the Church said many things for
which she had no Scriptural warrant. Consequently he attempted to foster the study of the Bible by preaching—both
things forbidden him as a layman—and it was quite hopeless for
the Church to attempt to keep him within the bounds of orthodoxy by a qualified approval of his work, because he had attacked
the Church in the same way that the Reformers of three centuries later did. To open the Bible, till now forbidden them
except in so far as they heard certain selected passages read in a
strange tongue by the priest, could only lead, in men acquainted
with the elements of reasoning, to the setting up of their private
judgment against the authority of the Church; which is *ipso
facto* heresy, apart from any particular incorrect doctrines they
may have developed. It is this fact which makes the Waldensians in a sense more interesting than the Cathari, in spite of
their lesser success, because in their origins they had no false
doctrine whatever. This, too, would give some colour of reason
to Danzas' otherwise ludicrous attempt[1] to prove a connexion
between thirteenth-century heresy and Protestantism; but un-
wisely he takes the Cathari as Luther's spiritual ancestors, and
rather naturally makes out but a poor case.

Heresy proper—at this time almost entirely restricted to
dualistic beliefs[2]—flourished under the same conditions, and

from the lowest classes, and produces a great deal of evidence in support of
his arguments. As he pertinently remarks (p. 168), "Das Bekenntnis zur
freiwilligen Armut wäre verlogen gewesen, wenn die Armut aus Not ihm
vorangegangen wäre; das Bekenntnis zur *humilitas* wäre eine leere Geste
gewesen im Munde derer, die sich nicht tiefer erniedrigen konnten, als die
Not sie gestellt hatte." For an excellent account of heresy, see Kirsch-
Hergenröther, *Handbuch d. allgem. Kirchengesch.* (5th ed. 1913), ii. 524–55.

[1] Danzas, p. 432.

[2] Dualism, in spite of being a common characteristic of heresy, is often
found within the orthodox fold, e.g. the Processus Belial; cf. Coulton, *Five
Centuries*, i. 62–66. Another parallel with heresy is provided by Aquinas
(2a, 2ae, Q. 183, art. 4), who lists mankind under three heads, so far as concerns their religious advancement: *incipientes, proficientes, perfecti*. This
classification bears a resemblance to the *credentes* and *perfecti* of the Albigensian church.

had a vastly greater number of adherents than Waldensianism. It had been almost unknown since Patristic times, but began to get a firm hold in Languedoc and Lombardy in the late twelfth century. It was an importation from Bulgaria, and is ultimately traceable to the Manichaeism of the Near East in the third century A.D.[1] This line of descent seems proven; but Mani's synthesis of older beliefs with some new elements, all essentially Oriental in character, had as its central tenet an idea that has often proved attractive: that Good and Evil are warring forces within the human frame, the ultimate hope of salvation depending on the victory of the former. Naturally the two abstractions are easily identified with spirit and body, and original Manichaeism expressed this by the idea that a small portion of Light, the good principle, was mixed with a greater volume of Darkness in every man,[2] the Light always attempting to rejoin other similar scattered fragments to form once again the complete Light that had existed before the Fall. It is easy to see how this duality lent itself to perversion in the minds of opponents, leading them to find grounds for their accusations of immorality in the fact that the body (being, according to the Manichaeans, in origin evil) might be allowed to do anything here on earth: a good life was of no avail because it could not make the Light any brighter. But whatever foundation there may have been for this argument in Manichaean doctrine, there seems to have been little for the suggestion of immorality, which was in consequence of it continually alleged against the Cathari.[3]

It may be well to indicate here that this division of heretical movements into Waldensian and Catharist-Manichaean, though useful in giving a clear sketch of the situation in a few

[1] The most recent opinion agrees upon this, which was the view of the Cathari themselves. Some (e.g. Lea, *Hist. Inq.* i. 109) have denied the connexion. Cf. F. C. Burkitt, *Religion of the Manichees*, p. 11; he thinks it likely that "fragments" of their teaching were derived from Manichaean sources, but considers the original doctrines had become attenuated, so that to call the Albigeois Manichees is "misleading". S. Runciman, *First Bulgarian Empire*, p. 196, states that upon a comparison of Slavonic-Bogomil literature with that of the Albigeois "all doubt upon this matter must vanish". Quite lately, Grundmann, *Relig. Bewegungen*, p. 23, has reaffirmed the Oriental origin.

[2] Cf. *Anecdotes*, p. 301, on this belief.

[3] The Inquisitors themselves admitted as much. Lea was only able to find one case of this charge being made by Inquisitors—in 1387! (*Hist. Inq.* i. 101).

words, and though excellently justified in that it is a division commonly adopted by contemporaries, does some violence to historical accuracy. It disguises the historical origin of the revolt from orthodoxy. Dualistic beliefs were not at first the chief mark of heresy in the West (they do not appear, indeed, till towards the end of the twelfth century), nor was the Church's campaign against heresy ever directed solely towards combating them. The earliest manifestations of heresy (i.e. from the eleventh century onwards) were marked by an attempt to lead the apostolic life; that is to say, the life of poverty and preaching.[1] Waldo was, then, by no means the first to advocate this way of making Christianity a living creed once more; nor was Manichaeism, when it was later imported from the East and assimilated by a part of the heretic movement, ever the real gravamen of the Church's charge, however much the Inquisition may have directed its efforts towards discovering it. Quite apart from dualistic tenets, the heretics were already sufficiently convicted of error by their desire to live the apostolic life. Preaching was not even the regular duty of the parish priest, let alone of secular folk; while to advocate poverty was (as was pointed out to Waldo, and later to St Francis) to insult the whole of the hierarchy, which was "possessionate" throughout. The most recent writer on the subject[2] insists on this historical approach to the problem of heresy, and puts his conclusions succinctly thus: "Das Leben der Apostel zu führen, die echten Nachfolger der Apostel zu sein, das ist der eigentliche Anspruch der Ketzer und aus ihm hat sich ihr Bruch mit der Kirche entwickelt." A full appreciation of this point makes even more clear how thoroughly well calculated were the methods St Dominic adopted.

The wide diffusion which heresy now gained in Italy, France and Germany (especially the old Middle Kingdom) soon caused the Church to realise that new methods were necessary to deal with it. Since the doctrinal disputes of the first five centuries of Christianity and the development of an orthodoxy universally recognised and firmly entrenched in Rome, the sheer weight of the hierarchy had always been sufficient to crush any heretical

---

[1] St Bernard, for instance, takes this as their chief characteristic—see sermon 66 in Migne, PL. 183, col. 1098.

[2] Grundmann, *Relig. Bewegungen*. I quote from p. 21, but see the whole section pp. 18–28 on this paragraph.

tendencies. Perpetual imprisonment had silenced Gottschalk, official condemnation in solemn council had dealt successively with Claudius of Turin, Peter Abelard and Gilbert de la Porrée. While heretical opinions were confined to a few scholars who spent more time than was wise in meditating religious truth, and who had no party behind them, the said opinions could be adequately stifled by the prosecution of the offenders before an assembly of bishops who could be guaranteed to murmur "'namus, 'namus" between snores, even if they understood nothing of the matter in hand.[1] But the spread of dogmatic error to the large populations of the Midi made these methods no longer of any value. Mere condemnation might break the spirit even of an Abelard, but it did not suffice against the fanatical but unthinking multitude unless backed up by stronger measures.

Rome combated error in the thirteenth century by three new methods which circumstances forced her to improvise. The first involved, as so often, compromise with the enemy. Reason in theology, which Bernard had so strongly denounced, was applied by Aquinas to the defence of the faith and the closer definition of dogma little more than a hundred years after it had brought Abelard to disaster by leading him to question accepted beliefs. This surprising volte-face gave great trouble to the conservatives of the Church, who refused to abandon the Augustinianism of their early training for the Aristotelian teaching of St Thomas. Even his own Order looked askance on Aquinas for some time: within twelve years of his death the Dominican General Chapter had three times to issue injunctions against those "qui de scriptis ejus irreverenter et indecenter loquuntur".[2] The second method was to attack the evil at its root, by a revival of preaching, now an almost forgotten art, setting orthodox truth clearly before those who had fallen into error. It was realised that it was impossible to expect all be-

---

[1] "...When therefore the reader had stumbled upon some sufficiently thorny passage, he would cry to the deaf ears of those prelates: 'Damnatis?' Then a few barely awakening at the sound of the last syllable, murmured with slumbrous voice and nodding head 'Damnamus', while others, aroused by the chorus of the rest, caught only the last syllable and droned out '-namus, -namus'"—from the account of the Council of Sens, 1140, which condemned Abelard, written by the latter's pupil Berengarius: Migne, PL. 178, cols. 1857 sq., translated Coulton, *Life in the Middle Ages*, iv. 176.

[2] *Acta* 1279, cf. 1278, 1286.

lievers to keep to the straight and narrow path if that path were never shown to them. And when these gentler methods failed the appeal was made to a third force. The Albigensian Crusade and the establishment of the Inquisition were a last resort, the only remaining means to preserve the purity of the faith.[1]

Among these three the re-discovery of the virtues of evangelisation is our chief concern. Through centuries of barbarism the Church had been hard put to it to maintain life at all, and once the Teutonic races had been converted to Christianity evangelisation had ceased to be a primary need and had in consequence been in practice almost abandoned. Religion had hardened into a system which retained sufficient of the essentials to maintain itself in continued existence, but not one scrap more. It was this discarding of all excess burden which had led to the fatal concentration upon the political and feudal side of the Church which was noticed earlier. Faced with the danger of absorption by post-Carolingian Emperors and degradation into a very secondary position in that partnership of Church and State which was to be the *civitas Dei* on earth, the Papacy had developed its own strength along the State's lines and by using the State's own methods—purely worldly ones—from which the State in its turn later learnt much in regard to the detail and routine of government. But in consequence it, and the Church in the wide sense with it, lost touch with, and ceased to lay emphasis upon, the more purely spiritual side of religion. As a result, the successive waves of monastic reform affected Christendom at large to a surprisingly small extent. A few earnest souls in each generation were led to ponder upon the evils of the world and to try to counteract them by ever-increasing

[1] It is interesting to notice that new methods make their appearance almost exactly in 1200. The Church first took up a definite attitude to the problem as a whole with Lucius III's decree of 1184, which defined it, laid down tests by which it might be recognised, etc. Innocent III (1198–1216) introduced new ideas. He was prepared to listen to the claims of the wandering preachers, provided they did not attack Catholic dogma or organisation. Hence the rule created for the re-converted Italian Humiliati in 1199; the organisation of the "Poor Catholics" under Durandus of Huesca (a converted Waldensian), in 1208; the letter to the legate Raoul in 1204 (see below, p. 37); and Innocent's readiness to give Francis and Dominic a chance to prove their value in the struggle in defence of the Church. See a detailed examination of Innocent's personal policy, and the way in which the ban on further Orders (Lateran Council, 1215) can be reconciled with it, in Grundmann, pp. 70–112.

austerities, but outside the walls of the monastery Mammon reigned unchallenged as before. Thus when Cluny's effort was over, Cîteaux took up the task; from Cîteaux a still stricter party went forth, and founded Clairvaux; and so the series went on, until at last the friars appeared, who had for a time direct effect upon the world, and remained true to their early ideals long enough to stave off the threatened disruption of the Church, and to preserve Christianity until reform found its only hope in secession at the Reformation.

But none of these efforts materially affected the Church as an organisation. Monasticism was essentially selfish, considered the outside world as almost irredeemable, and was content to think mainly of securing salvation to those within the cloister. The Popes, busy with diplomatic affairs, had no time to turn monastic energy into more profitable channels. Hildebrand did indeed attempt it, but with little success. Simony went on unchecked throughout the Middle Ages, fostered with the best of intentions by the rulers of Europe, because they quite reasonably regarded their bishops primarily as parts of the machine of government and only secondarily as ecclesiastics. Celibacy was enforced in so far as it was henceforward regarded as the only lawful state for a priest to be in. But it was a very doubtful gain to replace lawful matrimony by illegal but widespread incontinence. It made one more crime for the clerical calendar and wasted the energies of the more zealous bishops in countless inquiries upon their visitations into the cases of priest after priest who was "*diffamatus*" of keeping a concubine. Certainly contemporaries sometimes regarded it as a disadvantage that the clergy were not allowed lawful marriage. In Alsace about 1200 "almost all the priests had concubines; the peasants commonly urged them to this course, saying that a priest could not be continent, so that it were better that he should have his own wife than that he should solicit or defile the wives of all men".[1]

The Church organisation, having been satisfied for centuries with mere conformity and never having made any real attempt to ensure that the generality of mankind should be instructed in even the elements of the faith, had developed no technique for meeting the kind of crisis that was facing it at the end of the

[1] *Annales Colmarienses*, in MGH. xvii. 232.

twelfth century. Papal letters directed to the bishops of areas infested by heresy repeatedly deplore the state of affairs with customary medieval pessimism, but make no constructive suggestions for an improvement in the situation. Still less could the regular clergy re-orientate their ideas and come to the rescue of fainting Christianity. It was their ideal to keep themselves unspotted from the world by retiring from it. In spite of the great and beneficent influence which he was conscious of possessing outside his monastery, Bernard refused to be lured from its shelter save in cases of greatest need. He even went so far as to discourage preaching. An indication of the inability of monks to deal with the situation is given by their complete failure to prevent or check the spread of heresy in Languedoc. Episcopal efforts proving useless, the Popes had made a habit of committing the care of Languedoc to the Abbots of Cîteaux and Clairvaux, but no improvement had been noticeable. At the Council of Montpellier in 1205 Diego d' Azévédo and Dominic found the legate and the twelve Cistercian abbots in despair, and on the point of deciding that the case was hopeless and nothing could be done to better it. They were perhaps naturally sceptical that good results could follow Diego's harebrained scheme to attack heresy on its own ground by dismissing their equipages and itinerating on foot and in poverty. Their apathy was profound: the position in Languedoc was beyond their experience and they had no new ideas, nor any inclination to set about the task committed to them by Innocent.

But besides this inability to deal with the pressing demands of the times, there was a general decay amongst the monastic Orders, so that they no longer gave an example of virtue in a wicked world. The ordinary man did not even respect them. For by 1200 the most recent reforms had begun to lose their original character; their own hard work and the gifts of the faithful had made the Cistercians wealthy; it is about this time that their churches begin to be referred to as "opus sumptuosum". Like the older foundations, they allowed their religion to be overlaid with too many temporal interests.

Monachi sunt nigri
Et in regula sunt pigri.[1]

[1] *Carmina Burana*, ed. Schmeller, p. 15.

Hugh de St Cher was one of the best of medieval churchmen, one of the few who managed to touch pitch without being defiled. No one considered that Satan was rebuking sin when, as a Cardinal of the Order, he wrote a letter to the Dominican General Chapter of 1257[1] urging the stricter enforcement of discipline—a letter the more impressive to us in that it is infinitely less hysterical and contains more reasonable suggestions for improvement than the generality of its kind. Yet Hugh's Bible Commentary is full of outbursts of anger against monastic degradation. Commenting on Matthew xxviii. 6 ("He is not here; for he is risen", etc.), he says: "This can truly be said of many in the cloister (*de multis claustralibus*), that he is risen and gone forth and is not there, yet his garment and the place where he was remain."[2]

It is the same tale of the secular clergy. From the Roman court to the simple parish priest, the majority were idle and corrupt where not actually vicious. All ranks bowed down to the god of money. That bitter but perfect parody, the "Gospel according to the Silver Mark", and Walter of Châtillon's

> Das istis, das aliis,
> addis dona datis:
> et cum satis dederis,
> quaerent ultra satis.

are well known.[3] St Cher is equally severe upon the bishops. The spirits of pride, luxury and avarice have ascended to the mountains, "id est in prelatos...et parvuli eius [sc. Dei] ducti sunt in captivitatem ante faciem tribulantis, sequentes prelatos suos qui debuerunt eos ducere in caelum et ipsi ducunt eos in infernum". None can be found to reprove evil in the people: "Ipsi prelati nolunt reprehendere, quia in hoc condemnarent se."[4] It was the archbishop of Narbonne of the time who called forth Innocent III's famous remark that "his God was money".[5]

In the parishes the priest was seldom respected. The ill-success which had attended insistence upon celibacy is well

---

[1] Printed in Humbert, ii. 507, note.

[2] St Cher v. 89 col. 3. For further judgments on the clergy, see below, Chap. IX.

[3] *Carmina Burana*, pp. 20, 22. The ascription of the latter to Walter is not certain, but it is probably by him; cf. Raby, *Secular Latin Poetry*, ii. 206.

[4] St Cher i. 200 col. 3.   [5] MPL. 214 col. 905.

shown in an early French *fabliau* quoted by Luchaire.[1] A
certain priest spent all his money on clothes for the "priestess"
and refused to take proper care of his mother, who lived with
them. She appealed to the bishop, who threatened the priest
with suspension if he did not look after his mother better; he
made no attempt to secure the dismissal of the other woman.
The general lack of education among the clergy is amply
demonstrated in the visitations of Odo Rigaldi,[2] or in the lament-
able answers of the priests to the simple questions asked them in
the contemporary Salisbury visitations. This evidence is due to
the preservation of the records of efforts made by exceptional
prelates. Many made no attempt to carry out their obligations;
the same Berengar of Narbonne of evil memory, though appointed in 1190, had not even visited his diocese by 1204, but
dwelt contentedly in Spain where he possessed large incomes
from an abbacy and the bishopric of Lerida.[3]

Added point was given to clerical failings by the superior
excellence of the heretics' life. In manners, morals and learning
the Catharist "Elect" deserved the respect of the populations
they served to an infinitely greater extent than the orthodox
bishops and clergy.[4] During the whole of the Middle Ages the
question of the validity of sacraments in polluted hands was
always recurring, and had purity in the ministrant been demanded, many Catholics would have found themselves deprived
of the means of grace. A far smaller proportion of the Albigenses
needed to have such doubts when receiving the "Consolamen-

---

[1] Luchaire, *Ph. Augustus*, trans. Krehbiel, p. 57.
[2] Coulton, *Five Centuries*, ii. 218–227.
[3] Lea, *Hist. Inq.* i. 15.
[4] On the pre-eminence of the heretics in learning, cf. *Anecdotes*, p. 307 sq.
Giving examples of it, Étienne de Bourbon compares (p. 309) "their diligence
in evil and the negligence of the Catholics in good. Many of the latter are so
careless of their own and their relations' salvation that they scarcely know
the Paternoster or the Credo, nor teach them to their dependents." On p. 311
he shows how the heretics employed their "sophisticacio" to defeat inquiries
into their beliefs, and admits that even clergy and University men found
difficulty in dealing with their subtlety. "They used, when they dared and
there were fewer trained and educated men in the Church, to defend themselves with false reasoning and arguments; but now, because by these means
they cannot prevent their foolishness from becoming manifest", they take
refuge in sophisms, "some of which we are able to bring to light, though not
all" (p. 312). Étienne clearly believed that the learned nature of his Order
had served some useful purpose.

tum" at the hands of an "Electus", or when performing the
ceremony of adoration. But apart from the respect with which
they were regarded as individuals, the heretic ministers gained
an enormous power by the practical monopoly which they held
over preaching. This was never the duty of a Catholic priest—
indeed the bishop was the only official preacher in the whole
diocese, though he was supposed to enjoin it upon his subordinates when necessary. In any case, adequate preaching was
not to be expected of one who could hardly read, much less
understand, his breviary; sheer lack of knowledge prevented it.
Congregations lacked spiritual food in consequence, did not
understand the faith in which they believed, and were easily
worsted in argument by the relatively well-instructed heretics.
It was not until the Lateran Council—in other words, after the
beginning of the Albigensian Crusade had recognised implicitly
that stronger measures were now called for; and after the entry
into the field of the volunteer troops of St Dominic and St
Francis—that the official Church tardily admitted that the
bishops had no time for preaching, and ordered the appointment of special deputies to relieve them of this work.[1]

To attack medieval Catholicism for the many things it did not
do, without having first admitted both its tremendous difficulties
and the good it did succeed in accomplishing, always savours
slightly of the unfair; there are so many vulnerable points for its
opponents to seize upon. Yet it is not unreasonable to suggest
here that the Papacy, having, as illustrated above, deliberately
chosen politics rather than proselytising as its main interest in
the earlier medieval centuries, had not even managed to sub-
stantiate its claims in that direction. Its political interests
rendered it slow to listen to non-political demands; but having
at last given ear and determined that something must be done
to cast out the virus of "heretical depravity", it lacked strength
to bend the episcopacy to its often-expressed will. It is a fearful
indictment of the inefficient building of earlier times to realise
that Innocent III, strongest of medieval Popes, could not get
rid of the archbishops of Narbonne and Auch, who were among
the worst of medieval prelates, until twenty-one years after each
had been enthroned. Yet the case against them was regarded as

---

[1] Cap. 10 of the Council's decrees.—Mansi, xxii. col. 998.

proven by the whole of Christendom and their dioceses were in the full glare of the limelight. Feudalism in the Church as in the State was at once the prop and the chief impediment of the ruler.[1]

Once again, then, the conclusion is reached that in and about 1200 it was becoming clear that existing methods would not work. If Innocent III, with all the weapons at his command, could make no appreciable headway against the attacks of innovation from without and the deadweight of feudal conservatism from within, it is clear that any attempted reform of the existing machinery must be ineffectual because it could not possibly be radical enough. It was not as if Innocent was the first to have to tackle the problem of heresy. It had appeared in France from the middle of the eleventh century and had grown steadily more powerful. Peter the Venerable had remarked upon it at length, and discussions had taken place between Catholic and Catharist Bishops as early as the Council of Lombers (1165). A Cardinal-bishop, Henry of Albano, had been sent to conduct a missionary campaign in 1177, and two years later the Lateran Council had made the first appeal to the secular arm. Since forty years of effort had produced an entirely negligible result, it was clear that either defeat must be admitted or some entirely new measures devised.

Before describing these it now remains only to indicate the special importance of Languedoc and Provence in the matter of heresy. In the first place commercial development due to the passage of important trade routes through the country was producing that more educated middle class to which reference was made earlier. But in addition the court of Toulouse— "Tolosa la gran"—was the centre of a higher type of civilisation than existed elsewhere in Europe. Set beside the knights of the Midi, Richard Cœur de Lion loses most of the glamour which is usually accorded him in this country, and appears little better than a rough warrior, unpolished and without skill in the gentler arts of polite society. Even Richard, however, perceived the shortcomings of the northern races in the arts of chivalry, and by making Arnaut Daniel his court troubadour tried to bring himself more into line with southern standards.

[1] Coulton, op. cit. ii. 300-4.

Shallow, erotic and highly-conventionalised though it may have been, the Provençal civilisation thought less in terms of force and more in terms of the mind than any other contemporary society. Because of this Toulouse merited William of Tudela's praise—

"Tolosa
Que de totas civitatz es cela flors e roza"[1]

(incidentally almost the only line in his section of the *Chanson de la Croisade* which rises above the merest doggerel)—more than London merited Dunbar's—"the floure of cities all"—three hundred years later. Since it was the home of this relatively advanced culture but lacked adequate instruction in Catholic dogma, in common with the rest of Europe, it was the more open to the seduction of heresy.

In the second place the Church of Provence was particularly bad. The two archbishops before quoted were worse than the general run of their contemporaries, and the lower clergy of their dioceses were only too much like them. Ill-instructed and degraded, they were the mockery of the surrounding population. And since nothing is so destructive as mockery that is justified, so it was with the Church in Provence. The heretics soon enjoyed a complete monopoly of education; St Dominic's foundation of Prouille was to meet the needs of Catholic women who had found it impossible to acquire the elements of learning anywhere but in the schools of the heretics. It is significant too that when the Albigenses recognised that Diego was a good man and yet a Catholic, they suggested that he had come amongst them to learn the true faith.[2] The common opinion in Provence is summarised in the remark of Thierry de Nevers, relapsed priest and heretic: "'Diu me detinuit meretrix, sed de cetero non tenebit'; hoc dicens, dicebat Romanam ecclesiam meretricem."[3]

A final cause of the predominance of heresy in the South was its separation from the rest of France. The history of the French monarchy is the history of the gradual expansion of the royal domain: Toulouse was outside the royal boundary and owed

---

[1] *Chanson de la Croisade*, 79.
[2] Jord. Sax. p. 10.
[3] Vaux-Cernay, cap. vi, in Migne, PL. 213, col. 555.

the most nominal allegiance to the King, until the Albigensian Crusade and the marriage of Raymond VII's daughter to Alphonse, brother of St Louis, ended its independence for ever. Cut off from the rest of the country, Provence was left to its own devices and behaved differently from the North in face of the advent of heresy. When it first became prominent, Raymond V adopted that policy of toleration which was to prove so fatal to his son. None of his house seem to have been heretics themselves, in spite of allegations to the contrary, and the toleration of other opinion than their own appears to have been dictated partly by lukewarmness upon religious questions in general, and partly by a more modern reason—simply the avoidance of interference with opinion. The secular arm at Toulouse could in consequence never be enlisted wholeheartedly in defence of the Church, and years of fighting were necessary before Frederick II's heresy laws, the standard for all other countries from the time of their first draft in 1220, were inserted in the legal code. The final disastrous consequences of the separation were seen after the death of Simon de Montfort, when his son Amaury resigned all his claims to the conquered countries into the hands of Louis VIII, and the fine flower of southern civilisation was utterly crushed by the heel of a conqueror bent solely on unity and centralisation.

CHAPTER II

ST DOMINIC

ST Dominic is one of the most unresponsive of historical figures.[1] The documents from which we attempt to reconstruct his life and character are not notably lacking in any particular, yet all the while he escapes us as a man, while remaining clearly understandable regarded merely as the founder of an institution, a historical fact without flesh and blood or any of the normal attributes of a living being. Indeed, he provides a good case in point for those who, like Dr Johnson, maintain that "all the colouring, all the philosophy of history, is conjecture". It may be that this has been responsible for the hard and almost cruel character with which he is conventionally endowed.

Two difficulties occur at the outset. The evidence leads us to believe that in the space of the two years 1203–5 he discovered his life-work and set himself to carry out the duty which he felt had been laid upon him by Heaven. Therefore, it would seem, here is a fixed point, a certainty upon which to build. But we are cheated of our hope: while the end remains clear, the method by which that end was to be reached seems to have been long in doubt. For fifteen years Dominic maintained an equivocal attitude upon the question of poverty, and even the decision made at the General Chapter of 1220 is, as will appear later, open to a certain amount of interpretation. That this issue is a highly controversial one does not help matters; contemporaries and later writers alike have overlaid the surface of truth with more than a veneer of surmise, not always clearly acknowledged to be such. The second difficulty is one which is commonly met

---

[1] Just how unresponsive St Dominic is, is well shown by a consideration of the latest and most extensive biography:—H. C. Scheeben, *Der hl. Dominikus*, Freiburg i. B. 1927. In spite of the great length of the book, its painstaking chronological account of each stage in the saint's life, and a 14-page "character-study", the author never succeeds in making his hero "come alive". It is noticeable, too, that Walz (*Compendium*, p. 10 sq.) restricts himself in his (admittedly brief) account of Dominic to a purely conventional treatment, which does not go beyond the scope of dozens of medieval *Vitae*.

with in attempting a description of medieval personalities of all
kinds, but especially of saints; namely, the prevalence of
"common form". Certainly by the time of their formal canonisation, and very likely by the time of their death, what may be
termed the "normal miracles" begin to be related of them,
together with "normal sayings" and "normal austerities", and
these have, in almost every case, to be discounted. Very
frequently, of course, we find evidence additional to this conventional material, which by virtue of its very difference we
accept with joy; and if it happens to come from a source which
there is no reason to suspect, we have in it part of the skeleton
for a biography. But in St Dominic's case there is a surprising
lack of testimony of this nature as to his personality. There is
only one attempt at a sketch of him—perhaps it were better
termed the cartoon for a full-length portrait, since it gives the
impression that it could be filled in with greater detail—that of
Sister Cecilia.[1] Jordan of Saxony, Peter Ferrand and Constantine of Orvieto each tell us something, and the witnesses at
the canonisation more, but the value of the latter, in particular,
is decreased because "common-form" phrases constantly occur.
We really learn very little of St Dominic by being told in
phraseology that varies very little, that he was *verus amator
paupertatis*. Finally, the Lives of the Brethren, another source
of fairly early date, is unfortunate, like so much that has been
written about Dominic and his Order, in that it has an unspoken
comparison with a Franciscan composition—here the Little
Flowers—held over against it the whole time.

The material, then, is more suited to the historian than to the
biographer, and anything more than the barest generalities is
lacking. In consequence, we are forced to use material which
shows what he did rather than what he was, and attempt to
reconstruct the founder from the early history of the foundation.
"By their fruits ye shall know them" may answer a question in
morality, but it does little more than intensify a historical doubt.
Fortunately the Order does seem to have been to a larger extent

[1] However, Altaner (*Der hl. Dom.* p. 169) rejects this account on the
grounds that it conflicts with Peter Ferrand's, and suggests that it was taken
from a picture. It is in any case of late origin (*c.* 1280), though claiming to
come from a contemporary witness. Ferrand wrote 1235–41.

than might have been the case, the personal creation of Dominic, and so a possible complication is averted. But had there been one life-long companion to do what Leo did for Francis, much would be clear that is now obscure.[1] Danzas' comment on Raymond de Peñaforte is almost as true of Dominic; "il semble avoir fait un pacte avec l'obscurité".

The reason for this lack of information upon the individual man, as contrasted with the historical personage, may be that Dominic's life was fully taken up with fulfilling that need in the Church of his time which was outlined above; that his personality was completely sunk in his work; and that in consequence little else of importance remained over for contemporaries to see. We are, at any rate, forced to proceed under a handicap which amounts almost to assuming the truth of the suggestion.

St Dominic[2] was born either in or shortly after 1170 at Calahorra in Castile, a town already memorable as the birth-place of Quintilian and Prudentius. Of his early life we know little, apart from legend; according to the constantly-repeated stories, his birth was heralded by portents, and his boyhood marked by austerities and deep piety. We reach more solid ground with the assertion that at some time during his 'teens he went to study at Palencia, one of the most prominent cathedral schools in Spain, and remained there till about 1194. At about this date he returned to Osma, his native bishopric, and became an Austin canon under the capable and reforming bishop, Martin de Bazan. Here he took a prominent part in regularising

[1] It must be remembered that even Jordan of Saxony, author of the earliest and most useful book we possess (written 1232–3: see Altaner, *Der hl. Dom.* p. 7 sq.—I rely here and elsewhere entirely on Altaner for the dating and textual criticism of the various biographies), did not know St Dominic well. He entered the Order while still a University student in his early twenties, in 1219 or 1220 (Jord. Sax. cap. 38), and so cannot speak from personal knowledge of anything before then. St Dominic died in 1221. It is the more to be lamented that later biographers were content simply to borrow what Jordan had written; the amount and value of their new material is almost negligible. Even Étienne de Bourbon, who joined the Order in 1223 and knew most of the early friars well, makes no individual contribution. It would appear that there was scarcely any living tradition; this assertion "contains no exaggeration", remarks Altaner, op. cit. p. 127. Cf. the con-clusion reached in the text (below, p. 29) and the evidence for the neglect of the Saint's memory quoted there.

[2] It has become conventional to connect Dominic with the noble house of Guzmán; but scholars have never regarded the case made out by Brémond (*De Guzmana stirpe S. Dominici*, Romae 1740) as proven.

the Cathedral chapter, rising eventually to be prior, and came into personal contact with another of the canons, Diego d' Azévédo, who shortly succeeded Martin as bishop. It was through Diego that Dominic was introduced to what was to be his life's work. In 1203, and again in 1205, the bishop had occasion, for political reasons, to make journeys to Denmark,[1] and took Dominic with him as a companion. Passing through Southern France, they could not but note the hold which heresy had on the countryside, and it would appear that Dominic at once recognised the pressing need of doing something to correct the widespread influence of error. The story that on his first night out of Spain he did not sleep until he had converted his heretic host may be legend, and he appears only as a shadowy figure in the background at the Council of Montpellier where Diego made the startling proposal that the legate and the twelve Cistercian abbots, who were meeting in the town to discuss their missionary campaign, should adopt apostolic poverty to aid their preaching; but he did continue firmly in the mission-field when nearly all returned home discouraged on the deaths of Diego and Raoul de Fontfroide, the legate. Again, the evidence for his actions during the next eight years is meagre, being confined practically to two deeds in which, as the agent of the abbot of Cîteaux, he reconciles two heretics to the Church; and Lea's conclusion that his influence on the course of the Albigensian Crusade was "historically imperceptible"[2] may be inescapable; we are the more justified in saying that his persistence in the face of unimportance and probable ill-success— Languedoc was still as full of heresy as ever, long after this time—shows that his mind was made up. It is difficult to decide at what point Dominic determined on the formation of a preaching Order. Jordan tells us that after the return of Diego to Spain the Saint's companions were bound to him by no tie of obedience. Gifts made to him during the following years were made indiscriminately to the Prior of Prouille, to the

---

[1] Or possibly La Marche, in France?—The question cannot be finally settled, but I see no reason to reject the arguments in favour of Denmark produced by Mamachi (i. 126). However, Walz, *Compendium*, p. 3, and Altaner, *Der hl. Dom.* p. 141, take the opposite view.

[2] Lea, *Hist. Inq.* i. 249. Reconciliation of Pons Roger and another, Mamachi, *App.* 36.

brothers and sisters at Prouille, or to the sisters alone. The first definite indications are his journey to Rome in 1215 and the request for the confirmation by the Pope of an order "qui praedicatorum diceretur et esset", the establishment in the house of Peter Seila at Toulouse, and the appointment as licensed preachers of the diocese by Foulques (1215). It seems highly probable that it was much earlier than this, but certainty is impossible.[1]

At all events, the purpose of preaching was consecrated in 1217 by the dispersion from Prouille directly the Order had been approved,[2] and during the rest of his life Dominic himself continued with the work of evangelisation, when he was not engaged upon visits to Rome in the interests of the Order. From 1216 this seems the logical sequence in which to place the two purposes he had for himself henceforward: firstly, to establish his creation upon a firm foundation by the activities of a diplomatist, almost of a business-manager, at Rome and elsewhere, and secondly, to continue with the preaching as well whenever possible. But it is rather characteristic that there are few and brief accounts of Dominic's own sermons. Reginald of Orleans and Jordan of Saxony frequently receive praise, their master far less often.

In so far as this subordination to Rome was an essential part of the purpose of the Dominican Order, its founder can be brought into relation with one of the characteristics of his age:

[1] A related problem is presented by the inquiry: When did the plan of world-wide missionary activity replace the original sole concern with Southern French heresy in Dominic's mind? Altaner, *Persönlichkeit*, p. 403, clarifies the issue by distinguishing three stages in D.'s development: (i) 1205–15. D. the head of a body of friends campaigning without rule against heretics. (ii) 1215–17. D. the head of an official organisation in the diocese of Toulouse, working under the Augustinian rule, which they adopted in 1216 in response to Innocent III's demand that they should choose one of the existing rules. (iii) 1217–21. D. the head of a world Order, still under the Aug. rule but with its own "constitutions" in addition after 1220.—Dufourcq, p. 383, note, says: "Il obtient d'abandonner le Languedoc, où il reconnaît l'insuccès de son œuvre," in 1217; I know of no evidence for so categorical a statement. It would seem probable that a change took place between the first journey to Rome in Sept. 1215 and the dispersion of July, 1217, on D.'s return from the second; and it may well be connected with his experience of wider horizons during these two years. That the other friars had no thought of moving from Languedoc appears from their criticism of D. in July 1217 (Jord. Sax. cap. 27).

[2] By Honorius III's Bull of 22 December 1216.

the beginnings of centralisation in Church and State. Some anticipation of a later argument[1] is inescapable, but it is legitimate to say here that the case is quite sufficiently proven by the commonly accepted beliefs. Dominic's own constant requests for privileges from the Pope are undoubted: once he had jumped from a merely episcopal to a Papal sanction he turned Honorius' attention again and again to the Order and its aims; it may be fanciful to allege the words of the second and shorter Bull of 22 December 1216—"Nos, attendentes fratres Ordinis tui futuros pugiles fidei et vera mundi lumina, confirmamus Ordinem tuum..."—as proof that he had convinced the Pope as early as this, but in the light of later events it is at least not ridiculous. Inside his own creation, the constitution was clear, legalistic and definite, so that it worked smoothly and no energy that might have been spent on better activities was wasted in generating the heat of internal friction. Dominic's recognition of the benefits of centralisation and unified control has to be higher if we admit, as seems possible, a more autocratic view of the constitution of the Order than is usually accepted. The measure of the success of his subordination to the Papacy is the opposition it aroused. Pope and bishop had long been in sporadic conflict over the limits of their respective jurisdictions; the advent of the friars gave the former the man-power necessary to advance his frontiers, and on the friars fell the odium of the secular priesthood. It was as preachers and as Inquisitors that the Order chiefly crossed the bishops, in addition to the more general quarrel with the seculars in the University of Paris; in every case they represented efficiency, orthodoxy and one-man control against the older inadequate and centrifugal methods. And in every case the victory was to the Pope and innovation.

But Innocent III's fame rests on things other than the strength of his rule, Frederick II's on his claim to be an experimental scientist as well as on his absolutism; the years round 1200 are generally granted a qualified right to that title of Renaissance which is more properly reserved for a greater destiny. And here again, Dominic belongs very much to his age. The rationalism of Abelard and the rationalism of the earliest law schools of Bologna were nearly contemporary and probably

[1] See below, Chap. x.

interdependent; together they constitute the beginning of the
early Renaissance, and create two dominant trains of later medieval thought—scholastic philosophy and an interest in Roman
law. Dominic himself was not a lawyer—he had studied arts and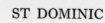
theology at Palencia—but he was, at any rate in later life, imbued
by the legal spirit, as his choice of Bologna as one of the two
"capitals" of the Order seems to suggest. Law was the basis of
his creation; as Mandonnet points out,[1] it is the emphasis on
law as against that on ethics in the older monastic Orders that
constitutes one of Dominic's chief claims to originality. It
was certainly this which made his purpose so clear, and his
creation so efficient an instrument for the execution of that
purpose. Law made the constitutions of 1220, which have
remained in many respects unchanged, and it was certainly their
legal character which made them the model for the imitation of
later foundations. It was only fitting that Gregory IX's edition
of canon law should have been drawn up by a Dominican—
though of course Raymond was a lawyer first, and only joined
the Order in middle life.

St Dominic's intentions with regard to learning are made
abundantly clear from the start. When the equipages were dis-
missed from Montpellier in 1205, one of the things the Cistercians retained was their books; the tithes granted by Foulques
were partly spent on books, and there is a strong tradition that
the first seven friars attended Alexander of Stavensby's lectures.[2]
But most significant of all is the command given to Matthew of
France when he was put in charge of the contingent sent to
Paris in 1217: "ut studerent et praedicarent et conventum ibi
facerent".[3] The order of the words themselves may be more
than accidental: if Aquinas arranged the three vows of poverty,
chastity and obedience in the ascending "canonical order", why
should Dominic not have done similarly in this case? But whereas the most difficult and essential vow comes last, the most
important injunction comes first: study is needful in order that

---

[1] *S. Dominique*, p. 71.
[2] Humbert, *Vita S. D.* in Mamachi, *App.* 283.
[3] Mamachi, *App.* 115. This is from the statements preliminary to the
process of canonisation; my references to them are always to Mamachi, but
they are also to be found printed in AA. SS. Aug. i. 632 sq. and Echard i.
44 sq.

preaching may be good, while the foundation of a convent simply fulfils an unavoidable but unimportant requirement—the need of the body for a place in which to rest and meditate.

Zeal for learning is reflected in two respects from the earliest times. One is shown again in the Constitutions: the prologue gives superiors power of dispensation in all cases where they think advisable, "in hiis praecipue, quae studium, vel praedicationem vel animarum fructum videbuntur impedire". This passage goes on to place the chief emphasis on "fruit of souls", but a later chapter is devoted exclusively to students: "Circa eos qui student, taliter dispensetur a praelato ne propter officium vel aliud de facili a studio retrahantur vel impediantur."[1] The history of the Order throughout the century, which will be traced later, shows the continuance of this devotion to study as a primary requirement for the business of preaching. It was a natural corollary that early endeavours should be made to attract University men into the ranks of the Order; Bologna and Paris were besieged very quickly, and the effect was remarkable. On the one hand the appeal was so strong that we find stories such as that of Master Moneta, who knew his only hope, if he wished to avoid conversion, was to keep away from Reginald of Orleans' sermons—and this was impossible; on the other hand, the influx of these men gave a predominantly University, and at times almost snobbish, turn to the outlook of the Order. Thus the Second Master-General, Jordan of Saxony (1222–37), was noted for the way in which he frequented University towns and drew the students after him, frequently not having enough habits to clothe the crowds of postulants, and we find him writing in triumph to Diana: "I have received thirty-three friars by the grace of God, and all are good men and competently lettered, except two *conversi*[2]", or again, "When I came to Vercelli, God gave many of the best and most educated men to us."[3] The same insistence on learning is found in Humbert de Romans, who was Master-General thirty years later.[4] Every "religion" is good, study is good: "ita et ordo cum scientia non immerito praefertur illis in quibus est sola sanctitas." This is the first of

---

[1] ALKG. i. 194, 223.   [2] Lay-brothers.
[3] Jord. Sax. ed. Berthier, pp. 69, 77; ed. Altaner, pp. 17, 25.
[4] 1254–63.

eleven reasons he gives for the usefulness of studies in the Order.
The second is more germane to our immediate point; many
good and important men (*multae bonae et magnae personae*) would
never have joined the Order were it not learned, and many who
were of no account at their entering were made of great value by
study. At the end he sums up: "Quis est enim qui noverit
statum fratrum praedicatorum qui nesciat has utilitates pro-
venisse et provenire ex studio litterarum?"[1]

'All this leads to the impression that Dominic, probably of
deliberate intent, fulfilled a pressing need in the Church of his
day. Religion was failing through the present attack of heresy,
the promised attack of learning, and the inadequacy of the
priesthood. Since attack is the best defence, the proper measures of recovery would adopt and adapt the strongest points of
the opposition: hence poverty and learning:[2] hence too, perhaps,
the staffing of the Order from just that class which was a chief
cause of offence—the clergy. (Previous Orders had been lay in
character; monks are laymen as a class, no matter how many of
their number may be in orders.) This suggestion, which is
Mandonnet's, can be nothing more than surmise, and cannot be
used as evidence to prove the main contention; the clerical recruit-
ment of the Dominicans may be attributable to nothing more
than the previous experience of Dominic as a canon-regular at
Osma under the Augustinian rule, and its continuance for new
purposes by him to the fact that it was material lying ready to
his hand and of proven worth. From this desire for the perfect counter-attack comes too the pre-eminence of preaching
over all else, the authoritarian principle,[3] and the comparative
neglect of choral services—they were to be said "breviter et
succincte".

The sketch further leads to the conclusion that if historical

---

[1] Humbert i. 433-4.
[2] To say this does not imply the attribution to Dominic of a more or less
Machiavellian outlook or an exclusive and sole concern with tactical considerations. No doubt he had, as a result of his early training, a general
predisposition in favour of education, and he may well have acquired a
similar feeling with regard to poverty; but the specific emphasis he laid on
both leads to the conclusion that some more precise explanation than this is
necessary to account for his attitude in these matters.
[3] See below, Chap. x.

comparisons must be made, then Ignatius Loyola rather than
Francis of Assisi, beside whom Dominic is eternally placed,
must be the parallel. Circumstances were similar in their respective centuries: Catholicism was being attacked in ways that
were not very diverse, both appear to have reacted in much the
same way and to have adopted much the same methods—all
those characteristics of Dominic just listed will serve equally
well for Ignatius. Where differences must be made, they can
fairly adequately be described by saying that Ignatius was
simply more extreme: e.g. his insistence on absolute obedience,
even to "perinde ac cadaver", and in the abolition of corporate
services in favour of private devotions. But to push too far into
detail is to show up the truism that analogy is the worst way of
treating history. No more need really be said than this: both
represent in different degrees the union of learning and
Christianity, which had been in danger; to use sixteenth-century
terminology, the union of Renaissance and Reformation to
produce Counter-Reformation.

To this mass of generalisation from material that is only
partially adequate to support it, there may be added what will
amount to little more than a catalogue of a few of Dominic's
more prominent characteristics. If only original sources are
used, in place of later views upon them, the figure of a mild,
upright and rather preoccupied man emerges. The gentleness,
which has so often been denied by non-Dominicans, is suggested
by the story of the heretic guide who led him through the thorn
bushes, by the legend that while still at Palencia he attempted to
sell himself into captivity, like Paulinus of Nola in an earlier
year, in exchange for the brother of a certain woman, and by the
fact that all the miracles recorded of him, with two exceptions,
are beneficent.[1] Humility seems unquestionable: he lived about
1210 at Carcassonne, where he was despised, rather than at
Toulouse, where he was held in honour; he refused at least two
bishoprics; at the first Chapter-General he wished to resign, and
when this was refused, insisted that the diffinitors should have

---

[1] He foretold the death of a certain nobleman who interrupted his preaching at Segovia (*Vit. Frat.* ii. cap. 9); and cruelly plucked a sparrow, saying it
was the Devil, in Rome. (Sister Cecilia, in Mamachi, *App.* 259–60: but this
may well be apocryphal.)

power over him as well as over the other friars.[1] Simplicity seems to follow necessarily from his personal poverty and willingness to sleep in any place he was offered and to eat anything that was put before him.[2] This last shows that Dominic himself ate no meat outside the convent, but it is by no means certain that this applied to other friars (it is recorded of Dominic as a special austerity) either outside or inside. General abstinence from meat must, in view of the witness of de Vitry to life at the Bologna convent about 1222, and of the chapter "De pulmentis" in the Constitutions of 1228, have been introduced by Jordan of Saxony during these six years.[3] There is abundant testimony to all other forms of austerity—prayer prolonged all through the night, the floor of the church used as a bed, frequent weeping, and so on. Yet with all this he was "semper ilaris et jocundus". Finally, there appears to have been a certainty about Dominic's acts that was derived from divine inspiration. So, at least, his followers thought; Jordan remarks on it, and thinks that the saint knew what would be the result of everything he did before it came to pass. Both Bonvisi of Piacenza and John of Navarre relate that when, as he sometimes did, their master sent an unlearned and so reluctant brother out to preach, he would tell him to have no fear, for God would provide the words. Bonvisi himself had this experience, preached extempore and converted three.[4]

This short description has, however, exhausted almost all there is to say about Dominic the man. Is this, within limits, all there ever was to say about him, or have important testimonies been lost? May we conclude with Lea, that "he made less impression upon his contemporaries than his followers would have us believe"?[5]

Several events in the later history of the Order will add to what has already been said upon the subject. A glance at the later Lives in the Acta Sanctorum support this view, for it is at

[1] Const. Orv. cap. 44, in Echard i. 35; Mamachi, *App.* 122.
[2] Mamachi, *App.* 101: "...in itinere ea quae dabantur sibi ad comedendum patienter comedebat, excepto quod non comedebat carnes."
[3] de Vitry, *Hist. Occ.* c. 28, in Echard i. 24. See Mandonnet, *Les chanoines-prêcheurs de Bologne*, in *Archives de la soc. de l'hist. du canton de Fribourg*, viii. pp. 16, 34–5 (1907).
[4] Mamachi, *App.* 114–5.   [5] Lea, *Hist. Inq.* i. 256.

once apparent that many of the traditional Franciscan stories, even to the Stigmata, have been bodily appropriated.[1] May this not have been due to a feeling of shadowiness, of impalpability, in the personality of Dominic? More convincing, because occurring within the lifetime of many who knew him, is the evidence we have on his cult in the thirteenth century. Jordan's Encyclical of 1237 complains that the glory of their blessed father has remained without veneration for twelve years; and from 1239, when a weekly mass was instituted in his honour, the first volume of the Acta Capitulorum Generalium contains no fewer than eleven instances of orders for the better honouring of his name, services in commemoration, etc.[2] This seems a little strange; in the early years there was no controversy to split the Order, no Elias, as among the Friars Minor, to draw away the respect of large numbers from their founder, and throughout the century no reason why his fame should have been allowed to become dim. The delay in the canonisation itself calls for explanation—thirteen years after death is a long time for so important a man, and compares ill with the few months that elapsed in the middle of the century between Peter's martyrdom at Como and his elevation to the altars.

Doubtless this comparative neglect does not belong to Dominic alone—in 1279 the friars had to be incited to remember adequately Raymond of Peñaforte and others—and doubtless part of the explanation is that the centre of the cult of any new saint was immediately the recipient of notoriety, reputation for miracle-working, and showers of gifts; all of which the poverty and humility of the early friars were eager to avoid. But the

---

[1] AA. SS. Aug. i. 365.
[2] Jord. Sax. p. 44, *Acta*, 1239, 1245, 1254, 1255, 1256, 1260, 1269, 1276, 1283–4–5. The following may also be of interest: Bromyard mentions St Dominic once, so far as I have been able to discover, notably failing to quote him either under *Paupertas* or *Humilitas*; he does not appear at all in the index to St Cher: this may perhaps be explained on the ground that the index was not meant to contain such things, but it is of enormous size, and the absence of mention of D. is fair indication that he is never quoted: certainly I have never come across his name in a fairly intensive reading of the work; Cantimpré ii. liii is entitled "De veneratione corporum sanctorum," and runs to 35 chapters, but there is no reference to D. either here or in ii. lvii, which contains a good deal about Jordan of Saxony and John the Teutonic; Étienne de Bourbon provides an exception by quoting him nineteen times (cf. seven references to St Francis, six to St Bernard).

well-known story of St Stephen of Grammont[1] will not serve as a complete explanation in the case of an institution incomparably vaster and more influential: nor is Mortier's suggestion enough—"Ce n'était pas l'indifférence...mais un certain dédain pour ce qui pouvait paraître une réclame tapageuse."[2] May not the true explanation be that which has already been put forward? The death of Dominic had less disastrous effects upon his Order than the death of Francis, because the personality of the founder counted for less and the organisation for more.

---

[1] Shortly after his death (1124) his tomb became such a scene of miracles and (in consequence) of offerings, that the simplicity of the brothers was offended; the prior solemnly adjured the saint to cease working wonders, and threatened that if he continued they would throw his bones into the river. Similar stories are related of St Pardulf of Sarlat, St Spinulus, St Robert of Chaise-Dieu and St Bernard. Cf. Coulton, *Five Centuries*, iii. 98–9, and Martène, *Comment. in Reg.* ed. 1690, cap. 66, p. 866.

[2] Mortier ii. 46.

CHAPTER III

POVERTY

SOME excuse must be offered, at a time when medieval studies have advanced so far, for writing at length on the subject of Dominican poverty, for the matter has long since been regarded as settled. The excuse is two-fold and complete. It will be freely admitted that poverty was, in some shape or another, of the first importance in every monastic reform, and in none more so than in that of the friars; it is on that ground alone, therefore, well worthy of close study. But there is another and greater excuse, namely that Dominican poverty has been widely and thoroughly misunderstood. Historians of varying shades of opinion have gone to the question with minds already made up, and their prejudice has, moreover, taken extreme forms; some have said the poverty of Dominic was as complete as it is possible to be, some have denied that he ever considered it until late in life. Both these views are entirely unsupported by the documentary evidence upon which they purport to be based.

The first of the two chief stumbling-blocks has been the failure to focus correctly the place that poverty took in the scheme of life which St Dominic laid down for himself and his followers. The organisation which he founded very rapidly became known as the "Order of Preachers",[1] a clear indication that both the founder and his contemporaries regarded preaching as their main purpose. Most historians have seen this plainly,

---

[1] The first use of the words Ordo Praedicatorum occurs in Honorius III's Bull of 11 Feb. 1218 (*Cart.* ii. 156–7, Laurent 98). Étienne de Salagnac has a story that Innocent III deliberately used the name in 1215, but this is probably legendary (see discussion in Mamachi, i. 390–3); Honorius III did not use the words in the two Bulls of 22 Dec. 1216 (Laurent 84, 88; BOP. i. 2, 4; *Cart.* ii. 71, 86). In the longer *Religiosam vitam eligentibus* he refers to "ordo canonicus, qui secundum Deum et b. Augustini regulam...", and the shorter one begins "Nos attendentes fratres Ordinis tui...." There are earlier uses to be found, e.g. in a letter of 11 Sept. 1217 (*Cart.* ii. 129; Laurent 94), Foulques of Toulouse speaks of "fratres praedicatores", but it is impossible to be sure whether these have a "technical" sense or not, i.e. whether they refer to "preachers" or to the "Order of Preachers".

but many have refused to admit the possible conclusion that, in consequence, poverty played but a subordinate and accessory part. There is, of course, no reason in the nature of the case why St Dominic or any other, instead of St Francis, should not have made the mystical marriage with the "Lady Poverty", and have been the real revolutionary; for it must never be forgotten that poverty in its relation to the Christian life was "in the air" at the end of the twelfth century, and that no special explanation is required for its adoption by a new movement which came comparatively late into the field. Sufficient has already been said about Waldensians, Albigenses, Poor Catholics and Humiliati for this point to be admitted without further discussion.

Many have been led astray, too, by a refusal to consider the possibility that St Dominic changed his views in the course of his life. Yet it is a very natural thing for increasing age and experience to bring a development in a man's outlook, and it is, moreover, frequently rather a disadvantage than otherwise to be a slave to fixed ideas, no matter how good they may be. Has this refusal to admit development and change in Dominic, then, been quite the undiluted praise that it was no doubt intended to be? It may be added that the likelihood of alteration is obviously very great, when we remember that St Dominic went to his life-work of missionary activity quite untrained, and had to teach himself the whole technique.

Historians of the foundation of the Order may on the whole be divided in two classes—Dominican and non-Dominican. The work of the former has usually been marred by misconceptions upon one of the points outlined above, and in many cases they have followed both false trails. The trouble really began in the seventeenth century, when Luke Wadding,[1] the historian of the Friars Minor, insisted that in all essentials St Dominic was dependent upon St Francis, and borrowed his main ideas from him. In the next century, Quétif and Echard[2] answered him, making out a case for the greater originality of the founder of

---

[1] Wadding, *Annales Minorum*, Lyons, 1625–48 (see vol. i. ad ann. 1219, n. 5).

[2] *Scriptores Ordinis Praedicatorum*. 2 vols. Paris 1719–21 (see esp. i. 77 sq.).

their own Order, and from that time the controversy has never really ceased. The Dominicans, desirous of maintaining their founder's glory, but conscious that the word "poverty" is indissolubly linked with the name "Francis" in the public mind, have maintained that both saints held the same extreme opinions on the subject, and have used Dominic's undeniably earlier vocation to make out a claim that he was the greater. It must be admitted that the reader is often left to draw this inference for himself, but constant harping on the theme leaves no doubt as to the intention. The most prominent examples are Mortier, in the first volume of his *Histoire des Maîtres-généraux*[1]; Balme and Lelaidier, in the commentary on the documents assembled in the *Cartulaire*;[2] and (to a lesser extent) the late Father Bede Jarrett.[3] More recent writers have slightly altered the emphasis, while retaining the same intention. It has clearly become impossible to secure for St Dominic the place that St Francis has attained as a result of the spate of modern publications upon him, and of the popularity which they enjoy; attention has therefore been directed to showing that in spite of the two different decisions (1216 and 1220) made upon poverty in the early history of the Dominican Order, the saint's own ideas never changed, and that he was always in favour of an extreme form. The interference of Innocent III has been blamed for any apparent inconsistency. It needs, however, to be pointed out that neither of these assertions rests on any evidence whatever. The principal authors who have written in this spirit are Walz,[4] Lambermond[5] and Scheeben.[6]

The standard non-Dominican view, on the other hand, is so

---

[1] D. A. Mortier, *Histoire des Maîtres-généraux*. Paris, 1903 sq.
[2] Balme et Lelaidier, *Cartulaire ou histoire diplomatique de S. Dominique*. 3 vols. Paris, 1893 sq.
[3] Bede Jarrett, *Life of St Dominic*. London, 1924.
[4] A. M. Walz, *Compendium historicae Ordinis Praedicatorum*. Rome 1930. See in particular pp. 10–12, 21.
[5] H. C. Lambermond, *Der Armutsgedanke des hl. D. und seines Ordens*. Zwolle, 1926, pp. 5, 10–12; see review by Altaner in *Theologische Revue*, 1927, p. 382.
[6] H. C. Scheeben, *Der hl. Dominikus*, Freiburg i. B. 1927. See esp. pp. 77, 163, 195–8. He commits himself expressly (p. 109) to holding a middle course with regard to the debt to St Francis, but hardly keeps to it in practice. —On him see also the criticisms of Altaner in *Zeitschrift für Kirchengeschichte*, Bd. 46, p. 396.

carried away by the poverty of the Friars Minor as to believe
that anybody who approximated to their practice must have
copied it from them. The view leaves quite out of account the
poverty of earlier reformers, and tends to regard it as a new
conception invented at the Portiuncula. Thus to the previous
maximising tendency we have to oppose a second so minimising
to Dominic that it claims all his glory for another. It is significant of the hold Francis still has over generations far removed
from his own that where the friars are concerned poverty is
regarded as in all respects equivalent to "glory" in this sense.
But this is to blind oneself to all that is best in Dominic's
character. Apart from Wadding, who has already been mentioned, we may list the editors of the lives of St Dominic
contained in the *Acta Sanctorum*;[1] Lea, the historian of the
Inquisition;[2] Sabatier;[3] and Mrs Galbraith.[4] The use of Lea's
book as a work of reference, and the popularity which Sabatier's
life of St Francis attained, may perhaps account for the wide
currency which this view has achieved.

Between these schools of thought stand the publications of
Dr Berthold Altaner,[5] who has done so much for Dominican
studies in recent years. He has seen quite clearly that neither
extreme opinion can be maintained, and that St Dominic was
neither an imitator of St Francis, nor, so far as poverty is concerned, so entirely original. He insists, too, on a development
in St Dominic's ideas from the time of his first preaching efforts
in Southern France, up to the Chapter-General of 1220. To this
extent, then, the present account claims to do little more than

[1] AA. SS. August i. 358 sq.

[2] H. C. Lea, *History of the Inquisition of the Middle Ages*. New York, 1908.
See esp. vol. i. p. 253.

[3] D. Sabatier, *Vie de S. François d'Assise*. Paris, 1894. See esp. pp. 247–
252.

[4] G. R. Galbraith, *The Constitution of the Dominican Order*. Manchester,
1925, pp. 35–6. It is only right to add that, as is clear from the title, poverty
is remote from the main subject of this invaluable book, and receives but a
very summary treatment.

[5] I am referring here especially to the article in *Theologie und Glaube*, Bd.
xi (1919), 404 sq.—For full list see Bibliography.—It is noteworthy that two
encyclopaedic publications, which make no attempt to treat the matter
thoroughly, also incline to a rather more moderate view.—Max Heimbucher,
Die Orden und Kongregationen der kath. Kirche, i. 479 (3rd ed. 1933); Kirsch-
Hergenröther, *Handbuch der allgemeinen Kirchengeschichte*, ii. 653 (5th ed.
1913); the latter, however, speaks of strict poverty after 1220.

repeat and extend conclusions which have already been reached. But it does seem possible to go further than Dr Altaner has done in pointing out the reasons which lay behind St Dominic's attitude to poverty, and to modify very considerably the position he has taken up with regard to the possession of property by the Order.[1]

It may be well to state the main conclusions of the present research, before embarking on the detailed argument. It is intended to deny at once the complete poverty of St Dominic and his early companions, and the saint's alleged supreme insistence on it, and on the other hand the suggestion that he borrowed it *en bloc* from Francis; and to maintain that the poverty of the first-named was not greater or less, but other, than that of the second. Their purposes were different, and so their views on this and other subjects were different. It is therefore clear that poverty is not the only "glory" of a friar, and that Dominic's "glory" is not different in degree, but in kind, from the other's. The main criticisms that will be made are that Dominican writers have neglected to take into account the large amount of property which their Order, and individual friars as well, possessed at the two crucial dates of 1216 and 1220, and which both it and they continued to acquire after that date; and that non-Dominicans have tended to forget the very considerable personal poverty of Dominic himself, and that he was living the life of poverty in Languedoc while Francis was still on the road to Spoleto with Count Gentile.

The history of poverty in the mission-field of Southern France may perhaps be dated back to 1204. On 28 May of that year, Innocent III wrote to the legates Peter and Raoul ordering them to inquire into the evil life of the Archbishop of Narbonne; the tenor of the letter is Chaucer's "If golde ruste, what shall iren do?" Three days later he wrote a second letter urging strong measures for the stamping out of heresy, and ended by commanding "that your modesty...shall put to silence the ignorance of imprudent men, and nothing shall appear in your words or deeds which the heretics may have occasion to reprove".[2] It is difficult to think Innocent meant the legates to go very far

---

[1] Id. 407, 409.
[2] Mamachi, *App.* 30; Migne, PL. 215, col. 358 sq.

towards diminishing the pomp and circumstance with which they were accustomed to travel, but we can at least say that such a suggestion from Innocent fits in with his known readiness to come to terms with the poverty-and-preaching movement which was so strong in that part of the country.[1]

A year later, at the council of Montpellier in 1205, Diego d' Azévédo made the first definite move when he urged the legates and the Cistercian abbots whom he found there to dismiss their trains of servants and attempt less showy methods of conversion. It is more than likely, though in the present state of our knowledge a direct assertion cannot be made, that this too is to be referred for its origin to Innocent. Diego and Dominic had come direct from Rome, where they had met the Pope and discussed missionary plans. Diego wished to lay down his bishopric and turn his attention to evangelising the heathen of the Near East. Innocent refused to allow this, telling him that he had more important work to do in his own diocese, and sent him back to Spain. He knew by this time that his emissaries had made little impression on the Albigensians, and he knew moreover that Diego would pass through Languedoc on his way to Osma; and finally he had just received proof that the bishop was ardent in the cause of conversion. What more likely than that he entrusted Diego with a message to the missionaries working there, of the delivery of which the council of Montpellier was the scene? But here, again, it is impossible with the existing sources to do more than point to a probability. We cannot be certain whether Diego acted on his own initiative or not.[2]

It is in any case clear that the proposal was simply and solely a piece of tactics.[3] Diego had noticed that the heretic preachers could show impressive poverty, and that a great deal of their success was due to the way in which their profession and their practice contrasted in this respect with that of the local Catholic

[1] See above, p. 9 and refs. quoted.

[2] Grundmann, p. 103, thinks it likely that the original suggestion was Innocent's. He points out that we have no documentary proof, and goes on: "Trotzdem darf man vermuten, dass an der Kurie zwischen dem Papst und dem Bischof von Osma die Frage der Ketzerbekämpfung besprochen worden war, und dass Innozenz entsprechende Weisungen gegeben hatte."

[3] Vaux-Cernay, cap. 3, in Migne, PL. 213, col. 549; Jord. Sax. p. 9. A similar account is given by Étienne de Bourbon, ed. Lecoy, pp. 79, 213.

clergy. Therefore he suggested that their own weapons should be used to defeat them, adding that, after all, only the poor could without hypocrisy preach the Gospel of Christ, which was to the Middle Ages pre-eminently the gospel of poverty. No one has attempted, as far as I am aware, to see more than this in the events of 1205. No justification can be found in Diego's previous history for suggesting that he had any but the normal monastic respect for poverty as a prime factor in the Christian life; he applied it here in an abnormal way for special purposes. At Montpellier it was no more than a means to an end; and a means which the assembled abbots distrusted, for if they agreed reluctantly to attempt the mad scheme, it was only on condition that the Bishop of Osma himself should give them a lead. Here, then, it must be emphasised, the element of expediency, of tactics, is met at once; example is good, but is not an end in itself. "Who can doubt", says Humbert de Romans, "that preaching of this kind is of greater effect, and is more becoming, in the mouth of a poor man than of a rich one?"[1]

Gifts followed immediately upon the establishment of the nunnery at Prouille, which St Dominic set up in the same year to house certain converted heretic women. The earliest we have is dated April 1207, when the Archbishop of Narbonne gave the church of St Martin at Limoux to Prouille.[2] This seems to upset the earlier poverty, and attempts have been made to avoid this conclusion by suggesting that the gifts were made only to the

---

[1] Humbert i. 51.—Innocent III took this view in a letter of 17 Nov. 1206, which Mandonnet (S. Dominique, p. 40) says would be the foundation-charter of the Order of Preachers were it addressed to Dominic and not to the legate. It is at once a definite papal recognition of the tactical value of poverty, and an indication that the preaching efforts were being maintained. Raoul, a little discouraged and doubtful of his instructions, especially with regard to the poverty of Montpellier, had written asking for guidance. Innocent replies: "Mandamus, quatinus viris probatis, quos ad id videris idoneos exsequendum, qui paupertatem Christi pauperis imitando, in despecto habitu et ardenti spiritu non pertimescant accedere ad despectos, in remissionem studeas injungere peccatorum, ut, ad eosdem hereticos festinantes, per exemplum operis et documentum sermonis eos, concedente Domine, sic revocent ab errore quod . . . spem per illud evangelii se gaudeant assecutos" (Migne, PL. 215, col. 1025).—But quite clearly this means little more than approval of the decision to avoid the pomp which had hitherto robbed preaching of its effect. How else explain Innocent's surprise at St Francis' desire to live in apostolical poverty in 1210 (I Celano 32–3; Leg. Maj. iii. 9; Tres Socii, 47–9) and the omission of poverty in the Bull of 1216? (See below, p. 39.)   [2] Mamachi, App. 34; Laurent 23.

nunnery, and so did not affect the friars; or, alternatively (anticipating the argument that some of the friars lived at Prouille as chaplains to the women), that these resident brothers were possessionate, the missionaries poor.[1] Two considerations destroy these theories, the second of which might otherwise prove attractive. Jordan of Saxony, commenting on the gift of Cassanel by Simon de Montfort (1214), states: "Quae vero de eisdem redditibus sibi [sc. S. Dominico et suis] possent sub-trahere, impartiebantur sororibus monasterii de Pruliano."[2] The sisters were not even the primary beneficiaries, and only received what was over. In the second place, most of the gifts in these years are made "to the brothers and sisters at Prouille", or "to brother Dominic, the brothers and sisters".[3] The number and extent of these endowments is great, but to them can be added a more significant item. We actually find Dominic engaged in the purchase of a mill and a tract of land, and exchanging one piece of land against another with Simon de Montfort: in other words, behaving as a normal estate-owner. Again, it ill becomes one who is said to have believed in utter poverty to have allowed the dispute which dragged on from 1218 to 1224 over the church at Linoux which has already been mentioned. In the end William Claret gained the day against the Abbot of St Hilary at Carcassonne, and retained the church in the interests of the nuns of Prouille.[4]

[1] O'Leary, 94, 117. Scheeben, 173, approaches very near this view.
[2] Jord. Sax. p. 13.
[3] In the following list a number of examples are collected. Between each pair of semi-colons the first figure refers to the page in *Cartulaire*, vol. i, the second to the same document in Laurent.—161, 25; 200, 26; 216, 27; 257, 32; 285, 36; 295, 37; 308, 39; 324, 42; 336, 45; 338, 46; 340, 47; 343, 48 (de Montfort); 381, 52. Land and mill-rights: 330, 44; 385, 53; 389, 54. Altaner (*Armutsgedanke*, p. 407) rightly points out that these gifts show that the idea of poverty was not fixed before 1215, but omits to add that the same is true of gifts *after* 1215. This upsets his whole description of the amount of property owned. The error becomes worse on p. 409, where he "will not lay much weight" on the fact that St Dominic is mentioned in the deeds of 1216–20, and hesitates over the possibility that the property was really given to the nuns in the first place.—But the quotation in the text shows that a few years earlier, at any rate, this was definitely not the case. Further, many of the later gifts are made direct to St Dominic or to the house at St Romanus, Toulouse: e.g. (refs. as before, but to *Cart.* vol. ii.) 48, 80; 58, 82; 60, 83; 250, 108; 112 (not in *Cart.*).
[4] Mamachi, *App.* 55–6, 82; Laurent 93, 106.—Claret had previously been left in charge of *temporalia*, as Dominic of *spiritualia*, by Diego when he went back to Spain to collect help a few months after Montpellier; this is in itself significant.

In May 1214 Foulques, bishop of Toulouse, released the lands of Fanjeaux from tithes, and in July of the next year granted a sixth of the tithes of his diocese to the missionaries to support them in their preaching. This was at the time of their appointment as official diocesan preachers, assistants of the bishop. Also in 1215, Peter Seila, son of a rich merchant of Toulouse, divided his inheritance with his brother and presented his share to Dominic, so that, as he delighted to recall in later years, it was not the Order that received him, but he who received the Order. This gift, according to Jordan, consisted of "sublimes et nobiles domos", in which they now began to live, and which constituted the first convent of the Order.[1] At this point Dominic journeyed to Rome to get Papal approval and confirmation of the work he had taken up. He found the Lateran Council in session, and discovered that in virtue of a decision it had made, Innocent would not give the required confirmation unless he first adopted one of the existing monastic rules.[2] He did, however, secure a Bull in which the Pope took under his protection Prouille, the brothers and sisters, *and their possessions, present and future*; a long and detailed list of the latter is given, and there is no mention of poverty. (This, indeed, does not occur in a Papal Bull till 1219.) On his return, Dominic assembled his followers and the meeting came to two decisions: to choose the Augustinian rule, as being wide enough and loose enough in its provisions to give them the required freedom of movement; and to abjure *immobilia*.[3]

The Pope, then, had assumed that the nascent Order was "possessionate"; the Augustinian rule assumes the ownership of corporate property; and the decision to give up *immobilia* implies that something had previously been possessed which was now abandoned. It follows as a natural consequence that there is a direct conflict between these facts and the theory which

[1] Release from tithes: *Cart.* i. 450, Laurent 62; Sixth of tithes: *Cart.* i. 515, Laurent 66; Seila's gift: *Cart.* i. 498, Laurent 69 and Jord. Sax. p. 13.
[2] Canon 13 of the Council. See Mansi, *Conciliorum nova et amplissima collectio*, xxii. col. 999, also reprinted in Laurent 74.
[3] I.e. landed property, houses, etc. Innocent's Bull in BOP. i. 1, *Cart.* i. 526, and Laurent 70.—Constantine of Orvieto (cap. 17, in Echard i. 27) says they gave up revenues as well. But he did not write till 1244–5, when a theory of greater poverty was already growing up, and is in several places suspect of tampering with his sources. See below, p. 46.

maintains that strict poverty and mendicancy were Dominic's
idea from 1205, and that he adhered firmly to them throughout.
An attempt to explain away this apparent contradiction has been
made by Lambermond and Scheeben,[1] but the attempt must
be held to have failed. It rests on two arguments. First, that
Innocent compelled St Dominic to make certain concessions as
a price of his confirmation. Of this, however, there is not the
slightest trace of evidence; and though the argument from silence
is a bad one, it must surely be obvious that Jordan, as ardent a
disciple of poverty as his master, would have been very likely
indeed to have given us some hint, had the compulsion taken
place. Second, that the adoption of the Augustinian rule and
the acceptance of revenues represented a retreat from an original
purity in the question of poverty, this retreat being solely due
to pressure from the Pope. This flies directly in the face of our
documents. The extent of the possessions already given to the
brothers by 1216 has been indicated above, while Jordan's
account says expressly: "Proposuerunt etiam et instituerunt
possessiones non habere...sed tantum redditus eis adhuc habere
complacuit."[2] It is plain that Jordan is not reporting this as an
academic decision, but as a measure designed with relation to
the existing situation, i.e. the ownership of such "possessiones".

Three considerations arise here. First, if it is to be maintained
that the restriction of property to revenues represents a real
poverty of any kind, it must be shown that a non-resident land-
lord drawing an income from his estates is in some sense less of
a capitalist than a resident owner; which does not seem possible.
Secondly, it has been suggested[3] that Dominic hoped for more
than the renunciation of *immobilia*, and only accepted the half-
measure as a concession to the uncertainty of the early friars.
But surely the earlier friars were likely to be the most enthusiastic, and the most willing to make great sacrifices of their

---

[1] Lambermond, p. 21, Scheeben, pp. 196, 309. The latter also tries to give
colour to the suggestion that poverty was now given up by saying that St
Dominic made a virtue of necessity and took over the property of the formerly
independent nunnery at Prouille. We have, however, already shown (above,
p. 38) that gifts had been by no means exclusively made to the women.
Equally unacceptable is his attempt (p. 163) to minimise the importance of
the grant of tithes by Foulques.

[2] Jord. Sax. p. 14.

[3] By Balme and Lelaidier, *Cart.* iii. 70.

personal comfort in what they felt to be a good cause? It is absurd to suggest that poverty could not be put into operation until the Order contained a large proportion of University men— the very class who wrecked Franciscan poverty.

Finally, we must inquire how serious this decision was. Its importance for us will decline when we see that gifts and acquisitions of lands went on as fast as before. This, it appears, must destroy Lacordaire's contention[1] that Dominic had accepted possessions "tout en gardant l'arrière-pensée de les abandonner un jour". If that *arrière-pensée* existed, now, if ever, was the time to carry it into effect. Yet on the dispersion which immediately followed, William Claret was again left in charge of *temporalia*, i.e. property. (Having quoted him twice, we must in honesty admit that he later found the poverty demanded of him too great, and eventually became a Cistercian, in which Order poverty was now interpreted in a lax sense.) The definitive Bull of 22 December 1216 again mentioned property. On 13 December 1217, Simon de Montfort issued an order to his seneschals of Carcassonne and Agen to protect Dominic's property as his own.[2] Dominic himself, when in Spain 1218–19, accepted endowments, and allowed the retention of those which had been received at Paris, when he visited the newly-founded convent there in the course of the latter year. Of Paris, again, John of Navarre reported in his deposition for the process of canonisation in 1233: "multae possessiones et redditus eis tunc datae fuerunt, et omnia cesserunt eis prospere." We are left in no doubt as to what he meant by the phrase "all went well". From 1217 to 1221 there was a quarrel over the interpretation of the grant of a sixth of the Toulouse diocesan tithes, which were finally surrendered in 1221 in return for the gift of Fanjeaux. In March 1219, Reginald of Orleans acquired the church of St Nicholas at Bologna, the previous church, La Mascarella, being by now too small; the saint did not upset this when he destroyed Odoric Galiciani's deed of gift. This will be mentioned later; here it is important to point out that neither it nor the decision taken at the General Chapter of 1220 prevented Dominic buying some land near

---

[1] *Vie de S. Dominique*, pp. 423–4.
[2] *Cart.* ii. 181, Laurent 96.

St Nicholas in 1221—a fairly large area, moreover, stated to be 6000 square metres.[1] So the list can be extended: the gift of St Jacques, Paris (1221); of £1090 Bolognese (1221); the arrival of the friars of Toulouse and district for the 1220 Chapter on horseback and with money in their purses.[2]

Against all this, all we have to set in the way of renunciation, either before or after 1220, is comprised by two cases where tithes were surrendered; by the abandonment of Cassanel in 1217—it had in any case been recently reconquered by Count Raymond of Toulouse; and by the retrocession of the sixth of the diocesan tithes to Foulques—which was a purely business deal, for the Order received the church of Fanjeaux, with its tithes, in return.[3]

It is now necessary to examine the already-mentioned events at Bologna, which constitute a kind of "leading case". Arriving there from Spain, by way of Paris, in the autumn of 1219,[4] St Dominic found that one Odoric Galiciani had just drawn up a deed of gift to the Order of land worth £500 Bolognese; "et fecit rescindi contractum et noluit quod haberent illas vel quasdam alias possessiones".[5] Here we have the first incontrovertible evidence of St Dominic's purpose with regard to poverty in his Order. So too we have the first mention of mendicancy—the quotation continues "sed solummodo viverent de eleemosynis et parce", and goes on to insist that if they had enough food in the house for the day, no further begging

----

[1] Spain, *Cart.* ii. 320, Mamachi, *App.* 56; Paris, *Cart.* ii. 250; Tithes and Fanjeaux, Mamachi, *App.* 53, 70, *Cart.* iii. 263, Laurent 94, 155; St Nicholas, *Cart.* ii. 257, Laurent 109; Land near St Nicholas bought from Lovello, *Cart.* iii. 406–9, Laurent 170. See Appendix I.

[2] Mamachi, *App.* 72, 74, 116, Laurent 168. The Monum. Conv. Bonon. (*Analecta* 1898, p. 609) add the picturesque detail that St Dominic sent round to all the inns of Bologna, seized the horses and sold them for the general purposes of the Order. Unfortunately the late date of the author (Borselli, d. 1497) and his inaccurate chronology do not allow much weight to be rested on his word. Further purchases in July 1220 (i.e. after the decision of the Whitsun Chapter of that year) in *Cart.* iii. 95–6 (Laurent 133–4), 173, 228, 316, 354, 413.—These are in Milan, Siena, Paris, Brescia and Florence respectively, and the last is after the *second* General Chapter (1221).

[3] Laurent 130, 132, 155, *Cart.* iii. 29, 263. To these may be added *Cart.* iii. 71 (quoted in Appendix I) and Jordan's account (p. 27) of the chapter of 1220: "ordinatum est ne possessiones vel redditus de cetero tenerent fratres nostri, sed et iis renuntiarent quos habuerant in partibus Tolosanis".

[4] Altaner, *Armutsgedanke*, 415, dates it a year later.

[5] Mamachi, *App.* 121, *Cart.* ii. 346.

was to be undertaken until the morrow. Was this a mere out-
burst on Dominic's part, or had his ideas developed recently in
the direction of a stricter way of life? The latter appears to be
without doubt the correct solution, in view of later events, and
we are entitled to regard the renunciation of revenues which
took place at the first Chapter-General (Whitsun, 1220) as the
carrying out of the new policy into legal effect.

There seem to be two possible reasons for this change of
attitude. The first is that in the past twelve months Dominic had
seen the advantages of the absolute poverty professed by the
Franciscans, and had determined to imitate it. The defenders of
this view allege that the saints had recently met at the Franciscan
"Chapter of Mats" which was the occasion of such striking
devotion on the part of the Assisans. This must at the best,
however, be characterised as exceedingly doubtful. The whole
history of the Chapter of Mats is shrouded in legend, and the
most acceptable chronology places Dominic in Spain at the time
it is said to have been celebrated.[1] Like the earlier supposed
meeting at the Lateran Council, so convincingly proved impossible by Luchaire,[2] the story flatters only to deceive. Still
we must not rule out of account the possibility of a meeting at
some other time or place (if the meeting recorded by Gerard de
Fracheto is to be accepted as historical—which remains exceedingly doubtful—then it may have occurred in Rome between
the autumn of 1216 and the spring of 1217[3]), nor must we forget
the practical certainty of contact with Franciscans everywhere.

[1] See Altaner, *Beziehungen,* 20, where this and all other possibilities of
meeting are fully discussed.
[2] Luchaire, *Innocent III et le concile du Latran,* 49–51. It is noteworthy
that Grundmann, *Relig. Bewegungen,* pp. 144–6, without referring to Luchaire, has attempted to revive the story that F. and D. met in Rome in 1215.
But his case is based solely on late and doubtful sources, buttressed only by
a questionable line of argument.—The dream of the falling Lateran supported by St Dominic belongs to the time of the same Council. It would
be pleasant to be able to assert that this story was borrowed from the Franciscans, on account of the most wonderful of Giotto's frescoes at Assisi. But
the two earliest authorities (II Celano 17; Const. Orv. 17) are of approximately the same date (1244–6) and it is impossible to decide between them.
Probability is perhaps on the side of the Franciscans; for in 1210 (the date
to which their vision refers) Innocent was approving Francis' plans in a wide
and general way, whereas in 1215 he was taking the Prior of Prouille under
his protection but deliberately refusing to confirm his Order.
[3] Altaner, *Beziehungen,* p. 18.

Alternatively, there is the chance that the sojourn at Segovia, which is slightly mysterious, was the scene of a spiritual crisis comparable with that of St Francis on Monte Alverno. Did Dominic return to his native land to debate some inner problem which was decided in the sense of greater austerity? Sabatier has given currency to this conjecture, but there is no documentary evidence to be found. Even the published archives of the Convent of the Holy Cross at Segovia show not the slightest trace.[1]

The new rule on poverty, then, must be taken as the more or less logical outcome of earlier events, and no peculiar character can definitely be ascribed to it. Franciscan influence is almost certain, but it cannot be proved to have taken the dramatic form which has been so often asserted. This view makes it a good deal easier to answer certain questions which will arise. Why, for instance, was the poverty of 1220 so imperfect, if Dominic was as insistent upon it as he has been made out to be? That it was imperfect cannot be doubted. The total extent of the evidence for renunciation of existing possessions after this date has already been indicated above, and it is necessary to emphasise that when Father Denifle wrote that a surrender of property took place in 1220–1, he was going beyond the authorities at his command.[2] Again, at that same Chapter of 1220, Dominic himself proposed[3] that the lay-brothers should look after the Order's property—which it was then engaged in renouncing! This event, like the rest of the evidence cited, is testimony at once to the sincerity of his desire for some poverty, and the partial nature of the poverty desired.

What little we know of Dominic's own actions strengthens this argument of imperfection. As an administrator, he was responsible for making purchases of land, etc. even after 1220. As a man, there are signs that he did at various times possess certain objects. We know that he had a knife and a seal, and the legend of the books that he dropped while fording a stream, refers to them as *his* books.[4] These are small details, perhaps, but

---

[1] Monum. Conv. S. Crucis Segob. in *Analecta*, 1895, p. 295 sq. Nothing is to be found here except the statement that a tradition exists of Dominic's contemplation, prayer and discipline in the crypt. Cf. Sabatier, *Vie de S. François*, pp. 251–2.   [2] ALKG. i. 182.   [3] Mamachi, *App.* 116.
[4] *Cart.* ii. 30, *Vit. Frat.* ii. cap. 4. Sister Cecilia relates (Mamachi, *App.* 259) that the saint brought back a little cypress-wood spoon from Spain for each of the nuns at St Sisto. But her account is unreliable, and, as Altaner (*Der hl. D.* 168) points out, she has just stated that there were 104 sisters! (col. 254).

surely enough to support the main argument that poverty did not mean the same thing to Dominic as it did to Francis, who would have resented even this tiny intrusion of personal ownership. The early Dominican sources never hold language comparable to that of the contemporary Minorite histories, which speak with such outright horror of the mere thought of private possession. There is, however, plenty of evidence that St Dominic was, apart from the farthest of extremes, himself definitely poor, and that he attempted to persuade his followers into a similar course. This material is well known, and needs little discussion. The main instances are Constantine's account of the dispersion (*magnas quidem sustinentes angustias paupertatis*); the story of John of Navarre and the twelve *deniers* which Dominic was so reluctant to grant him for the journey to Paris; Rudolf of Faenza's pittance[1] ("Why do you slay the brethren?" said St Dominic); the reproof administered to the same friar when as procurator he had caused over-large cells to be built—"Do you want so soon to abandon poverty and build great palaces?"; the seizure and sale of the horses of the Toulouse brethren in 1220; Dominic dying in Moneta's habit because he had none of his own; Jacques de Vitry's description of the Bologna convent in the early 1220's—"post Dominum currunt, et nudi nudum sequuntur"; while the Acta for the early years show that the Order took the idea of poverty seriously.[2]

Neither of the two extreme views can therefore be true, and some compromise is needed. One possible explanation, which covers a good deal of the ground, is that advanced by Mandonnet,[3] who sees in the years 1216–19 a trial period, during which Dominic was experimenting with a restricted poverty in order to see how it worked; finding it possible, he began to be definite in 1219. The drawbacks of this theory are obvious; it tends to misread some of the evidence during the alleged trial period, and assumes that after 1220 poverty was complete. Scheeben[4] goes further, and thinks that during these four years the Order

---

[1] An additional dish at the convent meal, which important visitors, and also, in certain circumstances, friars themselves, were allowed to present to the company.

[2] Const. Orv. c. 21; Mamachi, *App.* 115, 120, 127; *Analecta* 1898, p. 609; Echard i. 24. The *Acta* are discussed below, Chap. IX.

[3] *S. Dominique*, 68, 73.

[4] *Der hl. Dominikus*, p. 309.

gradually overcame the retreat forced upon it by Innocent in
1215, by means of "a re-establishment of the original plan".
But this is to draw deductions from what is, as has already
been shown, a pure surmise, and must remain in the realm of
fancy.

A much more likely suggestion, and one which can be adequately supported, is that Dominic's views on poverty were
indefinite. He saw in it a means to an end. All is therefore
relative, and what is right at one time and place will not be right
in different circumstances. The legend of the extreme insistence
on poverty was created shortly after his death, when for the first
time he had become a famous and saintly figure in the eyes of
the world, and under the influence of that Franciscan "complex" which has been the cause of so much confusion. This can
best be seen in actual operation by a comparison of the Life of
St Dominic written between 1235 and 1241 by Peter Ferrand
with the definitive version of Humbert de Romans (completed
1254). Humbert, like his contemporary, Bonaventura, set out
to fix discipline and liturgy for ever, and in consequence his
historical statements were coloured by the practical ideas of an
executive official. Ferrand's account provided the greater part
of the material upon which Humbert based his book. Large
sections of the two differ only in minor details, nearly always
grammatical improvements by the later and more skilful writer.
Yet Humbert omits certain passages which would have cast
doubt upon the already growing tradition of poverty. We may
compare with this the order of the Chapter-General of 1242 that
Dominic's dying words about always having preferred the conversation of a young woman to that of an old one, should be
deleted from the Legend; the saintliness of a marble statue is
beginning to replace the intense humanity, with its occasional
weakness, of the real man. Again, only two or three years later,
Constantine of Orvieto produced his biography, which was also
used by Humbert. We have already seen that his version of the
events of 1216 runs: "proposuerunt ex tunc terrenas possessiones et redditus prorsus abjicere", and this is not the only
place in which he tampered with his sources. On the evidence,
he must be accused of having done so with deliberate intent, in
order to enhance the poverty and originality of Dominic. To

support the suggestion of Franciscan influence, we may adduce, in addition to Humbert's necessary familiarity with the story of Francis' life, the close contact into which common misfortunes brought the Orders in the middle of the century, culminating in the issue of a joint encyclical by the Master-General and Minister-General in 1255.

The passage from Humbert's work which is in question runs as follows: an account is given of the gift of Cassanel by de Montfort, and it is said that Dominic had this and Fanjeaux to provide for his maintenance: so much is common to both. Ferrand continues: "de omnibus vero quae habebat beatus Dominicus, quidquid sibi suisque sociis subtrahere poterat, dominabus monasterii de Pruliano impartiri studebat."[1] We have already seen similar language, so clearly showing that complete poverty was not followed in about 1214–15, used by Jordan, from whom Ferrand had drawn the greater part of his material. Humbert, however, now omits this sentence completely; it is a justifiable conclusion that the reason was that a legend to the contrary effect had grown up. However wrong it would be to build too much conjecture on one passage, particularly as elsewhere the two accounts agree very closely, the above suggestion does supply about the only convincing reason why just this passage should have been omitted by Humbert.

Too much of the foregoing, however, has been destructive, and it is time to put forward a constructive view. What was Dominic's purpose in favouring poverty?—For it must be made clear that we have not destroyed his poverty, but merely altered the traditional emphasis.[2] The Montpellier resolution may be taken as a text, or the same idea as it is put into more compact

---

[1] Cf. Ferrand, cap. 25 (ed. Van Ortroy in *Anal. Boll.* xxx. p. 67), with Humbert, cap. 20 (Mamachi, *App.* cols. 274–5).—For another case, cf. the two accounts of the 1216 decision. Ferrand (cap. 28, p. 68) has: "Proposuerunt etiam, ne predicationis impediretur officium, se terrenas possessiones abjicere; verumtamen redditus adhuc jussum est eis quos acceperant retinere," i.e. he repeats Jordan almost verbally. Humbert (cap. 23, col. 277) writes: "Proposuerunt autem ex tunc, ne predicationis impediretur officium, a se terrenas possessiones abjicere; quod postmodum in primo capitulo generali Ordinis...affectu pariter et effectu, per constitutionem perpetuae fuit executioni mandatum".—Humbert's account is not so far from the truth as Constantine's, in that he says nothing expressly incorrect; but he deliberately omits the mention of *redditus* which is found in both Jordan and Ferrand.

[2] See Appendix II.

form by Humbert de Romans:[1] "ad praedicatorem pertinet ut
sic vivat quod non solum in verbis sed etiam in exemplis eius
glorificetur Deus", quoting Matthew v. 16, "Let your light so
shine before men". The contrast with the Minorite object, which
puts deeds *before* words, is clearly brought out in a story which
appears in Celano and the Mirror of Perfection.[2] A Dominican
doctor of theology visited Francis at Siena, and interrogated
him on Ezekiel iii. 18–20. (He mangled the text, but verse 19
says: "If thou warn the wicked, and he turn not from his
wickedness...he shall die in his iniquity; but thou hast
delivered thy soul.") Francis was reluctant to speak before so
learned a man, but under pressure expounded, saying that more
was required than mere warning: "servus Dei sic debet vita et
sanctitate in se ardere, ut luce exempli et lingua conversationis
omnes impios reprehendat. Sic, inquam, splendor vitae eius et
odor famae ipsius omnibus annuntiabit iniquitatem eorum."
The Dominican went away edified—"My brothers, the theology
of this man is like a flying eagle"—but it is not possible to
suppose that his Order as a whole ever subscribed to the
Franciscan interpretation of poverty. As a realist, St Dominic
chose a middle way, adopting neither the Franciscan extreme,
nor the possessionate character of the older Orders. His main
idea was to win the sympathy and trust of the masses to whom
he was preaching, and he used poverty strictly as a means to
obtain this. Any idea of poverty as an end or as a virtue in and
for itself alone never came within the scope of his thought.
There is therefore no need to look beyond expediency for the
origin of Dominican poverty, and to find out some historical
derivation for it, as, for instance, Scheeben does, with his constant reiteration of the influence of Peter Waldo's example.[3]

The reasonableness of the "means to an end" theory is surely

---

[1] Humbert ii. 455. In his *Vita S. Dominici* the same writer puts words
into the saint's mouth which imply both deliberate borrowing from the
heretics and the view that the main purpose of poverty is simply "ad proxi-
morum aedificationem" (Mamachi, *App.* 275). Here again he quotes "Let
your light so shine before men". Whether or not this perfectly represents
Dominic's own thought, it certainly represented the official view of the
Order at the mid-century.

[2] *Spec. Perfect.* c. 53; II Celano 103, cf. 153.

[3] Scheeben, *Der hl. Dominikus*, 142 sq. See Altaner's criticism, *Persönlichkeit*, 406.

borne out by the nature of the problem it was intended to solve. Poverty was needed in so far as it gave a "pattern of good works". When it hindered the apostolate it was given up; and it might easily be an impediment, by preventing the possession of books (which are specifically mentioned from 1205 onwards), by the immobilisation of forces in a heretic country which would not contribute to the friars' support, and so on. Humbert counts three "impedimenta fructus animarum, licet non sint contra ordinem":—mendicancy; "officia odiosa, ut sint inquisitiones"; and "nimia austeritas in consiliis et opinionibus; terrentur enim ex hoc homines in tantum ut salutem negligant".

Just as in the interests of a more immediate purpose Dominic gave up manual labour, the conventional method of monastic reform, and modified the choral services, so he subordinated poverty to preaching—or better expressed, used poverty as an adjunct to preaching.

The question has been viewed too much through Spiritual Franciscan eyes, and views have been attributed to Dominic to which he did not subscribe. A syllogistic form may make the matter quite clear. It has been argued:

> All friars believed in absolute poverty;
> Dominic was a friar, and moreover a saintly one;
> Therefore Dominic believed in absolute poverty.

But the major premiss is an arbitrary statement, unsupported by clear historical evidence for the crucial period. The assumption that a friar is a friar, no further specification being necessary, is invalid until the middle of the thirteenth century. It does not become trustworthy until we reach later years, when the original Franciscan enthusiasm had largely decayed in face of the rise of the Conventual party, the Dominicans had adopted a fuller poverty, the Franciscans had replied by borrowing the Dominican constitutions, and both were being regularly used as Papal instruments in the service of the Inquisition. The two Orders are essentially different in origin; the one naïvely enthusiastic, the other worldly in the best sense—the sense of Metternich's motto, *tout à terre, toute historique*, the statesman's virtue. It follows that the standards of one must not be used to judge the other.

[1] Humbert ii. 36.

Here another surmise is possible. Was the second Master-General, Jordan of Saxony, more insistent on poverty in Francis' sense than his more practical predecessor? It can be confidently asserted that he was of a more mystical turn of mind than the other, and that in his Generalate there had been more time for external influences to make themselves felt. The only chapters in Gerard de Fracheto's Lives of the Brethren which remind us of the Fioretti are those referring to Jordan.[1] He approved holy joy, even on one occasion to laughter; he loved animals; he gave away his own tunic more than once; like Juniper, he chose the side-streets to avoid popular acclamation. Moreover he conducted a correspondence of an almost Franciscan tenderness with Diana d' Andalo.[2] Even if many of Gerard's stories are borrowed, there still remains the query: Why attribute them to Jordan rather than Dominic? His successor in office, Raymond de Peñaforte (1238–40), was equally insistent on poverty, but in a colder and harder way, that of a strict disciplinarian, as the General Chapter Acts of his years plainly show.

Yes, it may be replied, but what does this prove? Humbert was just as insistent, and so was John the Teutonic; witness the same Chapter Acts. But with Humbert we are able to go deeper and discover his thoughts at greater length. With him poverty is again only a means to an end. He saw that disciplinary action was necessary to prevent slackness, and used strict poverty-legislation as a useful and convenient method of carrying out that action. Yet his books are full of reasoned defences of moderate relaxation. "The flesh must be fed, but vices rooted out. Therefore superfluities must not be given to the body, nor necessities refused." "It is certain that just as God created man to serve Him, so He created all things to serve man.... How then does it seem probable that He wishes His followers to lead so hard a life that they may the less abundantly be ministered to?" Of the essentials for a preacher, "the sixth is that he should temper the labour of his way".[3]

Most convincing of all, however, is Aquinas. "...perfectio non consistit essentialiter in paupertate, sed in Christi sequela

---

[1] *Vitae Fratrum*, iii. caps. 4, 13, 16, 22.
[2] See the correspondence, ed. Altaner, esp. pages 27, 36, 45, 46.
[3] Humbert i. 39, 93; ii. 455.

...paupertas enim est sicut instrumentum vel exercitium per-
veniendi ad salutem."[1] How much more reasonable is this than
extreme poverty, and yet in its less emotional way it is as attractive. How much more likely to be the view of a man like
Dominic, who, whatever he was, possessed statesmanlike qualities—shown, for instance, in his seeking continuous Bulls from
the Pope to make more certain the foundation and privileges of
his Order. The early failure of extremism, even among the
Minors, and its restriction to the Spirituals and finally to the
Fraticelli, with their ridiculous and un-Franciscan belief that
there was a positive virtue in wearing a ridiculously old and
shrunken habit, show that it never appealed to more than a
small, fanatical minority.

The view that has here been taken of St Dominic as an apostle
of "enlightened (and cultured) common-sense" withdraws most
of the sting from the possible argument that St Thomas's very
sanity leads us to appreciate him too much. Nothing Aquinas
said was inconsistent with the leading principles of St Dominic's
life. Finally, if the former could write these words in the middle
of the century, why should not Dominic have thought and acted
them less than fifty years before? Aquinas was not a relaxed
friar—the unbroken unity of the Dominican Order only
strengthens the argument. After all, moreover, it was a common
medieval quotation from Jerome: "Holy boorishness profiteth
itself alone, and howsoever it may edify the Church of God with
the excellence of its life, by so much it worketh harm if it resist
not those who would destroy her."[2]

Those who would destroy St Dominic's fame and originality
by imputing to him the views of another, may be answered in
the words[3] with which John of the Cells rebuked the Spiritual
Franciscans in the fourteenth century—"Voi fate uno vostro
idolo di questa povertà."

---

[1] *Summ. Theol.* 2a, 2ae, q. 188, art. 7.
[2] "Sancta rusticitas sibi solum prodest, et quantum aedificat ex vitae merito
ecclesiam Dei, tantum nocet si destruentibus non resistat."—*Ep. ad Pauli-
num,* Migne, PL. 22, col. 542.
[3] Quoted by V. D. Scudder, *The Franciscan Adventure,* p. 259.

CHAPTER IV

LEARNING

"ARCUS tenditur in studio, postea sagittatur in praedicatione."[1] "The bow is first bent in study, and then in preaching the arrow is let fly." Together with poverty, learning was one of the two methods—and in many respects the more novel of the two—used by the Dominican Order in carrying out its work of defending the Church against the dangers that beset it, and of extending its dominion over wider areas of the known world. The history of study in the Order dates right back to primitive times, if we accept the story that the saint took his first few companions to hear Alexander of Stavensby lecture at Toulouse.[2] Dominic himself was in any case an educated man before ever he left Spain, though it may with some show of probability be conjectured that his training had followed rather conventional lines. Palencia was not a *studium generale* of the type then beginning to spread over Europe, following the development of Paris and Bologna, but merely a Cathedral school, the germ from which a University might grow. Spain, too, was a backward land, hampered by the Moorish problem, divided into small crusading states which were forced to devote most of their energy to war with the infidel, and cut off by the barrier of the Pyrenees from the fountain of medieval theology, Paris.

There was, however, never the slightest doubt of St Dominic's intention to see that his sons were possessed of all the weapons that learning could give them in carrying out their work of evangelisation. On the dispersal of 1217 the largest contingent was sent to Paris to study, preach and found a convent.[3] The house, St Jacques, which they were given in 1218, soon acquired the dominant position which it retained for centuries. "Jacobins" became a synonym for "Dominicans" in France, though

---

[1] St Cher i. 13 col. 3.
[2] Humbert, *Vita S. D.* in Mamachi, *App.* 283.
[3] Mamachi, *App.* 115.

the modern world is more prone to connect the name with that
of the party which held its meetings in the convent during the
French Revolution. Bologna was "colonised" in the same year,
and with the entry into the Order of Reginald of Orléans, who
immediately took over the government of the house, leapt
straight into prominence, and may be reckoned the headquarters
of the friars during these early times. Reginald's power of
attracting members of the University, masters and students
alike, was only rivalled by that of Jordan of Saxony, who devoted the major part of his energies to the schools of the Lombard
plain. His letters to Diana d' Andalo show clearly enough the
success which attended his efforts.[1] In the Constitutions of 1228
a lector is as essential for a new convent as a prior;[2] the General
Chapter Acts throughout the century show continual care being
given to convent teaching,[3] the elaborate *Ordinaciones pro studio*,
which were incorporated in the Acta for 1259, being the most
striking piece of evidence. The value of the instruction was
ensured by insisting that no one should teach publicly unless he
had studied theology for four years.[4] Every convent had its
schools: a private class where the novices were given elementary
instruction, and a public course in theology for those who had
passed through this, and for the learned lawyers and artists who
joined the Order when of mature age. At these schools every
preacher received the instruction without which he was forbidden to exercise his functions, and it was by means of them
too that the Dominicans succeeded to a large extent in filling the
gap left by the failure of the bishops to carry out their duty[5] of
organising schools within their dioceses.

The importance of education and the determination to seek
it at its main sources being thus so definitely decided, it remained for the Dominicans to extend the part they were already
playing, and acquire a hold over University teaching. At Paris
this was secured as a result of the crisis of 1229, when by a
process of probable legality but doubtful wisdom, in view of the

[1] Ed. Altaner, *Die Briefe Jordans v. Sachsen*, pp. 17–18, 25, 42, etc.
[2] ALKG. i. 221.
[3] See cases quoted in this chapter, and below, Chap. ix.
[4] ALKG. i. 223.
[5] Laid upon them by canon xi of the Lateran Council, 1215.—Mansi, xxii.
col. 998.

hostility of the University authorities (who disliked being forcibly reminded, especially by upstarts, of their legal dependence upon the chancellor of the bishop), the chair of St Jacques was set up. During the period when the greater part of the University had left Paris, a friendly-disposed master, John of St Giles, transferred his lectures to the Preachers' convent and held them there long enough for friar Roland of Cremona to perform his year's course as a bachelor under him, and thus qualify for the magistrature. This done, John returned whence he came, leaving the Dominican school firmly established. Hugh de St Cher "incepted" as bachelor under Roland, and the line of masters was started.[1] In 1229, too, the new University of Toulouse, designed by the Pope to combat heresy, was handed over largely into Dominican charge. In the next year a start was made at Oxford, but this was not at once as successful from the administrative as from the legal point of view. The General Chapter of 1246 erected the Oxford school into a *studium generale* for the Order, along with others in France, Lombardy and Germany. Oxford resisted, however, and matters remained in an uncertain state for the next fifteen years. It was not till one of the greatest disciplinarian Chapters-General, that of Barcelona in 1261, took strong action, that Oxford was forced to capitulate, to accept the *studium* which it wished to avoid, and to admit the foreign students to whose burdensome presence it had hitherto successfully objected. The lesson that resistance to lawful authority is always foolish was driven home by the removal of the Oxford lector to Cologne and the imposition of penances all round.[2]

---

[1] See the full list, compiled from de Salagnac and Bernard Gui, in ALKG. ii. 203 sq.

[2] Since Dr Coulton mentioned my name in connexion with this question (*Camb. Hist. Journal*, v, p. 23 (1935)), I have unfortunately been unable to find sufficient evidence to clear the matter up. Dr Coulton, writing on "Nationalism in the M.A.," quotes the case, and comments: "This incident seems to bear equal testimony to English nationalism and continental disapproval." I am in a position to add only the two following remarks: (1) Oxford's refusal may well have been due to nationalism; but it may also have been due to the convent's unwillingness to bear the cost of maintaining students from outside, whether they belonged to other nations or not. We have ample proof that this burden would be very great: e.g. it was this cause which prompted the General Chapter to appeal for voluntary aid to the Paris convent, which found itself periodically in financial difficulties, in 1246,1261,

Between these two extremes, however, the convent school and the University, what opportunities of study were open to the Friar Preacher? By the time the full organisation of education had been standardised—that is to say, by the early fourteenth century—a long and elaborate programme had been drawn up.[1] He would begin with the study of arts, probably in his own or a neighbouring convent. For this purpose the houses were arranged in groups of three or four, and the school moved from one to the other, thus equalising the expense which the housing and feeding of a body of external students implied. Next came the *studium naturalium*; here the friar would extend his knowledge of natural philosophy, with special reference to Aristotle. Here again there was a *combinacio* of convents, each having the school in turn.

These two preliminary stages passed, the main business of theology was taken up. For this, as we have seen, each house made provision, and the lector held courses on the Sentences of Peter Lombard or on Aquinas, who was beginning to oust Lombard from his position by the turn of the century. Theological learning might be carried further either at a *studium bibliae et sententiarum*, which was concerned chiefly with textual criticism and scientific exegesis, or at one of the two *studia sollemnia* which served each province. There theology was taught by the scholastic method, and the application of philosophy to it made clear. Almost certainly at this stage, and very likely at an earlier one as well, there intervened a term of service as lector in a convent, and the control of its theological school. Finally, a picked number of scholars might reach a *studium generale*, of which there were eventually eight;[2] these served the whole Order, each province contributing its quota of students.

1283, 1289. (2) In a newly-founded Order, still preserving its original enthusiasm, the refusal to listen to the English complaint may have been due to a simple desire for administrative efficiency, and perhaps even also to a conscious internationalism, as well as pure "continental disapproval"; but this must remain at present pure conjecture.

[1] The following account is drawn from Douais, *Organisation des Études*, pp. 59–134.

[2] Paris, Montpellier, Cologne, Bologna, Naples, Oxford, Barcelona and Cahors; Toulouse may also have been among the number.—Since *studium generale* is also the medieval word for University, it must always be borne in mind that there is no necessary connexion between an *s. g.* in this sense and

Even this very brief sketch, however, gives a false impression of the education of the average friar; it has been included merely to show how varied were the possibilities and how carefully and intensively the scheme was worked out in its final form. Only a very limited number went through the whole course. By no means all were worthy of such an extended training, lasting probably fifteen years (three at each of the schools in turn), a considerable slice out of the active life of medieval man: and an evangelical, not a learned, activity was after all the purpose which the Dominican Order set clearly before itself. A rigid process of selection was enforced, by means of which only chosen men passed beyond the first three years' study of theology; after this the prior-provincial in the first place, and then the Master-General (under whose direct care all university students were placed)[1] exercised a strict control. Such men as gave promise of intellectual ability would be allowed to pass on to the *studium sollemne*, which was pre-eminently the training-ground for the teaching staff of the next generation. As the provision for one lector to each convent shows, the extent of this staff was comparatively wide, and was constantly increasing as new foundations were made; the expected attendance at a *studium sollemne* may be put in the neighbourhood of thirty. A further process of selection operated before admission to a *studium generale* was secured and the way laid open to a career of learned distinction. By the end of the thirteenth century the restriction on the numbers of those who reached the pinnacle, the Master's degree in theology at Paris, had made it possible for them to form a small and jealous aristocracy of learning within the Order.

But for most, the two conventual schools sufficed. There the essential knowledge of theology was acquired, which qualified for the main business of a friar's life. The training given here was directed chiefly towards edification, and within the three years which the course lasted a friar could learn ample for the needs of the simple village audiences he would for the most part be addressing; ample enough, too, it may be added, for his

in the restricted Dominican sense. The O. P. could clearly not create an *s. g.* in the sense of "University". In point of fact, however, all the places mentioned either were already Universities, or secured a University later, except Barcelona.

[1] E.g. *Acta* 1264, 1276, 1277.

learning to appear overwhelming in comparison with that of
most parish priests. It was thus unnecessary for the average
"limitour" to possess an extensive knowledge of the application of philosphy and reason to belief which that light of his
Order, St Thomas Aquinas, was engaged in making. For the
first half-century after the Lateran Council, moreover, the
average friar lacked even that preliminary study of philosophy
which has been described above as preceding the theological
course. Such study was only allowed in 1259,[1] as a result of an
evolution in the intellectual history of the Order which mirrors
that of the whole thirteenth century. It is upon the battle which
raged around the permission to study secular as well as divine
letters that the main interest of the history of learning in this
period rests.

"Arcus tenditur in studio. . . ." But what guarantee was there
that the bow, having been drawn in study, would then be used
to shoot the arrow of preaching into the hearts of the peoples of
Europe? Did not just these extended opportunities of study
leave the way open for the friar of literary, philosophical, or
scientific turn of mind to spend his whole time in the University
lecture-room or in the library, to the neglect of the purpose to
which all this was ostensibly directed? Within a comparatively
short time from its foundation, the Dominican Order included
an ever-growing class of men who were drawn to study for its
own sake, and not, or only to a very much smaller extent, for
the sake of the use to which it could be put in spreading the
Gospel and combating error. This was no new problem for
the Middle Ages, but it produced a very serious position. The
dangers of learning were obvious in a Church which, though it
had not yet reached the conservatism of the Trent and Vatican
decrees, yet regarded dogma as fixed, and any divergence from
accepted views as heresy. The controversies that convulsed the
Church in the East for the first post-apostolic centuries had
provided a warning which Rome and the West had taken to
heart. Subsequent events had only driven home the lesson. Too
much learning had always tended to make mad the best brains
of the Church. Some, like John Scotus Erigena, and, in more
recent times, Joachim of Fiore, had escaped the worst censures

[1] *Acta* 1259.

by their comparative obscurity; others, like Berengar of Tours
and Abelard, suffered because of their too-questioning minds.
When St Dominic set out to create an Order which should be
composed of educated men, he was, consciously or not, laying
his followers open to the temptations of learning: namely, that
it would eventually become a pursuit which absorbed too much
of their time, and that it might lead their thought to range too
freely. In so far as they fell victims to the first temptation, they
were false to their original purpose. As far as the second is concerned, the rigid adherence to orthodoxy, which was a permanent
characteristic of the Order, saved it from disaster, while its
leading thinker was of so great an intellectual distinction, and so
accurately embodied the best tendencies of the time, that his
views were before long accepted by the Catholic hierarchy
itself.

The attraction by deliberate design of the new legal and University class made the problem particularly acute. The Order
was forced to attempt a practical impossibility—to insist on
learning, and yet to insist equally that it should not be used to
criticise dogma or to occupy so much time that preaching suffered, while it was all the time intentionally filling its ranks with
just the men to whom speculation and the life of study most
appealed. Francis' vain and equally impossible command that
the instructed should cast away the whole of their past life and
become "fools for the Gospel's sake" is in many ways a more
defensible position, which possessed the added advantage that
the Minorites counted, in early days at least, a considerable
number of members who were prepared to construe the expression literally. Had the ruling party among the Franciscans
desired to maintain this part of their Father's teaching, it might
not have been beyond their power to do so. As it was, they,
along with the Preachers, attempted to serve two masters. And
since the lesser was the more immediately attractive and provided the better temporal rewards, disciplinarians had continually to take action to secure that the greater received anything
but lip-service.

Humbert de Romans puts the dangers very clearly. Under the
rubric "Of the evils of study without virtue" he explains that
this kind of learning not only generates evils, but by abuse is

itself turned into evil. He quotes Bernard's condemnation: "Some wish to know in order that they may know, and this is curiosity; some that they may be known, and this is vanity; some that they may be enriched, and this is covetousness." Many have grown old in study and yet have done no good thing, for study has corrupted them.[1] In an immediately preceding passage he goes into the errors which much learning may directly create. Yet in spite of this clear vision of the perils of his action, Humbert as much as any attempted to harness the pure Renaissance zeal for knowledge. Almost as much as the Italian Quattrocento, this period was searching for the Unknown God, and many thought to find him within the covers of a book. Students sometimes came many miles under appalling conditions of travel, and without means of support apart from begging or the possible profits of tavern-singing, and, arrived in Paris or Bologna, applied themselves to their work with a feverish intensity. But satisfaction often failed, and some turned to religion as a possible alternative. The early chapters of the *Vitae Fratrum* show this very clearly: Jordan rising at midnight for meditation in Church, Moneta going willingly-unwillingly to hear Reginald's sermon, because he knew that if he heard it he would be so moved that he would join the Order, and was not quite certain that he really wanted to do so; Humbert himself passing hours in meditation and finally forming a compact with his master St Cher that both should become friars.[2]

Much could be done with material like this, and much was done, within what may be called the specifically religious territory. Roger Bacon was probably justified in condemning the Bibles of his day,[3] but by the time he wrote (*c.* 1268) they were bad more from a failure of critical ability on the part of their correctors than from want of effort, and the greatest part of the work had been done by Dominicans. The revision of the text produced by the Paris theologians about 1230–6 had proved inadequate, and a *correctorium*, or list of improvements, was drawn up by the Dominicans of Sens. This in turn failed to bring satisfaction, so Hugh de St Cher undertook a further

---

[1] Humbert i. 444.
[2] *Vit. Frat.* iii. cap. 2; iv. cap. 9.
[3] E.g. *op. tert.* ed. Brewer i. 94.

revision, which was made the standard for the Order in 1256.[1] General Chapters are continually instructing priors to see that their convents possess copies of the latest editions both of the Scriptures and of the Office. This was by no means the full extent of the effort expended upon the Biblical text: the first useful concordance was made by English Dominicans,[2] while Hugh's great seven-volume commentary has already been quoted on several occasions. Languages, too, provided an opportunity for some to use their talents in the service of the Church. The Chapter-Provincial of Toulouse in 1250[3] ordained that eight friars should be chosen to learn Arabic, with a view to using their knowledge in the mission-field. Among them was Raymond Martini, who not only mastered Arabic, but also Hebrew and other Oriental languages, and wrote two of the most widely used missionary handbooks.[4] This is not the place to discuss the literature of preaching, because it will receive special treatment later,[5] but the extent of it may be pointed to as evidence of a very great activity.

All this and more, however, did not provide a sufficient outlet, and strong action had often to be taken to prevent unnecessary expenditure of time in the libraries, and the consequent dissemination of error. "Diligens est adhibenda cautela," is the warning in the Constitutions of 1228, "...in libris gentilium et philosophorum non studeant, etsi ad horam inspiciunt. Seculares sciencias non addiscant.... Sed tantum libros theologicos tam iuvenes quam alii legant."[6] Yet as early as 1236 no brother

---

[1] This was still a long way from perfect, however. St Cher's main object was to secure a good working text for preaching purposes, not to produce a scientifically edited result. Denifle (*Die Handschriften der Bibel-Correctorien des xiii. Jhdts.* in ALKG. iv. 295) thinks Bacon's comment ("Eorum correctio est pessima corruptio et destructio textus Dei, et longe minus malum est et sine comparatione uti Exemplari Parisiensi non correcto, quam correctione eorum vel aliqua alia") was not too hard a judgment.—On the whole question, see Denifle, op. cit. and Hastings, *Dict. of the Bible*, s.v. *Vulgate.*

[2] John of Darlington, Richard of Stavensby and Hugh of Croydon, about 1250. This was an improvement upon one made by a committee under St Cher's presidency about 1230.—Cf. Echard i. 203–9.

[3] Altaner, *Missionen*, p. 92.—On Raymond Martini, see id. p. 95.

[4] *Explanatio simboli Apostolorum*, and *Pugio fidei adversus Mauros et Judaeos*, the latter deriving largely from Aquinas' *Summa contra Gentiles.*

[5] Below, Chap. v.

[6] ALKG. i. 222.

is to read into the prophets or psalms "alium sensum litteralem
nisi quem sancti approbant et confirmant".[1] Seven years later
the prohibition was reinforced by reference to the constitutions and the added warning given: "And they shall not make
curious writings" (scripta curiosa). The same difficulty can be
traced right through the Acta—there are nine similar admonitions[2] before the end of the century. A censorship was set up in
1254, an example which the Franciscans followed at the end of
two years; both may probably be attributed to the "Everlasting
Gospel" controversy then raging. In 1255 the Master-General
complained in his annual encyclical letter[3] that the study of
languages was being unduly neglected, and attributed this,
among other things, to the prevalence of an excessive philosophical curiosity. The same writer condemns disputations in
another place[4] for a similar reason. Useless subjects are chosen,
too great ostentation is shown in the conduct of the disputants
and "there are some (aliqui) who are childishly more intent upon
winning in the disputation than upon discovering the truth".
How far afield some of the brother's interests went appears from
the legislation against alchemy (1273, 1287, 1289), whilst even
medicine is restricted. Internal patients only are permitted in
1251 (one more proof that the monasteries were not the hospitals,
as they were not the schools, of the Middle Ages), while in 1293
no one who was not already a practitioner on taking the habit is
to study medicine or in any way concern himself with it.[5]

Yet in spite of Aquinas, who was capable of reconciling
religion and philosophy, and harnessing the latter in the service
of the former, it was a hopeless task to try to enforce these

---

[1] Acta 1236.
[2] This word may be understood in its normal English meaning; but
legally an admonitio, which could be issued by any Chapter-General, is to be
distinguished from a constitutio, which required the consent of three successive Chapters before having the force of law.—Acta 1243, 1244, 1246, 1271,
1274, 1277, 1278, 1280, 1283.
[3] Litt. Encyc. p. 8.
[4] Humbert i. 464.
[5] Cf. Finke, Dominikanerbriefe, for cases of alchemy (p. 150) and medicine
(p. 160—this is after the prohibition of 1293). On medicine, see further a
story in de Bourbon's Anecdotes, p. 349. In a footnote on the next page,
Lecoy de la Marche illustrates the conflict between secular and spiritual
medicine by a quotation from de Vitry: "Dominus ait: Vigilate; medicus ait:
Dormite. Dominus dicit: Jejunate; medicus ait: Comedite," etc.

regulations. "The good of man consists in the knowledge of truth; yet the highest good does not consist in the knowledge of any truth, but in the imperfect knowledge of the highest truth." All knowledge must be related to its due end, the knowledge of God, in which is the greatest felicity.[1] But the writer's existence was the chief criticism of the writing. He it was who, following the lead of his master, Albertus Magnus, fought in the van of the "philosophers", and secured for the new Aristotle a place in religious teaching. The new learning was in the air of the thirteenth century, and the two great doctors had innumerable followers, whose devotion to this fresh interest the Chapters-General attempted to suppress. Time and a changing world were against them, however. Arts were being studied openly in Southern France in 1241[2]—in spite of its Dominican bias, the new University of Toulouse had all along been more notable for its philosophical than for its theological teaching[3]—and by 1259 the "modernist" movement had become strong enough to compel the legalisation of arts. The new regulations for study drawn up in that year were prepared by a committee of five Dominican masters of theology of Paris, led by Thomas Aquinas himself. We may legitimately suppose that a moderate party of non-Aristotelians, prominent among them the Master-General, Humbert, had by this time become convinced that a compromise with the forces of progress was inevitable, given adequate safeguards against abuse of the freedom of learning. "Laxandae sunt habenae circa studium huiusmodi," writes Humbert,[4] discussing secular philosophy, but goes on to lay down severe restrictions upon it. Some friars are quite unfitted to read it, others only to a limited extent; "but there are certain men from whose great aptitude for such things great profit and fruits of Holy Scripture may be expected." The first should not be allowed to touch it, the second only with discretion, but the last-named must be allowed freedom. Philosophy is good and evil mixed, and only those who can with certainty distinguish the one from the other should be allowed to concern themselves

---

[1] *Summa Theol.* 2a, 2ae, Q. 167, art. 1.
[2] Walz, p. 125.
[3] Denifle, *Universitäten des Mittelalters*, i. 336.
[4] Humbert i. 435.

with it. Its value is limited: it assists in understanding the Scriptures, in defending and corroborating the faith, but the chief purpose of studying it is to learn to despise it. "For many who do not know what the philosophers have written, think them greater than they really are; and when they do know, they hold them as of no value in comparison with theology."

Unfortunately the matter was not quite so easy as that; before long the Chapters-General are complaining again, in a similar sense; they are forced to demand that those reading arts shall at least be first instructed in the elements of theology.[1] By 1300 there were fifteen hundred Dominicans lecturing in the Universities and convents, only half of whom were teaching theology, and it has been suggested that the Order's total literary output between 1220 and 1350 was equal to that of the whole Church between Patristic times and the beginning of the thirteenth century.[2]

The real roots of the conflict, however, go deeper than any question of the origin or purpose of the Dominican Order, deeper than a prejudice of the Chapters-General against secular studies, spread wider than the Order itself, and draw their strength from the battle between the new and the old theology. The whole of Western Christendom witnessed the struggle, and was, like the Dominican Order, nearly split by it. It was not until the end of the thirteenth century that the Preachers fully accepted the teaching of Aquinas, not until the fourteenth that the Church as a whole followed their lead, set him among the company of saints fifty years after his death (1323; died 1274) and made of him the very canon of orthodoxy.

Early medieval theology was built upon the works of St Augustine. These in their turn owed much to Platonic conceptions, never clearly separated the domains of faith and reason, tended strongly towards mysticism, and believed in the direct illumination of the human spirit by the divine. Augustine's own "Credo ut intelligam" represented its attitude to the more difficult questions of dogma, and it was far more concerned with speculation upon the nature of God and his relations to man than upon reconciling practical knowledge with faith by the

[1] *Acta* 1283.
[2] Mandonnet, *S. Dominique*, pp. 114, 122.

exercise of a rational process. It accepted Jerome's adaptation
of the Scriptural injunction to "shave the captive maid and
pare her nails", and followed him in interpreting the text as a
reference to secular learning.[1] The greatest concession it was
prepared to make to the wisdom of this world is expressed in
Augustine's *De doctrina christiana*: "Such things as those who
are called philosophers, and especially the Platonists, may say,
which chance to be true and in agreement with our faith, not
only need not be feared, but may be taken from them as from
illegal ownership, and claimed for our own use," continuing
with the favourite simile of the spoiling of the Egyptians.[2] In
this strain speak all the medieval theologians down to the re-
introduction of Aristotelianism in the thirteenth century. As
we approach the time with which we are concerned, we find the
humanist John of Salisbury asserting that the main duty of
philosophy is to love God; the sacred page is queen over all
others:

Hanc caput agnoscit philosophia suum;[3]

while the new Franciscan mystical school of Bonaventura speaks
for the living nature of the tradition.

By far the greatest number of the leaders of the Dominicans
continued supporters of this Augustinianism they had been
taught in youth. Hugh de St Cher begins his Bible-commentary
at once by an attack on secular philosophy and its methods.
"We read that there have been many whose sole care was to
investigate the measure and order of events, neglecting to inquire why they occurred, being content with the scantiest and
vilest nourishment, whence they called themselves philosophers.
But by us they are more rightly called vain and curious."[4] He
proceeds then to talk of eliminating the errors of Plato and
Aristotle,[5] and a few pages further on remarks that the descent
of Abraham into Egypt "signifies the descent of a cleric to
secular wisdom, a descent which ought to be reputed a pilgrimage, so that he comes back quickly".[6] Later still, spoiling

---

[1] *Ep.* 66, in Migne, PL. 22, col. 644.—See Deuteronomy xxi. 12.
[2] *De doct. christ.* lib. ii. cap. 40, in Migne, PL. 34, col. 63.
[3] *Entheticus*, i. 444.—Migne, PL. 199, col. 974.
[4] St Cher i. *Prologue to Genesis*, col. 1 (this page is not numbered in the
edition published at Venice in 1600).
[5] Id. col. 4.　　　　　　　　　[6] Id. i. 17 col. 4.

the Egyptians is defined in exactly the same terms as those used by St Augustine.[1] We have already noticed Humbert de Romans finding it difficult to say anything definitely good about philosophy except the additional support it lends to faith; his statement that the best thing about the study of it is that only so can we understand and escape from the dangers of it, is paralleled exactly in Étienne de Bourbon, the famous preacher-general.[2] The gift of preaching is really the gift of God and study is only necessary in so far as it ensures that preaching shall be done *laudabiliter*;[3] the gift may equally well be granted to the unlearned.[4]

I remember the place and the time and the person, when Jordan of blessed memory, the second master of the Order of Preachers, a most strenuous preacher, had received into the Order at one time in Paris, sixty youths of small education (*parvae litteraturae*), so that many of them, as I heard, with much repetition could scarcely read one lection at Matins. Being severely accused about this, it is said, by the brothers at the Chapter-general, he replied in the Holy Spirit, 'Take heed that ye despise not one of these little ones; I tell you that you will see many, indeed nearly all of them, glorious preachers, through whom the Lord will work for the salvation of souls more than through many more brilliant and more educated men.' Which to speak truly, we have seen and do see to this present day.

The two things most feared were philosophical *subtilitates* and the dreadful dangers of all kinds that beset those attending the schools.

For the philosophers tore themselves to pieces (*se evisceraverunt*) to weave this web, and yet they catch nothing but flies, that is, the simple and foolish, whom they deceive with the perplexities of their words.[5]

Humbert de Romans pours scorn upon the *involutio verborum* to which teachers are prone, and says that it is reprehensible when anyone in expounding Scripture does not follow the interpretation of the Saints, but rather his own will.[6] The dangers attendant upon a University life are emphasised by the same

---

[1] Id. i. 78 col. 1.
[2] *Anecdotes*, pp. 276–7.
[3] Humbert ii. 394.
[4] Cantimpré ii. xix. 2.
[5] St Cher vii. 190 col. 4.
[6] Humbert i. 457.

writer in the *De modo prompte cudendi sermones*, where he gives notes for a sermon suitable for delivery to students.[1]

Although knowledge is good in itself, and of no small value to religious, yet the study of those who spend their time in the schools can more often be reprehensible, and may be turned into baseness for many reasons; for instance, through an appetite for too great a knowledge, through which the whole world is subverted, like Adam and Eve.... It is not fitting for a religious man to study such things as lead him to spend his time on secular business, like the Civil Law, or on the care of the flesh, like medicine, or on the delusion of the intellect through things which are useless or nearly so, like the philosophical sciences, but it is becoming in him to study the wisdom of salvation...[waste of time and bad company at the schools]... *Item*, by the abuse of learning, as happens in the case of those who on their return from the schools are proud of their learning, or disturb holy simplicity....

Item, he is a deceiver who pretends to hear God and does not hear him, like many religious, who say they are hearing theology,[2] when they are really hearing the decretals.[3]

The Acta for 1259 lay it down that all friars who remain overlong at the schools shall be severely punished. Our chain of evidence may appropriately end with a scriptural quotation. Both Humbert and Hugh quote Ecclesiastes i. 18 in this connexion: "For in much wisdom is much grief: and he that increaseth knowledge increaseth sorrow."[4]

Such, then, are the views of most of the prominent members of the Order in the middle of the thirteenth century; they typify the views of the countless provincial priors and elected "diffinitors" who attempted year by year as they met at the General Chapters to stem the advance of the suspected "modern" theology. This new body of teaching was created, and really won its battle, during thirty years of intense activity on the part of Albertus Magnus and St Thomas Aquinas, between 1245 and 1274. If it had to wait longer for final and complete recognition, all the important works had been written within that period, the

---

[1] *De modo cudendi*, i. cap. 28, in *Bib. Max. Pat.* xxv. 469.—He repeats the same kind of argument in cap. 65 "Ad Scholares in Logica," id. p. 488.

[2] I.e. attending lectures on it.

[3] St Cher iii. 9 col. 4.

[4] St Cher v. 41 col. 1; Humbert in *Bib. Max. Pat.* xxv. 469.

crucial debate with the Averroist Siger de Brabant[1] had taken place, and so large a number of adherents had been won that acceptance by the Church could only be a matter of time.

The new theology was based upon the use of Aristotle. The works of the Stagirite had come into Western Europe in three sections. Some had been put into Latin by Boëthius and others not long after the fall of Rome, and had been known and used since then. Further translations were made during the twelfth century, and, as the "New Logic", played a great part in the shaping of scholasticism. Finally, about the end of the same century, the Physics and Metaphysics, and, in time, all the remaining books of Aristotle, became known in Western Europe, and brought with them a much fiercer quarrel than that which had raged round the universals. Already in 1215 a papal legate, Robert de Courçon, had condemned these new translations, along with their heretical commentators, Averroes and Avicenna, but the struggle did not reach its height until the middle of the century, when Albertus Magnus (*nostra intentio est omnes dictas partes* [sc. *physicam, metaphysicam et mathematicam*] *facere Latinis intelligibiles*)[2] and his pupil, Aquinas, took up arms in defence of Greek learning. These two accepted Aristotle's dependence upon reason and the experimental method, and applying their criteria to theology, found themselves bound to reject large parts of the Augustinian system. In so doing they were not becoming unfaithful to the Catholic Church, nor were they attempting to upset the fundamentals of belief, but merely justifying what they did believe by the use of rational processes. It is difficult to-day to realise that the works of Aquinas can ever have appeared radical, but at the time his methods were revolutionary, shocked the conservatives in the Church, and represented the incursion of the secular sciences into the sacred preserve of theology.

In his commentary on Boëthius' *De trinitate*, Aquinas puts the position clearly. Philosophers who follow the order of natural conceptions put a knowledge of created things before a

---

[1] On Siger, see Mandonnet, *Siger de Brabant et l'averroisme latin*, 2nd ed. Louvain 1911.—My debt to this great work will be apparent in the pages immediately following.—On the discovery of a large number of previously unknown writings of Siger, see Grabmann, *Neu-aufgefundene Werke des S. von B.* in *Sitzungsberichte d. bay. Akad. d. Wissenschaften*, 1924.

[2] *Physicorum*, Lib. I, tract. i. c. 1.

knowledge of things divine; theologians, on the other hand, treat of the Creator before considering the created.[1] He then comes to close quarters with the problem by inquiring into the main Augustinian tenet: "Utrum mens humana ad cognitionem veritatis nova illustratione divinae lucis indigeat." After discussion, he comes to the conclusion that there are large areas of truth which the human intellect alone, aided merely by *divina operatio*, not by the Augustinian *illustratio* or revelation, is capable of understanding.

Sic igitur sunt quaedam intelligibiles veritates, ad quae se extendit efficacia intellectus agentis, sicut principia quae naturaliter homo cognoscit, et ea quae ab his deducuntur, et ad haec cognoscenda non requiritur nova lex intelligibilis, sed sufficit lumen naturaliter inditum.[2]

Both here and later, however, he expressly limits this area of truth; it does not include matters of faith. If natural reason were capable of proving the faith, then the merit of faith would disappear, for assent would not be voluntary, but compulsory, since what can be proved must be believed.[3] In a later division of the subject he extends this position, and asks whether philosophical reasoning may be used in matters of faith, which pertains to God. The answer is "Yes". Although natural reason cannot prove the grounds of belief, yet it is impossible that faith and reason should contradict one another, else God, who gave us both, must somewhere be teaching us untruth. If philosophy appears to contradict faith, then it is not true philosophy, but the abuse of it. He concludes, therefore, that the main uses of philosophy are

Ad demonstrandum ea quae sunt preambula fidei, quae necessaria sunt in fidei sciencia, ut ea quae naturalibus rationibus de Deo probantur, ut Deum esse, Deum esse unum, etc.,

and

Ad notificandum per aliquas similitudines ea quae sunt fidei.[4]

Novel as this is in some respects, it does not perhaps sound so

---

[1] *In Boëth. de trin.* Introd.—On the whole question of Aquinas' attitude to secular philosophy, cf. Grabmann, *Die Bewertung der Profanen Studien bei T. v. A.* in *Philos. Jahrbuch*, Bd. 37 (1924), pp. 311–328.
[2] *In Boëth. de trin.* Q. 1, art. 1.
[3] Id. Q. 2, art. 1.
[4] Id. Q. 2, art. 3. The same views as those summarised in the text may also be found in the *Summa contra Gentiles*, Lib. i. caps. 3, 7 and 8.

much when expressed carefully in this way as it would be in practice. Possibly the strictly rationalistic method of the Summa Theologiae constituted quite as radical a condemnation, from the conservatives' point of view, of the new methods, as did this direct statement of principles. But sharply as Aquinas distinguished the realms of reason and belief, philosophy and theology, natural and supernatural, he remained in the highest degree a theologian. In its broadest sense the earlier idea that philosophy aids theology is still true for him; he is revolutionary in the extent to which he is prepared to accept that help, and in his interest in philosophy in and for itself. The search for truth led him to cast his net as wide as possible to secure all possible assistance in prosecuting his inquiries.

The conflict between old and new can be illustrated further. In so far as St Thomas was a philosopher, he was dangerously near being classed with the heretical Siger de Brabant and Boëthius of Dacia, who were teaching at the same time, and who used their Aristotle to such an extent that they actually attacked the orthodox faith. Within the specifically Aristotelian territory, Aquinas and Siger went a very long way together, completely though they disagreed upon final results. This put the whole of the new movement into the most acute danger, and made it possible for its enemies to lump it together with obviously heretical teachings in a general condemnation, and so identify the two that both would be relegated to a limbo outside the Church. For Siger was the chief representative of the school of Averroes, the twelfth century Spanish commentator of Aristotle, whose teaching laid emphasis upon the points in which Greek thought conflicted with Latin faith. Right from the time of de Courçon's condemnation of 1215, and even before, it was Averroes rather than Aristotle that Rome had feared; the latter was welcomed, if only he could be purged of certain heretical elements,[1] and was in fact taught and read to a very considerable extent both in Paris and outside, despite the ban.

Albert combated Siger de Brabant directly (so far as we know) he began teaching in Paris, by writing the "De unitate intellectus contra Averroem" (1256), and twelve years later Aquinas re-

[1] Various attempts were made to "edit" him. See, for instance, Mandonnet, *Siger de Brabant*, p. 20 sq.

turned to his chair at Paris (a very unusual occurrence) for the express purpose of holding debates with him and exposing his errors. All was in vain, however; the opposition was too convinced of the rightness of its own position and too distrustful of the powers of the unaided human intellect to take heed of nice distinctions, and when the storm broke in 1270 it opened the campaign with an attempt to condemn both Averroists and Aristotelians alike. The Franciscan, John Peckham, and his Order were in the front rank of the opposition, and they made the first moves.[1] Étienne Tempier, Bishop of Paris, gave vent to the dispute by publicly condemning fifteen philosophical propositions in the same year. Seven years later he extended his condemnation to 219 propositions, nine of which did not come from Siger at all, but from the works of Aquinas.

There is no necessity to follow the conflict in detail, but its direct application to the Dominican Order is of interest. One of the strongest of Tempier's supporters on the second occasion was Robert Kilwardby, previously Dominican prior-provincial of England, and now Archbishop of Canterbury. So violent was his championship of the older ways that the Chapter-General, for all its still-lingering distrust of philosophical novelties, was forced at its next meeting to send a special commission across the Channel to inquire into his attitude,[2] and reproved the detractors of Aquinas in 1278, 1279 and 1286. Many years passed before the matter settled itself in a new generation— Peckham, for instance, on succeeding to the Archbishopric of Canterbury (1279–93) was particularly active—but as far as the Black Friars are concerned, the first step towards reconciliation was taken in the Chapter of 1286, when the teaching of Aquinas was accepted in full. But the "Sentences" of Peter Lombard were still the ordinary book read by the convent lectors, and it

---

[1] Evidence in Mandonnet, *op. cit.* p. 100. Opposition from the O.F.M. was natural, in view of the extreme contradiction between Bonaventura's mysticism and Aquinas' rationalism. Peckham even wrote "...cum doctrina unius ordinis sit tota pene contraria doctrinae alterius, exceptis fidei fundamentis". (Quoted, Mandonnet, *Siger*, p. 102.) This dogmatic disagreement lasted long: cf. the opposing stands taken up by the two Orders on the question of the Immaculate Conception of the B.V.M. in the fourteenth century. The O.F.M. supported the popular (and eventually victorious) party which affirmed it, the O.P. the scientific party which denied it.

[2] *Acta* 1278.

is not till 1309 that we find them commanded to teach in accordance with St Thomas's views. By this time disagreement was slowly fading, and as was noticed earlier, the canonisation of Aquinas in 1323 marks the end of serious opposition.

So far we have kept strictly to the main lines of development in treating the question of study, but there is also a certain amount of evidence to hand for the existence of a minority who had quite different grounds for dissenting from the emphasis on study in general and Aristotelian philosophy in particular. A brief discussion of this will also present an opportunity to indicate the difference between the main interests of the Dominican Order in the thirteenth and in the fourteenth centuries. By about 1300 the primitive enthusiasm for preaching and conversion had died down, the decay of discipline was already obvious,[1] and the best minds of the Order are found devoting their attention mainly to mysticism. St Catherine of Siena, Eckhart, Suso and Tauler are as characteristic of the second century of Dominicanism as are in their various ways Jordan, St Thomas, Humbert de Romans or Étienne de Bourbon of the first.

The mystic and the scholar are frequently opposed. Certainly, to take a parallel contemporary example, the strength of the Spiritual party came from the more ignorant members of the Order of Friars Minor. The typical Spiritual scorned erudition and refused to wash his clothes, although his leaders could write long theological works like Ubertino da Casale's ponderous Arbor Vitae. To a far less extent the Dominicans show the same tendency, and the origins of fourteenth-century mysticism can be seen in the earliest years of the Order. It was a latent tendency which became ever more prominent as time progressed.

Some of the first friars had been drawn from a very uneducated class, quite likely from the peasantry; though it must be remembered that here, just as in contemporary heresy, there is no evidence of a general movement of the lower classes, and in any case it was from the Universities and the educated generally that the greatest number of the Dominicans were drawn. Jordan tells us that St Dominic's first followers were "paucos...et ut

---

[1] See below, Chap. IX.

plures exigue litteratos et simplices", and Peter Ferrand repeats
him.[1] Deliberate purpose soon changed this—the multiplication
of young and unlearned friars was forbidden by the Chapter of
1240—but we have already seen even Jordan, the apostle of the
Universities, being accused of indiscretion in accepting postulants, and successfully defending his action in admitting sixty
very ignorant novices. Life was made hard for the unlearned,
however. They had no power in the government of the Order,
which was entirely in the hands of the learned majority. Entry
was difficult: "ut non personis de ordine, sed per personas ordini
sit provisum",[2] writes the provincial of Germany in 1270, demanding recruits with a legal training; and, once in, there was
the aristocracy of the Order to contend against. Humbert has a
passion for describing the dangers and evils which arise if
"minus sufficientes" are allowed to cross the threshold of learning. Only confusion to themselves and others can result.

Nevertheless, the existence of a less learned body within the
Order can be traced throughout the century. Peter of Sweden,
whom we shall have occasion to quote at more length shortly,
seems to have been among them, although he was appointed as
lector at Skenninge in his native country. He relates that he and
Brother Nicholas, on one of their visits to Christina of Stommeln, went to her house and read the offices of the Holy Ghost
and of the Blessed Virgin in her presence "because we did not
know the office without a book".[3] From an earlier time we have
several stories in Gerard de Fracheto's Lives of the Brethren.
Gerard tells, for instance, of the vision of a certain English friar
to whom in a dream Christ showed a Bible with a soiled binding;
on the brother remarking on this, Christ opened it, showed that
the pages were clean, and said: "My word is fair enough, but
you have defiled it with your philosophy". To another friar a
vision revealed that an endless number were damned on account
of philosophy.[4] It is this more strongly condemnatory note
which makes it possible to see in these tales evidence for a
different line of opposition to that of the educated party who
were opposed to innovations in theology. This very severe

[1] Jord. Sax. p. 19; Ferrand, p. 74 (in Anal. Boll. xxx).
[2] Finke, *Dominikanerbriefe*, p. 71.
[3] AA. SS. June iv. p. 245.   [4] *Vit. Frat.* iv. cap. 20.

attitude comes out most clearly in an old story which Étienne de Bourbon repeats[1] telling of the conversion of the famous English scholar, Serlo of Wilton, from the follies and frivolities of the schools. A pupil of his died and appeared to Serlo in a dream, weighed down in a cloak covered with the sophisms he had used during his studies. Its weight was intolerable, he told Serlo, "et intus incomparabiliter ureretur". A touch of his hand showed Serlo by its torment what the pains of Hell must be like, and he left Paris and became a Cluniac.

There is no necessary identity between the less educated section and the earlier mystics, but they provided favourable ground upon which mysticism might work. The "Great Alleluia" of 1233 and the Flagellants of 1259 are but the most obvious signs of the state of spiritual tension prevalent in the thirteenth century, and this kind of appeal would be much more attractive to those who did not possess the ballast of sound scholarship. However, the extent to which this type of religious enthusiasm spread among the early Dominicans was comparatively small. John of Vicenza, the evangelist and bellicose peacemaker of Lombardy, is not really typical of his Order, but far more resembles the early Franciscans. It was not solely because the Dominicans were calculatingly orthodox that Joachism gained few convents among them; the parts are correctly cast when Hugues de Digne enmeshes the Franciscan Peter of Apulia in his own vaunted logic,[2] or when Hugh de St Cher presides over the commission which condemned Joachim.[3] Yet in so far as there was support for these less rational lines of thought among the Preachers, it is possible to distinguish in it a different sort of opposition to the growing part secular learning was taking in the Order.

So too the very beginnings of mysticism are to be found among unimportant friars, who were concerned with the government and spiritual welfare of the many women's houses that were confided to the Order during the century.[4] Their own efforts

---

[1] *Anecdotes*, p. 19.
[2] See Coulton, *St Francis to Dante*, p. 157 (quoting Salimbene).
[3] Anagni 1255.—ALKG. i. 88.
[4] Even earlier, the mystical element in the correspondence of Jordan of Saxony with Diana d' Andalo may be noticed. See the letters ed. Altaner, and his comments, pp. 119–20, 134.

and more especially the political action of the Papal Curia had brought the women into this position of close dependance and connexion, against the will of the greater part of the men; once finally under the men's control, the organisation of the nuns' houses passed out of their own hands, and they found an outlet for their religious ideals in mysticism, which in turn reacted upon those in whose charge they were.[1]

The strange nature of the friendships that could result from this mystical tendency is clearly shown in the case of Peter of Sweden and Christina of Stommeln. Visions and demonological visitations make up a large part of the biography of Christina which Peter wrote. He was seeking, he relates, for some revelation of Divine grace to inflame him with devotion, and exalt him out of the accidie which had oppressed him from childhood, and not feeling himself capable of original action in this sort, hoped that God would show him one of his servants "that in the conversation of his saints I might learn more accurately and openly not only by words but by deeds and examples".[2] So he was a willing subject for Christina's strange and hysterical revelations, and greeted the first manifestations—groans and wounds—with the cry "O dulcis et delectabilis nox, in qua mihi primum est degustare datum quam suavis est Dominus".[3]

Peter's relations with his spiritual daughter were above suspicion, in spite of the passionate language of love which he used in his letters, and the frank description she gave of the dream in which their friendship was revealed to her. But eroticism was a constant characteristic of the women mystics at this time, quite apart from evidence we possess which suggests that lower motives often came into play.[4] Many did with evil intent what he did in all innocence. As long as the strictness of the early times lasted among the governing body, mysticism was repressed, partly for this reason, partly because it did not advance the faith of others than the parties concerned in each experience. It only became a dominant trait in the Order in the next century.

---

[1] On this whole question see Grundmann, *Religiöse Bewegungen*, Chaps. IV–VII.

[2] AA. SS. June iv. p. 239.

[3] Id.

[4] See, for instance, cases in Finke, *Dominikanerbriefe*, pp. 132–3.

CHAPTER V

THE DOMINICAN PREACHER

THAT an enormous success attended the Dominican Order from the time of its inception cannot be doubted. The official figures account for 60 convents in 1221, 404 in 1277, and 582 in 1303;[1] while 50 houses of women in 1277 had become 149 by 1303. This shows a great rate of progress well maintained for a century. The number of convents may perhaps be illusory, because the number of inhabitants of each might vary very greatly; the Chapter-General had on more than one occasion to legislate against unnecessary foundations, and it has been shown that there was often a large time-lag between the sanctioning of a new convent and its construction, the reason being, almost certainly, lack of man power. "The benevolence of the faithful which cannot be withstood" was so continuous as to be embarrassing, as the early history of poverty has shown. But alternative figures, a conjecture of Mandonnet's based upon a statement of Humbert's regarding the number of clerics in the Order, tells much the same tale: 7000 members in 1256, 10,000 in 1300.[2]

What, then, were the means by which this success was attained? How did the Order carry out the purpose for which it was founded? What was the Dominican preacher like? How did he preach, and what did he preach? What kind of congregations did he have, and how did the world seem, when looked at through his eyes?—These and a host of similar questions immediately arise, directly we begin to inquire into the business of the new organisation. The following pages contain an attempt to answer them.

One great difficulty arises at the start, and remains to some extent insurmountable. It is to distinguish the Dominican preacher, his ideals, his work and his congregations from those of other evangelists. It has, for instance, already been stated that Friars Preacher and Friars Minor are almost indistinguish-

[1] *Acta* 1221, Mandonnet, *S. Dominique*, p. 93.　　　[2] Id.

able after about the middle of the thirteenth century; yet it is only from just that time onwards that we possess Dominican sermon-manuals and collections of sermons that can help us to answer the questions posed above. Over and above this, however, there is the further complication of separating even this mixed, or, as we might call it, Mendicant material, from that intended for, or emanating from, all the other members of the Church who were engaged, contemporaneously with the Friars, in giving spiritual guidance and instruction to the masses.

For preaching underwent a revolution about the end of the twelfth and the beginning of the thirteenth centuries. The increase in education which has led to the coining of the phrase "Twelfth Century Renaissance", together with the rise of seriously threatening heretical movements, caused a great revival in the art of the pulpit. Populations that had previously been unthinkingly content with the very occasional sermons of their parish priest, augmented by the words of a greater man on the infrequent occasions when the bishop or a papal legate might pass through the district on visitation or journey, now began to ask for more regular and more substantial food; and in some parts of Europe began also to indicate that they were only too willing to supply their unfulfilled needs from some non-Catholic source, if the hierarchy could not or would not do the work itself. As was earlier indicated on broader and more general lines, the Mendicant movements are at once a sign of and a corrective to this; upon the narrower ground of preaching, they are the result of the greater demand and the chief cause of the enormously increased supply.

This new volume of sermons took on a rather different nature, shown most clearly in the use of the anecdote or *exemplum*,[1] which illustrated the point the preacher was trying to drive home, and so made it at once clearer and more interesting to the congregation. With the history of these *exempla* we are in no way concerned; it is sufficient to point out that the change makes itself felt about 1200, and principally at first in Cistercian

---

[1] On the history, nature and use of the *exemplum*, see J. Th. Welter, *L'exemplum dans la littérature religieuse et didactique du moyen-âge*, Paris 1927; Dr Owst's two books, *passim* (cf. Bibliography); Lecoy de la Marche, *La chaire*, p. 298 sq.

circles. Alan of Lille (*c.* 1128–1202), Hélinand de Froidmont (1170–1220) and Caesarius of Heisterbach (*c.* 1180–1240) are prominent in this respect. More successful than any was Cardinal Jacques de Vitry (*c.* 1180–1240), whose collection of sermon-stories was continually drawn upon by later writers; of him we are told "praedicando per regnum Franciae...adeo totam commovit Franciam quod non potest memoria aliquem ante vel post movisse".[1]

It is, then, very difficult indeed to single out the specific Dominican contribution to this new sermon-literature, since they neither invented it nor were its sole exponents. The best that can be done is to examine material from Dominican sources, and attempt to draw some conclusion from these; for we are entitled to assume that anything written by a Dominican will be intended, unless otherwise expressly stated, for use by Dominicans in the first place, however wide the circle for which it is also suitable.

This is the method which will be followed in the succeeding chapters, where material will be collected from various Dominican authors of fame and reputation both in their own age and ours. Among those from whom the bulk of the material has come, Humbert de Romans, Master-General, chief organiser of the Order, and a prolific writer upon preaching and other subjects, and Hugh de St Cher,[2] the first Dominican Cardinal and commentator of the Bible, have both already been frequently quoted, and their suitability for our purpose requires no further demonstration. The same is true of Étienne de Bourbon and Thomas de Cantimpré, who were both preachers-general in the middle years of the thirteenth century, and may be held to give a fair picture of the work and reflexions of these important officials during the earliest and best period of the Order. Finally, John Bromyard, English Dominican and sometime

---

[1] Quoted Dufourcq, p. 412.

[2] If any further excuse is needed for treating the work of any thirteenth-century Dominican as mainly concerned with preaching, when the title of his book does not give an immediate right to do so (as in this case), it can be found in the frequency with which preaching is mentioned throughout Hugh's commentary (the notes to this and succeeding chapters are a pale indication), and in the weight which he lays at the very outset upon a correct understanding of the Scriptural text as an essential part of the preacher's equipment. (Prol. to Genesis, col. 2—page unnumbered in the 1600 edition.)

THE DOMINICAN PREACHER

Chancellor of the University of Cambridge, does call for a little
explanation, in that he lived and wrote in the late[1] fourteenth
century, and so falls outside the period with which we have
mainly been concerned. By his time, however, preaching and
preaching-manuals had become standardised, and Bromyard's
Summa Praedicantium, one of the largest of such "aids to
preaching" which we possess, is filled not so much with the
records of his own experience as with material and anecdotes
collected from a large number of earlier sources,[2] among them
many dating from the thirteenth century; and he presents us, in
addition, with a picture of preaching in as complete and highly-
developed a state as it ever attained during the Middle Ages.

It remains to indicate briefly the causes which led to the immense multiplication of collections of sermons, outlines, guides
and eventually complete alphabetical compilations like the
Summa Praedicantium, all intended to lighten the preacher's
work for him. Humbert de Romans writes:

Concerning the material of sermons or collations, note that it is
sometimes more difficult, for many men, to find useful and praise-
worthy material, than, the material being found, to compose a sermon
from it. And so it is expedient that the preacher should always have
at hand the materials for preaching or speaking about God, suitable
for all types of men, for all kinds of occasions, for various times of the
year or for the different feasts.[3]

It was his consciousness that the average preacher felt this, that
led Humbert to draw up his two tractates, each consisting of
notes for a hundred sermons; that it was a need very widely felt
is clear from the immense number of collections, infinitely
larger than Humbert's, that were made within the next two or
three centuries. A friar might be called upon at short notice to

---

[1] I am inclined to abide by this adjective. M. Welter (pp. 328–9) has given
good reasons for supposing that the *S. P.* was written between 1360–8
(briefly: B. was a prominent anti-Wycliffite; Wycliffe is not mentioned in the
S. P.; Wycliffe's *De dominio divino* appeared in 1368). Dr Owst (*Lit. and
Pulpit*, p. 224) accepts this as "approximately correct". However, the *S. P.*
is clearly the product of a life-time's experience, and Bromyard was apparently still active in 1409 (Owst, *Pr. in Med. England*, pp. 68–9).—But in
any case, the exact date is of no importance for our purposes.

[2] See, for instance, Owst, *Pr. in Med. England*, pp. 303–5, *Lit. and Pulpit*,
p. 224. Cf. the first reference especially for the plagiarism and impersonality
of Bromyard, as of most others.

[3] *De modo prompte cudendi sermones*, i. Prol. in *Max. Bib. Pat.* xxv. 456.

preach at a wedding-feast, at the election of a bishop, in cities or towns to the rich and poor or on countless other occasions, and needed some assistance in adapting the words of the Gospel to the needs of the situation. From the books that were written to help him, and from actual sermons preserved, we can reconstruct to some extent his methods and the social life of his times.

The education of the Dominican preacher has already been treated in sufficient detail. It is worth remarking, however, in elaboration of the picture already given, that the whole organisation of the Order was constructed with the purpose of preaching always in view. Convents were so placed as to cover the countryside to the best advantage, and by the mid-century each had its fixed limits of preaching,[1] so that on the one hand every inch of ground was covered, and, on the other hand, two houses did not attempt to draw their support from the same population, thus bringing begging too strongly into the minds of the people and nullifying the good work of the Gospel by the annoyance that might in consequence be excited. So, too, when at the end of the first fifty years the existing division into provinces was attacked, the reason urged by the progressive party was that the number of convents within each province had increased so much that the provincials could not adequately carry out their duty of supervision, and that efficiency of preaching was thereby impaired. Unfortunately, conservatism was too strong, and many schemes got no further than inchoation,[2] as succeeding chapters had different views. It was only at the end of the century that the general principle—to divide each province into two—was carried out piecemeal.

What, then, were the requisites for the preacher? It well becomes the disciplinary character of the Dominican Order that one of the most constantly repeated is that none should preach unless expressly commanded to do so;[3] clearly, a check was required by the authorities to prevent the countryside being flooded with newly-converted friars in the first flush of their

[1] For details, cf. Galbraith, pp. 79–82.
[2] I.e. the first of the three annual stages through which all legislation had to pass (the others are approbation and confirmation. Cf. Galbraith, pp. 106–7).—See, on division of provinces, *Acta* 1269, 1301, 1303.
[3] For instance, St Cher vii. 114 col. 2, 138 col. 4, 223 col. 2, 224 col. 2.

enthusiasm, more certain of the need to express themselves in words than of what they had to say or how they were going to say it. Next, the preacher must be of ripe age; nobody less than twenty-five, it was laid down in 1228, should be allowed to preach outside his own convent.[1] "None ought to be sent to preach save those mature in age, manners and conversation," repeats Hugh de St Cher,[2] emphasising what is clearly another very wise precaution, and one which, taken in conjunction with even the minimum necessary amount of study, went a long way to ensure that sermons carried some weight. Thirdly, the preacher must be an enthusiast for his work: "talis potest alios inflammare qui prius fuerit inflammatus, quia qui non ardet non incendit", writes the same author.[3]

With characteristic care, the preaching staff was arranged in three groups.[4] A young friar, straight from the convent theological school, was first put to preach to his brother-friars. If he passed this test satisfactorily, and had acquired sufficient experience, his prior might appoint him a preacher-in-ordinary (*praedicator communis*), when he was restricted in the exercise of his office only by the "limits" of his convent. Finally, the most successful were elevated at the provincial chapter to the rank of preacher-general, and could then travel at will within the province and preach to all and sundry. This system combined the virtues of intensity and flexibility with the maximum of skill and knowledge; an essential qualification for a preacher-general was three years' study of theology.[5]

All preachers were given special privileges, since they were regarded as the most active members, specially engaged in carrying out the Order's purpose. Dispensations were more easily granted them,[6] they need not conform to the rules of the cloister, though they were expected to keep fasts; those who had the gift were not to be appointed to any other office, whereby they might reap less profit of souls. Moreover, they were not

---

[1] Galbraith, p. 164; ALKG. i. 224.
[2] St Cher vi. 377 col. 3, cf. vii. 224 col. 2.
[3] St Cher ii. 272 col. 2.
[4] See Galbraith, pp. 162–174 on this and the following paragraph.
[5] ALKG. i. 223.
[6] Humbert ii. 33–4. The succeeding references are to: id. ii. 36, ALKG. i. 223, Eccleston, *De adventu F. Minorum...*, ed. Little, p. 58.

expected to go in search of alms—indeed, the "quest" was one of the hindrances to successful preaching. The constitutions laid a particular ban on preachers carrying or receiving money or gifts except for immediate necessities, thus attempting to keep preaching and money as separate as possible. This, of course, was difficult, but its failure had disastrous consequences. Brother William of Abingdon turned his talents towards collecting money for building the house at Gloucester. In consequence, the visitor of the province told him he had lost the grace of preaching, "and the king said to him 'Brother William, you used to talk most spiritually, but now, when you speak, it is Give, Give, Give.' And another time...the same prince called him a serpent".

Heavenly privileges were promised to the preachers, over and above these earthly ones. They would enter Heaven in triumph, they were told, leading behind them the souls of those whom they had won to salvation.[1] Even those who had had little success, in spite of continued efforts, would receive an equivalent glory. "A nigger comes out of the bath as black as he entered it," quotes Bromyard from Gregory the Great, "and yet the bath-man gets his pay."[2] Best of all was the assurance of receiving an aureole in Heaven, the possibility of which so excited the Franciscan Salimbene. There seems to have been a certain amount of doubt and debate about it, but Aquinas, Humbert and St Cher all decide that it will be the preacher's eternal reward.[3]

As a result of all these advantages, the office of preacher-general, which possessed them in the highest degree, became at once coveted and debased. As early as 1240 the Chapter-General ordered that their numbers should not be increased "without careful and proper caution", and six years later there was an abortive attempt to abolish them altogether. In 1255 the number of preachers-general in any given province should not exceed that of the convents by more than one-half; but all legislation of this kind failed in the face of a universal demand

---

[1] St Cher vi. 308 col. 4—309 col. 2; cf. Humbert ii. 385-9.
[2] Bromyard, V. ii. 4.
[3] *Summa Theol.* Suppl. Q. 96, art. 7; Humbert ii. 32, 388, 433; St Cher ii. 34 col. 4.

for the position. If one chapter "absolved" all the preachers-general in a given province, the provincial chapter would institute as many at its next meeting, and the position was as bad as ever. Humbert advised humility in accepting the office, and complained bitterly of those who were not only too ready to accept it, but actually sought for its burdens. Yet even he spends more time in the *De officiis* in explaining the legislative functions which the preacher-general possessed as an *ex officio* member of the provincial chapter, than in directing aspirants towards the best means of evangelisation.[1] As will be seen in more detail later, this is but one symptom of an aristocratic tendency which was developing throughout the Order.

Preachers, who "as it were sustain the whole fabric of the Church",[2] were exhorted to imitate St Paul, the *optimus praedicator*, and edify their audiences with their sweet and wholesome words. Persistence was among the greatest of the virtues for them; it would not be too often if they preached every day,[3] and they should continue their efforts even though the listeners might seem most unpromising ground for the seed of the Word. The value of a sermon can never be judged merely from appearances; there are some who play at chess or dice while the friar is in the pulpit, saying, "'Why should we listen to the sermon? Each of us has his five senses, and knows when he does ill, and when good.'—For he knows that when he commits adultery, or steals, or gets drunk, that he sins; yet it behoves him to listen to the preacher's moral tales, because terrible stories of the death and punishments of sinners may perhaps more quickly draw him back from similar punishment."[4] Hand in hand with perseverance must go patience. Many, writes Hugh de St Cher,[5] become impatient if their hearers do not mend their ways immediately, and think they are being held in contempt; but if they do convert anyone, they withdraw the credit from the divine

---

[1] Humbert ii. 414, 356, cf. Raymond of Peñaforte's edition of the Constitutions, Dist. ii. cap. 1 (ALKG. v. 560): "nullus fiat praedicator generalis antequam theologiam audierit per tres annos; et nisi sit maturus et discretus ad negotia ordinis in capitulis pertractanda".
[2] St Cher vii. 381 col. 3.
[3] Id. vii. 141 col. 1.
[4] Bromyard, E. vii. 9.
[5] St Cher iii. 90 col. 2.

wisdom, and arrogate it to their own eloquence, not sufficiently realising that they are themselves no more than the means by which God's grace works.

Yet, considered rightly, the preacher's is the highest of callings.[1] Humbert de Romans, giving a sketch for a sermon to be addressed to Dominicans, writes:

...consider how excellent this office is, because it is apostolic; how useful, because it is directly ordained for the salvation of souls; how perilous, because few have in them, or perform, what the office requires, for it is not without great danger.... *Item*, take note that this office calls for excellency of life, so that just as the preacher speaks from a raised position, so he may also preach the Gospel from the mountain of an excellent life.[2]

The necessity of giving a good example is continually insisted upon. Without it, preaching is "inanis et inutilis".[3] Like Saul, the preacher should stand higher than the people "from his shoulders and upward";[4] like the cock which beats itself with its wings before it crows, when he announces the near approach of the Day of Judgment and calls sinners to repentance, he must show that he himself is ready, lest the people say, "Physician, heal thyself".[5] When these conditions are fulfilled, the result is

a sweet harmony; then are the people more moved to penitence, and then the preacher himself, seeing the movement among his audience and that they begin to turn away, is raised to a higher state of life, and is filled with a wider spirit.[6]

This is the usual attitude taken up by those who set out to instruct the preacher in his duties, but some go on to say that even if the preacher's life is not as good as his words, he should none the less continue to announce the Gospel message. Wine is not any the worse because it is kept in earthen vessels; the preaching of St Paul was not any the less valid because he had

---

[1] See Appendix III, "Sermons and the Mass," for an attempt to estimate how far this exaltation of preaching led the Dominican Order into unsacerdotalism.
[2] *Max. Bib. Pat.* xxv. 461.   [3] St Cher iv. 138 col. 4.
[4] Id. vi. 377 col. 2.   [5] Bromyard, P. xii. 14.
[6] St Cher v. 15 cols. 2, 3. Apparently by the "movement" he intends to convey the ill-at-ease shuffling which denotes the oncoming of repentance, and by the "turning away" that they will go to confession or to restore ill-gotten gains.

been a sinner,[1] and the common folk will warm themselves in the heat of the words themselves, even though the speaker may be cold: "just as a man warms himself in the sunlight, though the sun in its nature is not warm"(!)[2] "...it does not matter with what intention the sermon is preached, so long as Christ is announced...preaching is useful in whatever manner it is performed."[3]

Armed with a competent knowledge of the Bible and of at least the fundamentals of theology, and fortified with the virtues described above, how did the ideal preacher set about his task of "extracting the devil from the hearts of men, as the enchanter draws serpents out of a cave with the words of his incantations, according to Isidore"?[4] Following Lecoy de la Marche,[5] we may distinguish two classes of sermons, roughly according to their age. It may reasonably be assumed that the early Dominicans, like the early Franciscans, preached quite simply and straightforwardly, setting forth the story of the Redemption and calling on men to change their lives at the call of the Gospel. In the early years of the Order, and in the early years of the century, neither preacher nor congregation required much more; the emotional temperature of both was high enough for surprising results to follow such simple teaching. But as the years drew on the Order fell, if not at once into an ignominious decline, at least from the heat of passion into the coolness of reflection, and placed more weight upon cogent argument than upon burning conviction; this is but the natural result of the establishment of a permanent organisation, and a continuance of the first enthusiasm in its primitive form could not have been expected. After the age of the Great Alleluia[6] the peoples of Europe lost, to some extent, that passionate craving for the Christian message which had characterised the years between the conversion of

---

[1] St Cher iii. 60 col. 4.   [2] Bromyard, P. xii. 37.
[3] St Cher vii. 180 cols. 2, 3.   [4] Id. iii. 195 col. 2.
[5] *La chaire*, pp. 111–12.
[6] The extraordinary wave of religious emotion which swept over North Italy, in particular, in 1233. Old feuds were healed, laws brought more into accord with Christian ideals, preaching became immensely and unwontedly popular, and hordes of the enthusiastic and newly converted paraded the streets. John of Vicenza played a large part in the movement. The best account of it is given by Salimbene (MGH. *Scriptores*, vol. 32); large excerpts are translated in Coulton, *St Francis to Dante*.

Peter Waldo and the preaching of John of Vicenza, and, over-whelmed by the political confusion which the mid-century brought, especially to Germany and Italy, dropped back into a more passive state in which they were to remain until the preaching of Huss ushered in the age of Luther and religious discord. As far as the centres of learning were concerned, the progress of philosophy made educated minds, if not really more acute, at any rate better armed against the specious attractions of the simple Gospel, and the number of instantaneous conver-sions among University masters and students grew less. Parallel with this gradual alteration in the general state there proceeded a change in the quality of sermons. At first in all probability simple and unadorned, they tend later to be constructed on a rigid scheme, to be tricked out with learning, and to follow the precepts of the sermon-books. The very manuals which were intended to help the preacher assisted in drying up the sources of personal inspiration by making it too easy to reproduce stereotyped forms.

In asking, therefore, how preaching was done, and what were the rules for a preacher's conduct, we are inevitably turning our attention to the later period, when rules had been thought out. In point of fact, the material for a study of the earliest phase of Dominican activity is lacking. Neither Jordan of Saxony nor Raymond of Orléans, not even St Dominic himself, has left records of his sermons, and we can only see faint traces of the earlier simple style in the sketch Humbert gives for a sermon to be addressed *Ad omnes homines*:

Every man is to be exhorted to beware of evil and to do good, that he may come to the celestial abode...just as a man who wishes to get to a particular place must leave the wrong road and follow the right, in order to reach his destination. Here is much material for speaking of the avoidance of evil and the doing of good. *Thema*, Depart from evil, and do good; and dwell for evermore (Ps. xxxvii. 27).[1]

Among later writers, Bromyard offers the best motto for preachers when he adapts II Timothy iv. 2—"Primo, argue frequenter; secundo, obsecra importune; tertio, increpa perse-

---

[1] *Max. Bib. Pat.* xxv. 456.

veranter."[1] All alike agree, however, that the work of rebuke
and exhortation must be limited by certain essential pre-
requisites, and that of these none is so essential as to construct
the sermon according to the needs and understanding of the
audience. Directly he arrives at a new town or village, the friar
should find out, from the parson or some other, all details he can
about the people of the neighbourhood,[2] and should draw up
his sermon in the light of this information. "And note", writes
St Cher,[3] for instance, "that the preacher ought to take care to
temper the nature of his preaching to the nature and capacity of
his audience." This may seem advice so obvious that it scarcely
needed to be given; but there was on the one hand the danger
that the preacher would display the extent of his knowledge
rather than restrict himself to the simple exhortations which
were more suitable to an assembly of peasants, and on the other
that boredom or sheer inattention would cause the hearers'
minds to wander. Special effort was needed to capture the
attention of audiences such as Humbert describes:[4] "There are
others who, now standing, now sitting, now going out, now
coming back again, are so careless in listening that they take
little trouble to hear or understand what is said.... There are
others who raise disturbances" (*qui tumultum faciunt*). If, as we
have every reason to believe, this is a not unfair sketch of a
typical congregation, then the preacher's task was no light one.

Respice quid, cur, ubi, quo, quomodo, quando loquaris,

writes an unknown hand;[5] summarising this all-important
teaching for the benefit of preachers-in-ordinary, Thomas of
Cantimpré emphasises very strongly the need for moderation
and care, lest the congregation be excited, scandalised or pro-
voked too much,[6] and relates an unfortunate experience of a

[1] Bromyard, P. xii. 22. The text in the A.V. runs: "Preach the word; be
instant in season, out of season; reprove, rebuke, exhort with all longsuffer-
ing and doctrine."
[2] Bromyard, P. xii. 32.
[3] ii. 40 col. 3, cf. his instructions for speaking "breviter et distincte et
utiliter" (vii. 172 col. 1), and on the moderate use of gestures (vi. 47 col. 3).
[4] Humbert ii. 447.
[5] Printed id. ii. 371, but this section, "De officio praedicatoris communis",
was anonymously added to Humbert's work later.
[6] Cantimpré II. xxxiv. 4, 5, xlviii. 1.

friend of his, one Joannes Polinus, as he preached at Cantimpré "presentibus Beghardis[1] multis cum populo". Joannes waxed eloquent on the text "He that abideth in me", and a certain little old woman (*virgo quaedam anicula*) became unduly excited with the ardour of her devotion, and began to wave her arms about. She was repressed three or four times by the blows of her neighbours, but as the preacher dilated upon the mingling of the souls of the blessed with God, she screamed out loudly, and died in the sight of all those present "with a great effusion of blood".[2]

Probably the chief thing which led the Dominicans more than other religious to forget the necessity of considering the capacity of their hearers was the temptation to excessive philosophical subtlety. Apart from the obvious cause of this—the extensive education which they went through—another historical reason can be suggested. Heresy was the Black Friars' earliest enemy, and it was the medieval belief, presumably based on experience, that the best way to convert a heretic was to entrap him in verbal confusion. Dominic himself had done this during the ten years previous to the Lateran Council; the famous story of the rejection by the fire of his book containing a statement of faith shows this.[3] The test by burning was only taken after orthodox and heretic had each failed to convince the other at the end of a long argument. To this extent subtlety was legitimate, but anything further is repeatedly condemned. Many preachers, says St Cher, and especially doctors, make themselves barbarians, although they are not such by birth, by expounding difficult propositions.[4] A simpler method is more effective; the arrows of the Word should be directed at the hearts rather than at the ears of listeners.

Where a preacher much given to subtleties scarcely converts one, the other [i.e. using directer methods] converts many. Nor is this to

---

[1] Disorganised, or at least only roughly organised, semi-monastic bodies of men, analogous to the Humiliati or the Dominican and Franciscan Tertiaries.   [2] Cantimpré II. xlix. 2.

[3] Jord. Sax. cap. 14. Cf. Aquinas, *Summa contra Gentiles*, i. cap. 2, where he laments that the Mohammedans have no Scripture in common with the Christians, out of which they can be confuted, as the Jews can from the O. T.; "Unde necesse est ad naturalem rationem concurrere, cui omnes assentire coguntur."

[4] St Cher vii. 112 col. 3.

be wondered at; for a doctor who is diligent about the cure heals more than one who is talkative and full of words, but does not come down to detailed remedies.[1]

Secular learning must therefore be used sparingly in the pulpit; it must assist, not dominate, and we must "regulate philosophy according to the rule of faith, and not the other way round.... He who seeks to deck the faith of Christ out in words, obscures it with the splendour of verbiage, so that not it but he gets the praise".[2] A limited value as an aid to the apostolate was, however, freely admitted to learning, else the Order would never have taken such pains to educate its members. Humbert has an ingenious way of getting round the point which St Francis urged so often, namely that the Apostles were rough, uneducated men, filled only with a divine fire, so that the true imitators of the Gospel life should require no book-knowledge: "...And so the Lord, though he called simple men to the office of preaching, yet gave them knowledge of Holy Scripture, as appears from their writings, in which the authorities of the Old Testament are frequently cited."[3]

The constantly repeated advice, and the widespread use of the homely *exemplum* do, however, show an awareness of the need to take notice of the capacity of the listeners and to "get down to the level of the people", but it may reasonably be asked whether the medieval preacher was very often successful with his amateur psychology. The "distinctions" and divisions of his matter, so entirely reminiscent of the modern subject that "falls under three heads", were, admittedly, much more useful than they look. The preacher could count up the five species of *Luxuria*,[4] for instance, on the fingers of his hand, and might hope that his audience would go home and remember, or even repeat, this part at least of his sermon, by virtue of having so simple a mechanical aid to memory. But to us, reading the sermons to-day, the effect is inexpressibly dull and boring, and the question arises, "Was it not also boring seven hundred years ago?" The same is true of the *exempla* themselves: constant

[1] Bromyard, P. xii. 28, 30. [2] St Cher vii. 75 col. 1.
[3] Humbert ii. 400.
[4] *Anecdotes*, p. 400. Further examples in St Cher i. 36 col. 2, vi. 324 col. 2, etc. On the use of the fingers for this purpose, see Lecoy, *La chaire*, p. 324.

repetition must have worn most of them utterly threadbare, like a good joke that gains too wide a currency. (Repetition is vouched for by the way in which stories found in Jacques de Vitry, for instance, turn up again in the *Summa Praedicantium*, having gone through the collections of de Bourbon and half-a-dozen others.) Does not the increasing dreadfulness of the emphasis upon death and Hell tend to show that a sharp weapon lost its edge by too much use? We know that in the political sphere the sentence of excommunication, powerful in the hands of Hildebrand, had little terror for Frederick II when Innocent launched it against him a century and a half later, and the reason is well known. Again, the friars and others constantly denounced feminine adornment, tournaments, over-indulgence in food and drink,[1] and so on; and these things were, of course, expressly condemned by Popes and Councils, so that the preacher had no option, perhaps, but to follow in the footsteps of his superiors. But by such constant reiteration did not the Church dull the effect of its own attack? Would the Glutton of Piers Plowman have been so ready to stay with evil companions in the ale-house if his parish priest had not denounced all the things that amused the Glutton and many better men? Is not this once again the tragedy of the "black-or-white", "good-or-bad", so characteristic of the medieval outlook? Reason recoils from the attempt to put everything into two categories—one worthy of praise, one of condemnation. In so far as medieval preachers did this, can we not accuse them of faulty psychology, and suggest that they hindered their own efforts?[2]

Be this as it may, the friar was instructed to do his best to fit his matter and his treatment to the specific needs of the situation.

[1] See below, Chap. VII.
[2] This is, perhaps, only one side of the argument. Cf. evidence in the preachers' favour, and Dr Owst's views, *Preaching in Med. Engl.* pp. 70, 331. See, however, what Dr Owst himself says (*Lit. and Pulpit*, p. 287 sq.) on the responsibility of Bromyard and others in helping to cause the Peasants' Revolt. "His motif is nothing more than a powerful spiritual and moral corrective, wholly innocent of any revolutionary intent.... [But the preachers tried humanity too high; they denounced the rich and great, and yet said the poor were to put up with it, for they would have their reward in Heaven.]... We must forgive the *psychological blindness* which failed to see that injured and impatient folk, confronted with such a picture, would not be for ever content to exchange the practical opportunities of the moment for the somewhat uncertain sublimities of a future existence in the unknown." (Op. cit. pp. 292–297: my italics.)

In this connexion, Bromyard brings out very clearly the need for being direct and definite. "Come down at once to hard facts," he says, "and attack particular vices: he who strikes all the strings of a lute at once produces but a confused noise...."

So in preaching, he who deals with everything in a general way at the same time, and warns men against vices in general, saying "Do not be proud, do not be covetous, do not follow the lusts of the flesh ", does not make an effective preacher.[1]

One theme at a time is sufficient, and this should be treated simply and shortly, for to be tedious is the best way to fail: "results depend more on the manner of speaking than upon the substance of what is said ".[2] Sermons must not be too long, too repetitive or too complex. Too much rain causes a flood, enough is enough; "as the brevity of the divine office makes for devotion, so excessive prolixity induces sleep". Nor should virtue be made out too hard a way, but austerity should be relaxed as far as possible and men treated gently (benigne).[3] Hugh de St Cher rather curiously expounds the feeding of the five thousand as "against those who preach to unwilling ears, and produce tedium in their listeners by giving them too much.... And note that it is written 'And likewise of the fishes': the preacher should not only offer bread, but also fishes, mixing consolation with harder things...the two fishes are the examples of the saints which may be propounded, and the rewards of the blessed which are promised ".[4]

This last quotation suggests further consideration of the use of exempla in medieval sermons, but no useful purpose would be served in going into the question in detail. It does not come within the scope of the present work to treat of them for their own sake, though considerable sections of this and succeeding chapters are built largely upon series of exempla, for these are, after all, the most interesting part of the sermons to us, in that they give a picture of contemporary social life. Their main purpose is well known: to give point and illustration to the various lessons which the pulpit was trying to teach; to this end, their usual place was at the conclusion of the sermon, where they pointed the moral and sent the congregation away in good

---

[1] Bromyard, P. xii. 25.   [2] Humbert ii. 44.
[3] Id. ii. 36, 395.   [4] St Cher vi. 324 col. 2.

spirits, more especially if the tale were a new one. Étienne de Bourbon's preface, in which he says that he collected his stories from every conceivable source and wrote them down "because they very greatly instruct the rudeness of simple men",[1] is the most complete explanation of the *raison d'être* of the *exemplum*. Its chief interest for us, apart from its immense value as a mirror of social history, is that through the *exemplum* have been transmitted many of the fables of antiquity, while the actual origin of many of our favourite fairy-stories is to be found in these medieval sermon-tales.[2]

So far we have made no mention of the language of the pulpit. This was, naturally, the vernacular wherever the lay-folk were concerned, and nearly always Latin when the sermon was delivered to a clerical audience.[3] Any other language would have been useless, because only their native tongue was "understanded of the people", and comprehension was an obvious preliminary to action upon the precepts which were poured forth in such multitudes in the pulpit, in the market square, on the "scaffold" in the churchyard, or by the roadside to a casually collected group of labourers. From Dominican sources we have specific evidence that Jordan of Saxony, for instance, although a German, took pains to acquire a knowledge of French,[4] and that Thomas of Cantimpré was also master of both these languages.[5] The General-Chapter of 1254 ordered that the lay-brothers were to have a sermon in the vernacular on the day of their communion; the Chapter of 1236 had already commanded the friars in each convent to learn the language of the neighbourhood, while one of the most outspoken of the Master-

---

[1] *Anecdotes*, p. 4.
[2] As an example taken at random, the story of the King with the Three Lazy Sons, which appears in Bromyard (A. viii. 17), probably originates either with the *Gesta Romanorum* (c. 1300) or with the Dominican Robert Holcot (d. 1349).—See Bolte and Polivka, *Anmerkungen zu den Kinder- und Hausmärchen der Brüder Grimm* (Leipzig 1913 sq.), vol. iii. p. 207. On the question of the origin of fairy-tales in general, see id. iv. 127 sq., Lecoy de la Marche and Owst.
[3] See the arguments establishing this in Lecoy, *La chaire*, pp. 233–69, and in Owst, *Preaching in Medieval England*, p. 224 sq.
[4] *Vit. Frat.* iii. cap. 31.
[5] Evidence assembled in Berger, *T. Cant....*, p. 25. Cf. the many proverbs and quotations in English and French that are to be found embodied in Bromyard's text. (Fully discussed, Owst, *Lit. and Pulpit*, p. 41 sq.)

Generals' encyclicals (most, especially after 1263, limit themselves to the most guarded and vague generalisations) is
concerned with the reluctance of the friars to learn languages.[1]
Defect of latinity or of the vernacular is *indecens*, writes Humbert;[2] preaching is only useful when it is understood, therefore
it must be given in the mother-tongue of the hearers; only
foolish pride makes the preacher use Latin or the people
demand it.

This does not mean, however, that there was an edifying
literature in existence in the vernacular. Indeed the General
Chapter of 1242 expressly forbade the making of translations,
almost certainly with the intention of checking the spread of
heresy, which was too closely connected with the beginnings of
religious literature in the vulgar tongue, and with the sudden
spate of French Bibles which appeared in Paris in about 1230.[3]
All the sermon manuals were written in Latin, because the
preacher naturally understood it, and always used it for what
may be called "business" purposes; but he translated the
material he took from them when he actually went into the
pulpit, in the same way that he expanded the arguments and
filled out the stories which his hand-books nearly always gave
him in compressed form.

Difficulties and dangers without number beset the friar as he
went about within the "limits" of his convent, or upon the
highways of his province. Devils impended him at every turn,
drying up the sources of his inspiration, causing his words to
fall on stony ground,[4] even misleading him upon the road and
causing him to lose sight of the *socius* from whom he was supposed never to be separated.[5] When he did mount the rostrum,
further discouragements lay in his way. The net which he cast,
fishing for the souls of men, had so wide a mesh that many
escaped through it.

[1] *Litt. Encyc.* p. 19.   [2] ii. 402.
[3] Grundmann, p. 462, connects the 1242 ban directly with the fear of
introducing heretical opinions *via* the incorporated nunneries, and suggests
that the forbidden books were used as edifying literature for the women.
[4] St Cher vii. 198 col. 1, cf. Bromyard, S. xi. 14.
[5] Cantimpré ii. lvii. 35. Hence he proceeds in § 36 to give a warning
that the preacher and his companion should never separate for a moment,
lest even worse befall. On the rigidity of the rule regarding *socii*, see Galbraith, p. 165.

One silly woman, tricked out with foolish ornaments, and walking through the village, catches more men than the preacher crying the whole day.... The fishers of God seem to fish with a line, for as the fisherman casts his line into the water not knowing what he will catch unless God sends him something, and sometimes makes a catch, sometimes gets nothing; and when it is more than nothing, it is only one fish...[Even if he obtains this tiny success] it is some small or poor thing, and nothing great; because the great fish either do not come to the line, or, if they do come, will not take the bait; if they do take it, and begin to be drawn in, they break the line and escape the hand of the fisherman, etc.[1]

He might meet with strange adventures, like Étienne de Bourbon, who held a secret meeting with a brigand in the depths of a wood, in an unsuccessful attempt to convert this disturber of the country's peace;[2] or he might be mistaken for one of those begging preachers who, belonging to no Order, peddled false relics round Europe and earned universal execration.[3] But at the end of the day's work he could expect to be entertained to a meal by one of the faithful,[4] and, when his tour of duty was done, look forward (it would appear) to a wash and a shave on his return to the convent,[5] and a period of rest and recuperation in the cloister.

[1] Bromyard, P. xii. 6.
[2] *Anecdotes*, p. 369 sq.
[3] Denunciations of *praedicatores quaestuarii* in St Cher vii. 341 col. 1, and at greater length in Humbert, *Op. Trip.* iii. cap. 8 (Brown, p. 227).
[4] St Cher vi. 163 col. 1.
[5] So it would seem from a remark of Cantimpré's; he is relating a miracle, and says: "Paucis post diebus quo haec gesta sunt evolutis, de praedicatione fratres undique convenerunt. Quibus lotis et rasis...."—ii. liii. 4.

CHAPTER VI

THE PREACHER'S CONGREGATION

SUCH, then, was the Dominican preacher in his ideal form, according to the views of the great and the experienced within the Order's ranks. It is now time to take a different view and inquire into the nature of the congregation which listened to him. How did the people look when viewed from the height of the pulpit or the platform in the market square? What was their attitude to the pious exhortations of the wandering friar? What were their characteristics, their virtues and their vices, from his point of view? The sources offer a considerable amount of material which makes some kind of an answer to these questions possible. This material is in the highest degree instructive and enlightening; but one warning is necessary in re-creating a picture of social life from the sermon-manuals. The preacher's duty was to bring people from their evil ways to an active and willing service of Christ. Therefore he gave more of his attention to the wandering sheep than to those already within the fold, and blame for the wicked takes a larger part in what he says than praise for the good. Like his kind in all generations, he preached quite as much for the benefit of those who were so sunk in their sins that they were not among his audience, as to the faithful few who were hanging respectfully upon his lips, in the hope that if his words were strong enough they would make so great an impression upon the minds of those who did hear that they might later be repeated in the presence of those who had been absent. Moreover, the Dominican represented an age and a class which exalted the narrow and precise piety of the monastic calling in its almost unattained ideal form, and regarded it as in some sense the standard by which everyone should be measured, even though he did not expect all his hearers to enter the cloister. A small acquaintance with medieval religious literature does leave the impression, however, that the only way in which the constantly repeated precepts could logically be carried out was to embrace the religious life, at least to the extent of joining one of the Tertiary Orders and keeping its rule in the strictest possible way.

The truth is that the concepts of St Augustine's City of God, the second Bible of the Middle Ages, had bitten very deeply into the thought of the times. St Augustine's own interpretations of the *civitas Dei* and the *civitas terrena* were not fixed, but varied in the course of the argument contained in a book, the writing of which took him over ten years to complete. But he had at times spoken as if the *civitas Dei* was the sublime City of God in Heaven, the *civitas terrena* the evil world here below, and this was of course the most easily comprehended and most direct interpretation. In consequence, moralists had the best of authorities for denouncing all human affairs in round terms as simply wicked, and even the saints of the cloister received undiluted praise for putting their bodies through the severest tortures in order to fit themselves in the most limited way for the life above. The ordinary man, therefore, stood little chance of gentle handling from those who were responsible for his soul's health; even if he did good, he was living in so excessively dangerous an environment that, from the clerical point of view, it was most likely that he would be to some extent defiled by the pitch he was touching every hour of his life.

Looking through the preacher's eyes, therefore, we see good and bad defined by clear, hard lines; and indeed there is very little of the former to see. As will appear in the course of the following pages, Humbert de Romans (who expressly says that people should not be handled too severely from the pulpit, lest more harm than good be done)[1] is the only one of our five chief authorities who is prepared to make the slightest concession to human weakness and imperfection. There is at times a certain warmth and geniality to be sensed behind the words of de Bourbon and Cantimpré, but in their didactic moods they are completely inflexible; and this in spite of the fact that each had years of experience of the rough-and-tumble of daily life in French and German towns and villages. What they thought, we know not; as far as their published works go, they remain severely official in their outlook.

From this follow two conclusions. The first, which need not

[1] See above, p. 90 and ref. there.

detain us here, is that in some such way as this we can explain the terribly impersonal nature of most of the sermon *exempla* still preserved; Cantimpré is the only writer used in the present study who has largely drawn upon his own experience. Far more immediately important is the realisation that these sources present us to a certain extent with a biased view of social conditions. The standard by which virtues and vices are measured is superhuman; and the preachers could be convicted out of their own mouths, were it of any profit to do so, of setting forth a way of life they knew to be impossible to the larger number of their hearers. Therefore, when they castigate the failings of mankind, the twentieth-century reader is very often justified in toning down considerably the sharpness of the outlines. The thirteenth-century preachers have left us an invaluable picture of the social life of their age; but still more have they left us a picture of their own minds.

In seeking to visualise the appearance of a typical medieval congregation, we must put out of our minds all notions gained in Protestant or English surroundings. Within modern experience, at least the respectful simulation of attention and wakefulness is never grudged even to the dullest and most uninteresting speaker. Even in the eighteenth century, the most spiritually dead age the Church of England has ever experienced, high-backed pews, which hid the members of the congregation from each other and also to some extent from the preacher, were common; and the squire might be expected at least to refrain from snoring during morning service in the village church. Some, like Sir Roger de Coverley, rose to their feet at intervals and sent a servant to reprove those of their tenants whose heads were nodding dangerously.

The wandering friar of medieval times could expect no such maintenance of the outward proprieties. If he spoke in church, he might have a congregation seated in pews or seats of some kind, but more likely they would crowd round his pulpit, as in most continental Catholic churches to-day. If he spoke in the open air, the people would most probably be standing, or at best seated upon the bare ground, with consequent movement and fidgeting due to the resultant discomfort. In any case he would practically never have attentive silence, but must raise his voice above normal pitch to overcome the surrounding noise.[1] There would be a constant to-and-fro; people would come in and go out again for a variety of reasons totally unconnected with the sermon; for the church was the centre of village life as well as the house of God. We have already seen[2] Humbert complaining of those who create "tumults" during a service; this might well be due to a heated discussion about the excesses of the bailiff of the manor, or the fairness of that year's division of the communal meadowland. In Flanders or the north Italian towns it might be caused by argument respecting the price of the latest consignment of English wool, while in England itself, on Bromyard's testimony, the friar would be lucky if he secured an audience at all: "Not only the Queen of Sheba, but all the nations of Christendom", he writes, "can rise in judgment against the English, for there is not a Christian people which so rarely or so unwillingly hears the word of God, *experto crede magistro*."[3] More spiritual interruptions were caused by argument with the speaker upon some debatable point in his sermon, or, like the Puritan divines who were in so many ways his real successors, the medieval preacher might expect to hear the commotion caused by the "working of the spirit": "Just as a stone thrown into a crowd makes him cry out upon whose head it falls, and by the cry may be known where it fell, so when the word of the preacher is cast at random (*generaliter*) into a multitude of people, murmurs and abuse show who has been touched."[4]

For a present-day parallel to the average medieval congregation we must go outside these islands to countries like Italy, for example, where the reverence of those present is apparently not in the least disturbed even by visitors walking past the steps of the High Altar itself, Baedeker in hand, and under the charge of a clerical guide, while an important service is in progress.[5]

With these things in mind, we may attempt a sketch of a typical congregation. If the friar was a popular and successful preacher, able to catch the minds of men by his oratory or by his shining poverty and devotion, there would doubtless be some

---

[1] See further on this point in Owst, *Preaching in Med. England*, p. 173 sq.
[2] Above, p. 86.
[3] Bromyard, A. xxvi. 29.   [4] Id. A. xxvi. 21.
[5] Personal observation at a Palm Sunday service in the Basilica of St Francis at Assisi.

present at the sermon who had followed him from the village where he had made his last stop, or from even farther away.[1] These, it may reasonably be assumed, would be among the most devout listeners. Of the local population, who are in the great majority, some fulfil the friar's ideal of a good congregation, and are "attentive, devout, docile, and believe the good master's words";[2] they retain the speaker's words in their hearts, and are not found wanting when judged by the standard of the first "condition" which Bromyard expected to find among those listening to him, namely to be "like a glass window-pane, which lets in the light and keeps out the storms".[3]

Unfortunately few succeeded in living up to these demands. Many of those present pay no heed to what is said;[4] others fall asleep during the sermon, and the preacher may be granted a vision of four devils at their fell work which is thus nullifying all his efforts.[5] More come with bad intent, to criticise the life or doctrine of the preacher.[6] They excuse themselves for this by a specious application of logic: "Why should I listen to him or to what he says, for he is such, and such". For such rashness (bordering so closely upon the attitude of heretics in Languedoc or, indeed, everywhere) they shall answer at the Day of Judgment, and in the meantime it is pertinent to ask them if they would accept the help of an evil-living priest in escaping from prison.[7] Most discouraging of all, from the earnest friar's point of view, is the little success he has with the Gospel message among people who will listen greedily to those who bring interesting or exciting news of earthly affairs:

And this is a thing meet for wonder and sorrow; Hippocrates[8] speaks of the things which pertain to the body, and he has many hearers who believe in him; Justinian speaks about earthly justice...; some trifler, a silly old woman or a fortune-teller, speaks about those

---

[1] *Anecdotes*, p. 75.   [2] St Cher ii. 198 col. 3.
[3] Bromyard, P. xii. 35.   [4] Id. A. xxvi. 16.
[5] Id. § 10. The four devils are *obturans aures et oculos, indurans cor, obturans os, obturans bursam.*
[6] Id. P. xii. 38, St Cher v. 51 col. 4.   [7] Bromyard, A. xxvi. 23.
[8] I.e. the medical profession.—The 1586 edition of the *Summa Praedicantium* correctly follows the MS. (Brit. Mus. Roy. 7. E. iv.) in printing "Ypocras", but this form seems well-authenticated from the thirteenth century onwards. It occurs, e.g. in Vincent of Beauvais, *Spec. Hist.* iv. 54 and in Walter Burley's *De vita et moribus philosophorum* (ed. H. Kunst, p. 180).

things which lead to the damnation of souls, and they have many hearers who believe in them; the heretics speak, saying that God will lose none of those whom he has redeemed, and they have many hearers who believe in them; Christ and his ministers speak...a poor man, I say, speaks, and they answer, "Who is this?"[1]

Innumerable too are the excuses for not coming to hear a sermon. Some say they cannot come because they are entertaining company, others that they are busy, that they live too far away or are too ignorant to understand what is told them, while a few are even brave enough to say boldly "Why should I come and listen? I don't intend to give up my sins".[2] If they had not taken bodily food for three days, they would run ten miles for something to eat, but although they may not have heard the word of God for a month, they will not stir a foot outdoors when the opportunity is given them.[3] If they do actually succeed in getting to church, they try to hurry away as quickly as possible. On feast days, for example,

most people rise late and come to church later. They only want to be there a short time, and say to the priest, "Get it (meaning the Mass) over quickly, because we have a friend coming to dinner and must hurry back". If there is supposed to be a sermon about the soul's health, they either try to prevent it by various excuses, saying "It's getting late", or something of the sort, or at least make a burden of it. If they cannot get away altogether, but do stay a short while in church, they pass the time with absurd stories or in useless gossip, not remembering that the house of God is the house of prayer. Afterwards they go home and then to the tavern, and there they do not hurry away, but some of them spend the rest of the day, and until late at night, eating and drinking and having a great celebration.[4]

It is even worse when they are urged to repentance, and to give some visible proof that they intend to reform. Then the answer is that it is not the right time or the right day, or "I'm busy with something else". They say they cannot fast because of their delicate health, nor restore unlawful gains because of their poverty, nor pray because of a "tight feeling in the chest" (*pectoris artitudinem*).[5] The preacher's very choice of subjects is severely limited, if he wishes to hold his audience's attention. There is only one popular topic—the vices of others. Especially

---

[1] Bromyard, A. xxvi. 6.   [2] Id. §§ 27–31.
[3] Id. § 18.   [4] Id. F. iii. 11.   [5] Id. C. ii. 8.

popular is preaching to clergy about the wickedness of laity who do not pay tithes, or to a lay congregation against clergy who give a bad example; yet this is expressly forbidden, because it leads not to profit but to scandal. In the same way husbands are pleased when the sermon attacks the extravagance of wives, and the way in which they spend half their income on dress; while the wives are glad when the men's waste of time and money in ale-houses is exposed to criticism. Each and every one, says Bromyard, is angry when his own short-comings are attacked, and since only in this way can good come, they show thereby that they are more concerned for the salvation of others than of themselves.[1] But it was cold comfort for the discouraged preacher to demonstrate logically that it was foolish of people to be wicked; it was his business to get over these difficulties in one way or another.

It is interesting to advance now a step farther, and separate this unwilling and inchoate congregation into some of its component elements, and see how the man in the pulpit regarded them and their occupations. It is not surprising to find that the poor, the lower classes generally, composed mainly of villeins in the country but including a certain number of artisans in urban districts, were considered the most fruitful audiences. They are ignorant, writes Humbert,[2] and may have to be taught the Lord's Prayer and the Ave Maria, and instructed in their duty of coming to church and of confessing to the priest; they have many vices, of which the greatest is the ease with which they are led astray, especially when someone of a higher social rank condescends to them for his own purposes; yet they show a greater devotion to Christ than the classes above them, and possess faith in greater measure. Let the sermon be simple and straightforward, using stories to drive home its points, like the parables in the Gospels, and the preacher may expect to be richly rewarded for his efforts. The praises of poverty are a commonplace of the thirteenth century, but it is strange in this connexion to find Humbert de Romans, the incarnate official and organiser, the apostle of the golden mean, diplomat, statesman and once nearly Pope, going almost to the lengths to which

---

[1] Bromyard, A. xxvi. 14, cf. St Cher vi. 249 col. 2.
[2] *Max. Bib. Pat.* xxv. 499, cf. 493.

John Ball went, in his attempt to bring consolation and assurance of heavenly reward to the poorest classes.

[Those who live on the fruits of others' labour are for the most part wicked]...there are some who live by honest labour, and these are the peasants dwelling in villages...*Item*, note that this is the life which we were put into the world to lead from the beginning...but again note that since this life is pleasing to God, such people have no ground to murmur against God because he has made them poor labourers in this world, as a certain man used to do, who, when he was overburdened in his work, continually cursed Adam, because through him he had come to such wretchedness.[1]

They have but to live virtuously on earth and then they will win the joys of Heaven; they may be compared to the chicken, which leads a hard and hungry life, but is eventually carried to the king's table.[2] All agree in this, and the poor are continually bidden not to envy the rich their worldly pleasures, because they are a sure sign of coming penance; it is impossible to receive good things in both lives, therefore those who receive them here will suffer later, and conversely, the poor shall receive an eternal reward.[3]

The great ones of the earth, on the other hand, come in for severe handling from every preacher. In the first place they are wealthy, which is alone very nearly enough to condemn them straight away; in the second they show very little devotion, seldom come to church, and are in consequence very much in need of improving sermons.[4] They are very nearly always evil. They lead idle and unprofitable lives; in town and country alike they spend their leisure quarrelling among themselves, and in consequence oppress the poor, both because they disturb the peaceful occupation of agriculture and because the common man has in the end to foot the bill.[5] The manorial lord encroaches on the peasants' rights by engulfing the common pasture,[6] but worst of all his offences are those of having around his table hordes of sycophants who urge him on to new means of extorting money from his tenants, and of employing ruthless and

---

[1] Id. 494.   [2] **Bromyard, P. iii. 13.**
[3] E.g. id. § 11.—See also below, pp. **126–7.**
[4] *Max. Bib. Pat.* xxv. 497.
[5] Id. 492. Bromyard, H. iv. 7.
[6] Id. M. i. 1.

oppressive underlings. The flatterers whisper in the lord's ear, when his money is gone as a result of a riotous youth spent in tournaments and feasting, "You have so-and-so many tenants; you can take twenty marks from them without oppression, for they have many sheep and cattle", and then go on to get something for themselves by making the lord promise a benefice to their ne'er-do-well nephew—*nepotulus*, as Bromyard scornfully has it.[1] The order goes forth for the twenty marks; but the officials charged with its collection have been appointed more for their voracity and skill in extorting money than for their powers of administration or consideration of the peasants' interests, and in any case they always take something for themselves as well.

And so the common people (*minutus populus*) are first oppressed by the great prelates and lords, who take excessively large exactions and tallages, to marry their eldest daughter, to make their eldest son a knight, for their expenses in the pretences of war (*in belli simulacris*) and so on, for their misfortunes and for the horses they have lost in war, and to redeem prisoners from their enemies' lands, and for many other causes.[2] [But this is not all; there come others and yet others to batten on the fruits of the poor man's labour.]

Small wonder, then, that the pulpit resounded to the friar's denunciation of the rich and great; small wonder if a fierce murmur of agreement echoed back at him sometimes from his peasant congregation, or if a Peasants' Revolt or La Jacquerie sometimes sent up the neighbouring castle in flames.

Besides these two divisions of society, we are granted a glimpse of the class with whom the future really lay, the wage-labourer. The rival merits of time-work and piece-work are discussed,[3] and the obvious conclusions drawn, as true to-day as when they were written. Carpenters and masons can be seen vying for praise for the part they have taken in building a house, each grudging his mates a word of commendation from the owner,[4] though all alike are accused by the preacher of careless

[1] Bromyard, A. xv. 11, cf. D. xii. 19.
[2] Id. M. viii. 18.—The three aids (knighting of eldest son, marriage of eldest daughter, ransoming lord's body from enemy) were, of course, expressly permitted by Magna Carta.—For further attacks upon the oppression of the poor by the great, extortionate baronial officers, etc., see M. viii. 20–41, M. xiii. 11–13, I. ix. 19, R. i. 19, 20.
[3] Id. O. iv. 1.   [4] Id. A. xv. 2.

and wasteful work.[1] Most interesting of all is a picture of the workmen at leisure, and the way in which the passing friar may take advantage of the opportunity.

Note that sometimes workmen are found in the market-places of a morning, before they are employed, or in the evenings, when they come to demand their wages, or actually at leisure while at their work. It is a good thing to make some kind of salutary address to such men, because many of them are very ignorant of matters which pertain to salvation.[2]

In the larger towns, and at fairs—where the friar was also bidden to preach if he could find occasion[3]—merchants might be met, carrying on their business of buying and selling on a large scale by means of methods which were repeatedly condemned by the Church, but which defied all her efforts to stop them. It has become fashionable to-day to justify the daily deceptions of the business world by appealing to a "business morality," admitted to differ in many respects from ordinary ethical standards, but held to have no real affinity with those uncompromising words "cheat" and "lie". This is but a poor attempt to explain away conventional bargaining methods, which are so well known that in most cases the deception is discounted almost before it is practised. Perhaps the defence would do better if it were more frank with moralists who attack it; but in the Middle Ages the trader suffered from the disadvantage that his methods were not taken for granted, like those of his modern brother, but practically the whole body of educated opinion was against him. There can have been hardly one favourable word about merchants spoken in a medieval pulpit.

This is no place for a full statement of the thirteenth-century doctrine of usury, but it is necessary to indicate in outline the nature of contemporary beliefs. The earliest Christians had banned indiscriminately, as mortally sinful, all taking (or even expectation) of interest for money lent. The enormous revival of trade in the twelfth and thirteenth centuries rendered this doctrine untenable, though traces of it survived throughout the Middle Ages. The teaching of St Thomas Aquinas on this subject finally became quasi-official: it bears the stamp of his

---

[1] E.g. Bromyard, O. iv. 9, *Max. Bib. Pat.* xxv. 500, etc.
[2] *Max. Bib. Pat.* xxv. 500.   [3] Id. 561-2.

usual balance and moderation. Interest might lawfully be charged in respect of *damnum emergens*, that is, of any actual loss which the lender had suffered through his loan, but not in cases of pure speculation or investment with an eye to profit. Again, in cases of partnership, if the lender took his share of the risks of loss, he had a right also to his share of the profit. But this concordat, however reasonable in theory, was very commonly neglected in practice; and, while the Canon Law upheld these logical distinctions, Civil Law was content with merely insisting that interest should be kept down to reasonable rates. In 1312, for instance, this was 20 per cent., except at the great fairs of Champagne, where securities were probably sounder, and therefore only 15 per cent. was permitted. In certain districts, however, official licences were granted for 40 per cent. or even 50 per cent. All through the Middle Ages this was a very thorny subject for moralists and confessors, as the divergence between theory and practice became wider. We must remember, therefore, that the Dominicans of our period were dealing with a Canon Law in which many "usurious" transactions, though rooted in mercantile custom, were officially banned. Equally forbidden was any attempt at securing more than a moderate profit, or at regulating prices by the relation between demand and supply. The "just price" reigned supreme, but as an idea too vague to be seized by mortal minds. Bromyard, who constantly insists on the observance of this rule, says as much quite expressly: "...it is held unlawful if the equality of justice is not maintained in the buyer and the seller; and he who has more is held responsible to recompense him who loses...because the just price of things is sometimes not exactly determined, but consists rather in a certain estimate"[1] (*in quadam aestimatione*). This being the accepted theory, it was of no avail for the merchant to plead "A man deceived me, and so I want to deceive another who has done me no wrong";[2] he had no right to look at things in that way at all.

Consequently condemnation from the pulpit was frequent and heavy, irrespective of any specific deceit committed in our sense of the word. Even when all possible allowances have been made, however, the conclusion remains that there was a great

---

[1] Bromyard, M. vi. 14.   [2] Id. § 12.

deal left for the preacher to denounce. Dr Owst refers to "the accusing language of Bromyard, who, like others, would wellnigh damn the merchant and his kind with charges of lying, perjury and the baser forms of deceit, chiefly at the expense of rustics and the unsuspecting poor".[1] He lists the extent of this indictment as including: profiteering in corn, using false weights and measures, tricking the balances with the hand, etc. To this catalogue may be added tampering with the coinage[2] and the sale of bad meat[3] (the mind recoils at the thought of how bad it probably was to merit this description seven hundred years ago!), and the picture of the merchant who has just successfully concluded a good "deal", sitting at his ease in his inn or at the fair, little thinking of the fate that is shortly to be his when robbers fall upon him as he proceeds on his way,[4] just as Falstaff, Poins and Prince Hal fell upon the "chawbacons" on the forest-clad slopes of Gad's Hill.

To return to the village, however; in the course of his *exempla*, or even in casual remarks—which, to adopt stage terminology, are often no more than "asides"—the compiler of the sermon-manual gives us a momentary glimpse of many sides of daily life. The parochial nature of the village-community comes out, for instance, in a reference to those who make trouble with strangers,[5] even though they come from only a few miles away. They look upon them with suspicion, saying (no doubt with a world of scornful implication) "You're a northerner", or "You come from the east"; just as still to-day in the more remote parts of the English countryside the "furriner" is always regarded with the greatest distrust. Then there are the manifold petty adventures and incidents of the year. Horses get stuck in the deep

---

[1] *Preaching in Medieval England*, pp. 123–4.   [2] St Cher v. 189 col. 1.

[3] *Anecdotes*, p. 377.—There are also several other forms of trickery listed here.

[4] Bromyard, M. xiii. 17. See also the whole of A. xii (*Acquisitio*), and F. i. 6. One of the most attractive of Bromyard's tales occurs in A. xii. 17.—A man, on pilgrimage overseas, carelessly left about on the deck of his ship the purse containing money his wife had given him for expenses; a monkey seized it and ran with it up the mast. From this height it proceeded to throw two pennies into the boat and one into the sea, repeating the process till the money was exhausted. On his return, the man discovered that his wife had earned the money by selling milk into which she had put one-third the quantity of water!

[5] Id. C. iv. 25.

mud of the rough tracks, and are only persuaded out with the greatest difficulty;[1] the thoughtless make themselves ill by drinking water too far down the stream, where it has become polluted; in winter the fire smokes—there are only two things equally bad, a quarrelsome woman and water trickling through the roof;[2] in foggy weather it is very foolish to carry much money with you, lest robbers take advantage of the excellent cover it offers; maid-servants turn sulky, and make excuses to avoid doing their work; beggars come to the doors, complaining of the hard times they have been through, and so on.

Petty thieving and cheating are apparently fairly common. Cut-purses engage men in conversation to distract their attention while their hands are busy with the victim's wallet,[3] and there is always a supply of wandering rascals who invite people to drink with them at the inn, and then mysteriously disappear as the host is about to call for the reckoning.[4] The ordinary man is not above a little mild poaching, and tries to quiet his conscience by arguing: "God will not condemn me for a little theft like a chicken or a sheaf of corn, nearly everybody does that".[5] The common man, too, is very liable to talk scandal, destroying his neighbours' characters behind their backs, and will even on occasion actually give false witness against them.[6]

Among the evils most frequently castigated, however, are those of gluttony and drunkenness. Any excuse is sufficient for too much eating and drinking, especially at a wedding.[7] Some drink themselves into a state of insensibility,[8] or so near it that they think they see two candles in the room, and, putting the

---

[1] Bromyard, I. iv. 5. The succeeding references in this paragraph are to: D. v. 2; St Cher iii. 42 col. 1; M. xiii. 16; I. iv. 9; and R. v. 58. The exact text of the last is worth repeating because of its felicity: "sicut tempora deteriorantur illis qui contributionem petunt...."

[2] St Cher iii. 42 col. 1. He quotes the "Versus"

Sunt tria damna domus
Imber, mala femina, fumus.

This appears to be a versification of Proverbs xix. 13, which Hugh is here commenting; but the lines do not resemble the A.V. so much as the Vulgate.

[3] Bromyard, A. xii. 6.   [4] Id. C. ii. 3.   [5] Id. A. xii. 54.

[6] See id. D. vi (*Detractio*), *passim*, and a pleasant little story of retribution for talking scandal in A. xxvi. 34, cf. St Cher ii. 89 cols. 1, 2; iii. 41 col. 2 and 140 col. 3; vii. 327 col. 1.

[7] *Max. Bib. Pat.* xxv. 539.

[8] *Anecdotes*, p. 395.

apparently superfluous one out, are left stumbling about help-lessly in the darkness.[1] Yet after all this, and conscious that the preacher regarded their vices as sufficient to send them to Hell after death, they have the hardihood to argue "God made wine and bread and other things that we might eat and drink", and to believe that this is a sufficient defence of their conduct.[2]

Drunkenness and gluttony are the usual accusations levelled against men, and when the sermon touched upon them, the wives among the congregation could be counted upon to endorse the preacher's words with warmth. The turn of the women comes, however, when the subject is that of superstition. It is very significant of the medieval attitude to women that they are scarcely mentioned in the sermons, except in connexion with superstition and luxury in all its forms, and on these occasions they naturally come in for the heartiest and most unsparing condemnation. When their sons are ill, or are a great distance away and no news of them has been received for many months,[3] we may perhaps understand anxious mothers seeking super-natural aids to calm their fears, though the preacher did not. But there was no need for such serious matters to send them off to the witches or "wise women" (*carminatrices*) who pretended to be able to help in the discovery of lost property, produced written charms which were to be worn round the neck or sewn into the clothes, or told them to go to a certain place or walk round a particular tree or other object a certain number of times.[4] In all this, people are deceived and their money taken under false pretences, as Étienne de Bourbon clearly shows with his story of a mother and son who worked a very successful "racket", whereby the son stole cattle and took them to an agreed spot, to which his mother later directed the unsuspecting owner in her character as "wise woman".[5] Best of all, perhaps, is the same writer's tale of a priest who challenged a parishioner to make good his (for it was a man on this occasion) claim to

---

[1] Bromyard, M. ix. 42.
[2] St Cher vii. 200 col. 1. See also id. vii. 185 col. 2; Bromyard, D. xi. 10; *Anecdotes*, p. 409 sq.
[3] *Max. Bib. Pat.* xxv. 505; St Cher iv. 103 col. 1.
[4] Bromyard, S. xi. 3.
[5] *Anecdotes*, p. 314, cf. the curious superstition of "St Guinefort" (a dog unjustly slain by its master), which Étienne himself was called upon to investigate—id. p. 325.

ride about the skies with witches at night, by taking him, the priest, with him. He did, and they saw wonders. After a while the two were led into a great hall, and invited to take their places for a banquet. The priest, as was his custom, made the sign of the Cross before sitting down, whereupon "the demons [for of course they were such] fled away with great violence, and left him naked in Lombardy, shut up in a lonely cellar, and sitting upon a certain cask of wine" (*et illum nudum in Lombardia, in quodam cellario solo inclusum, super quoddam vas vinaticum reliquerunt*).[1]

Apart, however, from the regular business of addressing lay-folk everywhere, the friar might under special circumstances come into contact with two entirely different types of congregation. Most of them would be called upon at some time or other to address meetings of clergy, at a diocesan synod or on some similar occasion, while a few picked men were engaged upon the task of converting the heathen to the South and East of civilised Europe. When speaking to other Religious, the friar seems to have confined himself very largely either to denunciation of their evil lives or to prosecuting the standing quarrels which his Order had with the secular clergy, and this material may most conveniently be noticed later when we have occasion to consider these matters briefly; but a short sketch of the missionary activity of the Dominican Order may find a place here.[2]

Missions received attention from the start, as a natural corollary to bringing back wandering sheep to the Christian fold from which they had strayed. The Bishop of Osma's visit to Rome in 1205 was for the purpose of securing the Papal approval for his project of laying down his bishopric and proceeding to the Orient to convert the heathen. Dominic likewise always intended to visit the "Cumani",[3] and the beard with which he is always represented was grown with this intention in mind. One of the first Dominicans to become a bishop was John the Teutonic, who was placed over the missionary diocese of Bosnia in 1233.

---

[1] *Anecdotes*, pp. 88–9.
[2] On this whole question, see Altaner, *Die Dominikanermissionen des xiii. Jhdts*. Habelschwerdt 1924, where an immense amount of information from numerous sources is assembled to present something like a complete picture.
[3] I.e. Tartars.

As soon as civilised Europe had been provided for, attention was directed to the outer lands. St Hyacinth and his brother were given the habit at the hands of St Dominic himself, and immediately sent to plant the Order in their own country, Poland. In 1228, Scandinavia, Poland, Greece and the Holy Land became provinces of the Order (Hungary had been a province from as early as 1221), while three years earlier the Spanish friars had already pushed across the sea into Morocco. Schools of languages were soon set up to give the necessary training for missionary endeavour, and Raymond of Peñaforte was prominent in this respect. He had two schools of Arabic in operation by 1250, possibly at Tunis and Murcia respectively,[1] and in 1259 the province of Spain was commanded to set up another in Barcelona or elsewhere.[2] It is probable, however, that in spite of official encouragement, there were always too few properly-qualified men.[3] Humbert, in whose time missionary propaganda reached its highest pitch, lashes the friars in the Encyclical of 1255[4] for their slackness in learning foreign tongues. The work is hampered, he says, by two things: ignorance of languages, and a faint-hearted desire not to leave their native land. "Therefore if any find himself ready to learn Arabic, Hebrew, Greek or any other barbarous tongue, let him write to me about it." Next year he is glad to be able to announce that there has been a magnificent response to his appeal, and adds by way of encouragement that the friars who are on their way to the Tartars have sent back satisfactory news from the midst of their journey. It must not be forgotten in this connexion that Aquinas wrote the *Summa contra Gentiles* expressly to serve as a missionary text-book.

Success, so far as can be judged, was small. The friars were willing and conscientious enough, but used the wrong methods.[5] They were hampered at the outset by a curiously optimistic belief in the ease with which the infidel, and especially the Mohammedans, could be converted, and political events were always interfering with their work. But over and above this, they had no systematic plan. Sudden appearances in different

---

[1] Mortier i. 519, Altaner, op. cit. p. 92. [2] *Acta* 1259.
[3] Altaner, p. 236. [4] *Litt. Encyc.* pp. 19–22.
[5] On the contents of this paragraph, see Altaner, pp. 120–8, 230–6.

parts of the Tartar Empire, followed by equally sudden dis-
appearances, could hope for but little result. Brave as was the
journey of Brother Anselm to the Great Khan's headquarters in
1245,[1] successful as it may have been in lessening for a space
the pressure of the invasions upon Western Europe, it was
useless from the missionary point of view because it rested all
hope on the conversion of the Khan himself, which neither
Anselm nor any other achieved or were ever likely to achieve.
In the nearer lands where the secular arm added its aid, formal
baptism of an infidel population was sometimes secured, for
what it was worth; farther east, where the friars stood alone, the
irregularity of their efforts and their misunderstanding of
Oriental psychology prevented them from securing measurable
results.

They had, in any case, chosen a most dangerous and un-
comfortable dwelling-place. The Near East and even the
boundaries of Europe were overrun by the Tartar hordes, whose
leaders were characterised by a ruthless cruelty, and it was one
of the last invasions which wiped out in blood much of the good
work that had been done. In 1259 forty-nine friars were
martyred at Sandomir in Poland, and the General Chapter Acts
contain the simple remark: "Fratres de Ungaria, si a Tartaris
fugantur, caritative recipiantur ubique". This is almost a
parallel to the more naïve story which the Franciscan Jordan of
Giano relates[2] concerning a Friar Minor who preached in vain
to the fierce Hungarian shepherds, and as sole reward for his
efforts was fifteen times beaten and fifteen times robbed of his
breeches.

The Dominican friar did not regard the world in which he had
all these painful and discouraging experiences, and in which
men were so seldom brought to a true love of the Gospels and
the Christian life, with any great satisfaction. Bromyard especially views it with a very jaundiced eye.[3] Nobility, clergy, judges
and juries are incorrigibly corrupt, and the poor are oppressed;
evil seems triumphant everywhere. He even seems on one

[1] He was sent by the Council of Lyons, which was also responsible for the
better-known journey of the Franciscan Pian Carpini.
[2] *Chronica F. Jordani*, ed. Boehmer, p. 2.
[3] E.g. I. ix. 25–36.

occasion[1] to be directing his complaints against the throne, and making it chiefly responsible in that it does not secure more just and peaceful government. The world is evil, and has sadly declined from a former more happy state. The very trees and streams are not so fruitful as of old; as for mankind, he applies to his own generation the words of St Paul, "the ends of the world are come"; men do not live so long, and are neither so faithful nor so good as their ancestors.[2] This is a conventional medieval attitude; but Hugh de St Cher, writing a century earlier, when the outlook was a little more cheerful, was prepared to disagree.[3] He comments upon Ecclesiastes vii. 10 ("Say not thou, What is the cause that the former days were better than these?") and is capable of defending his text upon two definitions of the words "former days". If pre-Christian times are meant, it is easily proved that the hope we now have through the Redemption makes our age in every way the better. But even if the early Christian centuries are meant, the times of St Benedict and St Augustine, the sentence still remains true. Admitted, in those days peace gave opportunities of contemplation, whereas now the Church has become rich, and both it and the world are racked and divided by schism and war.

But that sort of question is foolish, though very common among men, for no age is better than another. Each virtue has its time, its harvest and its vintage.... Therefore it appears that no age is empty of virtues, but they are divided equally.

Even Hugh, however, when giving a list of opposites in the course of an argument upon an entirely different subject, can write: "Note that the flesh gainsays repentance, the world gainsays justice...."[4] Bromyard, writing under the shadow of the Black Death and the Hundred Years' War during its most unsuccessful period for England, goes much farther, and attributes famine and mortality through war and pestilence to "a public and general vengeance" which God is taking for the vices of mankind, as He did at the time of the Flood.[5]

[1] N. iii. 15.   [2] M. xiii. 2.   [3] St Cher iii. 89 col. 4.
[4] Id. ii. 211 col. 4.   [5] Bromyard, L. vii. 36.

CHAPTER VII

THE SERMONS

IT is clearly the purpose of the next inquiry to discover upon what subjects the wandering Dominican friar spoke. Here we are forced to plunge at once *in medias res*, because the amount of general information given by the sources is very small. In one place Hugh de St Cher expresses the four subjects which preaching must handle as "credenda aut operanda aut purganda aut assequenda",[1] and elsewhere extends this into more easily-memorable hexameter form as

Sacra, fides, virtus, vitium, laus, praemia, poena.[2]

while Bromyard would have the friar touch upon the goodness of God, as demonstrated in the Creation and the Redemption, the Kingdom and the Glory.[3] But these are clearly the widest of generalisations, and a real insight into the subjects can only be gained in two ways. A good superficial picture emerges from a glance at the table of contents to a book like the *Summa Praedicantium*, where the material is arranged under a hundred and eighty-nine heads in alphabetical order, ranging from *Abjecti* to *Xtus.* (i.e. Christus). Cross-references and innumerable repetitions, however, render this too complicated a plan to be used here, apart from the fact that not all the topics are of equal interest. The following pages contain, therefore, a selection taken from all parts of this and the other sources, and arranged so as to present a picture of what was said under a few typical heads, especially those which are of interest to a later age for the light they shed on the thoughts and beliefs of a past century. This involves no claim that they are necessarily the commonest subjects, or that the preacher would have presented them in just this way: for obvious reasons, admonition upon the need for abstinence, fasting, and a dozen kindred matters, which would take up a good deal of time in the pulpit, is of no special interest to-day, at any rate within the limits of a brief study.

[1] St Cher vii. 381 col. 3.   [2] Id. ii. 187 col. 3.   [3] L. v. 1.

Upon the method of delivery and the divisions of the sermon little need be said here; these questions will be found discussed *in extenso* in the established works upon medieval preaching.[1] Suffice it to say that, to judge from the sources, a somewhat rigid and scholastic method was adopted, and we may take an example or two of the way in which the sermon came into being in the friar's brain, with the assistance of his hand-books. Under the heading *Peccatum*, for instance, Bromyard enumerates the seven gifts of the "spiritus malignus" and the seven gifts of the Holy Ghost, and sets them over against each other: "The Devil expels the gift of fear by means of pride and presumption ...Anger expels the gift of knowledge...Jealousy expels the gift of piety," etc. Later he explains that each of these can be divided into four *genera*, that is to say, into sins of thought, word, deed and omission;[2] so that, with careful handling, the reader has already the skeletons of twenty-eight sermons, if necessary. A marginal note in St Cher's Bible-commentary[3] provides a similar example.

Theme for Advent: how the ancient Fathers awaited the Lord in certain ways which are noted in the antiphons beginning with O,

and the text duly contains a list of these antiphons (which were, or should have been, familiar to a regular church-going congregation), each provided with an appropriate comment. Quite often, too, he groups together[4] certain virtues or vices, qualities or states of mankind, ways in which the Devil tempts us or the tongue may err, within a large bracket, and illustrates each quality, etc. with a Scriptural text. Every one of these brackets must have represented a ready-made sermon to a man who knew his business, could expand the summary and illustrate it with appropriate *exempla*.

In spite of his desire to avoid being mistaken for one of the illegal and deceitful begging preachers, and of the reiterated commands that mendicancy and preaching were to be kept as

[1] Especially Lecoy, *La chaire*, pp. 289–320, and Owst, *Preaching in Medieval England*, p. 326 sq.
[2] P. v. 2.
[3] ii. 102 col. 4.
[4] E.g. St Cher ii. 101 col. 1; vi. 20 col. 3, 22 cols. 2, 3, 160 col. 1, 193 col. 3.

separate as possible, the friar might reasonably be expected to discourse on the virtue of charity.

> Cum sis in mensa, primo de paupere pensa.[1]

All alike share the obligation to support the poor; but this falls especially upon the rich.[2] Almsgiving is one of the greatest of the virtues, and is incumbent upon everybody. It must not be regarded as a burden; we should be cheerful givers, for through charity eternal rewards are obtained.[3] Like the quality of mercy, it is twice blest:

> ...the poor are necessary to the rich, because from the alms which he gives to the poor, a greater utility accrues to the rich man who gives, because where the poor receive earthly sustenance, the rich receive Heavenly.[4]

This element of reward comes out frequently; alms are enjoined not so much because to give them is an act of human sympathy or an outward expression of the Christian spirit, but because of the advantages to be gained thereby. Charity is made out to be a good investment, and in the language of trade, people are even urged to drive a profitable bargain with Heaven, buying in the cheapest and selling in the dearest market.[5]

St Cher[6] alone protests against this attitude, and rebukes those who think they can buy impunity for their sins in this way. A distinction should be drawn between the good and the bad, between the really needy and the fake; discretion is to be preferred to indiscriminate giving.

> God excludes no man from charity, but he shows that the righteous poor are to be preferred above the unrighteous, apart from the duty of giving to everyone who is in need.[7]

---

[1] Bromyard, M. ix. 33.   [2] *Anecdotes*, p. 124.
[3] E.g. St Cher v. 151 col. 4, vi. 22 cols. 2, 3, 204 col. 4, etc.
[4] Bromyard, D. xi. 35.
[5] Id. E. iii. 20. "Let us act, therefore, according to the custom of merchants, who purchase the goods which they wish to buy when they are cheap, and sell those they have to dispose of when they are dear. But the thing which we ought to prize most highly, that is, heavenly glory, is exceedingly cheap (as has been shown), and the things which we possess are dear, because for them God offers us something of infinite price, eternal glory. Therefore, 'Sell that ye have, and give alms' (Luke xii. 33)...." Bromyard can quote a letter (which I have been unable to identify) of St Augustine's as authority for using such language. Similar phrases are, however, to be found in MPL. 36, col. 387.
[6] St Cher vii. 134 col. 3, 137 col. 1.   [7] Id. iii. 194 col. 2.

This is somewhat exceptional, however, and the same author is
quite capable of writing that the first of the eight "fruits" of
charity is that by it "a man redeems his soul from the Devil's
prison".[1] The general attitude would seem quite clearly to be
that summed up by the doggerel poet Crowley in the sixteenth
century, in the words:

> Cesse not to gyve to all,
> Wythoute anye regarde;
> Thoughe the beggers be wicked
> Thou shalte have thy rewarde.[2]

It was a hard-hearted world, however, which wilfully or foolishly
misunderstood the plain words of the preacher. Some, by a
specious application of Scripture ("Let him that hath two coats
impart to him that hath none"), wish to restrict their charity to
those things of which they have a superabundance: a happy
state to which, of course, they never attain.[3] Others complain
that the poor are idle, wicked thieves, and do not deserve to be
given anything.[4] One rustic, a man of small learning, it would
appear, hearing his priest repeat the words of Christ "...and ye
shall receive a hundredfold", went straight home and gave his
cow to the priest, expecting to receive a hundred in return![5]

Before leaving this subject, it may be mentioned that exhortation to the prompt and cheerful payment of tithes occurs
fairly frequently, thus showing that the friars did make some
attempt to carry out their duty of strengthening the parish
system, and keeping on good terms with the local clergy.[6]

The other side of the medal is presented by contemporary
views upon the dangers of wealth. There can be little doubt that
the Middle Ages took the parable about the camel going through
the eye of a needle a very great deal too literally: "From which
it appears that the Lord has not chosen such (*tales non elegit*),
for if he had chosen them, the way into the kingdom would

---

[1] St Cher iii. 90 col. 1.
[2] *Select Works of Robert Crowley*, E.E.T.S. (1872), p. 16.
[3] Bromyard, M. ix. 31.
[4] Id. E. iii. 46.
[5] *Anecdotes*, p. 121. On the still superior virtue of giving to friars see a
story in Cantimpré II. xxv. 12.
[6] E.g. Bromyard, D. iii. 7, 10; St Cher vi. 240 col. 1.

more easily be open to them."[1] The reason is not perhaps far to
seek, and does provide a certain amount of justification for the
endless satire and condemnation upon the rich which poured
forth from the pulpit. In the first place wealth was very often
obtained by doubtful means; and, while the canonical restrictions upon trade and usury retained their force, it was quite
difficult for any but the landed baronage or the unscrupulous to
attain to riches. In the second, by whatever methods money had
been won, its possessors so often used oppressively the power
which it put in their hands, that the moralist was left with little
choice but to regard it as an agent of corruption.

In consequence, earthly riches are seldom mentioned except
as the prelude to eternal damnation.[2] They are usually referred
to in the same breath as covetousness, which is constantly denounced in Biblical terms as the root of all evil. Though pride
and self-indulgence are always close competitors, greed is nearly
always given as the means by which the greatest number of
mankind fall into evil, in that common sort of wonder-tale in
which "a certain religious woman" or "a saintly brother of our
Order", rapt into a vision, asks the Devil by what methods he
gains most success.[3] The most complete condemnation is
Bromyard's, who maintains that covetousness extends to all
classes and all ages, so that even a ten-year-old child will steal
from its mother.

It makes faithless workmen do bad work, turns the poor into
robbers, makes ordinary men into usurers, who hide away corn
while the poor are dying of hunger, makes lords into tyrants, etc.
...[It is a general plague, and completely insatiable]...the covetous
think to satisfy their greed by saying, "If I had such-and-such a
manor, or so many pounds' worth of merchandise, or a church, or
a prebend, I should never desire more". When they have it, they
complain that the air in the place is bad, or that it is so near the
road that they are over-burdened with visitors, or that it is too far
from a town (*a bona villa*), or that there are no pastures or woods
or fish there, and so they must have another place where they can
stay in summer for the pastures, a second for the fire-wood in

---

[1] St Cher ii. 207 col. 4.
[2] E.g. St Cher i. 33 col. 2; Bromyard, D. xi. 3.
[3] There is one, for instance, in Bromyard, A. xii. 34.

winter, and a third for the fish in Lent. Another must have a second prebend in his own country, etc.[1]

Even stronger denunciation was called forth when the sermon touched upon the daily enjoyments and pleasures of all classes. The puritanism of the medieval Church was almost, if not quite, as strict and narrow-minded as that of the Calvinist Church in the sixteenth and seventeenth centuries. True it was a great deal less business-like and successful in imposing its standards upon the subject populations; but certainly it often regarded all amusements with a very doubtful eye.[2] Rich and poor alike were told that if they persisted in enjoying themselves too much they were running the risk of an awful expiation hereafter.

Among the nobility, jousting and tournaments naturally took the first place. Not one good thing have our sources to say in their favour, not one reference is there to the glory of knighthood or the honourable nature of the profession of arms. A partial explanation is to be found in the decline of chivalry, which was proceeding during the whole period under consideration, but on the other hand the lives of Bromyard and the Black Prince (d. 1376) coincided, and the latter was but the foremost representative of an age in which men took the outward forms at least very seriously, and laid great weight upon keeping the letter of the chivalric law, no matter how much violence they might do to the spirit. The two days' abortive peace negotiations before Poitiers were enlivened by Sir John Chandos's anger at discovering that a French count[3] was bearing the same coatarmour as he.

None of this finds expression in Dominican teaching. Tournaments had been officially condemned by the Church at least from the twelfth century, and are denounced both on this ground and on the more humanitarian one of the evils they bring in their train. "Divitum torneamentum est pauperum tormentum,"[4] writes Bromyard, pointing out that it is the poor who pay in the long run for the nobility's pleasure. Lands are laid waste, heirs impoverished, the tenants reduced to such straits that they have

[1] Bromyard, A. xxvii. 4, cf. C. xiv. 24, D. xii. 18, G. iii. 17, M. xiii. 8.
[2] See Coulton, *Five Centuries*, i. 526–541.
[3] "The lord of Clermont, one of the French marshals."—Froissart, chap. 161 (Berners' trans.).
[4] L. vi. 3; but see the whole of L. vi (*Ludus*).

scarcely a crust of bread to eat, and all for the sake of empty applause and passing renown.[1] Many are killed on these occasions, and the birds of prey that in consequence appear are but the demons come to rejoice over the souls they have captured.[2] Tournaments take place, none the less, and the preacher may make use of the occasion to warn people against them.[3] Cantimpré gives us a picture of a Dominican, a certain Brother Bernard, attempting to do this at a great tournament held at Neuss. Just as they were about to begin, he appeared with his *socius*,

and begged them almost with tears (*quasi cum lacrimis*) that they would spare themselves, and desist from their foolish intention, and have compassion upon Christendom and afflicted Mother Church, at that time being wretchedly laid waste in Hungary and Poland by the Tartars. [All was in vain; the majority were for continuing with the arrangements, although] there were many who would willingly have desisted at their prayers.[4]

Rather less surprising to modern eyes is the condemnation of dice and all other games of chance at which one person makes money at the expense of his neighbour. They lead to lies, oaths and other evil consequences, and there are plenty of people who will dice away the very clothes off their backs. "Such a passion takes hold of gamblers that they lose all shame, even of going naked."[5]

Dancing and singing come in for very strong disapproval. In spite of the often repeated warnings against them, people would rather amuse themselves in this way than go to a sermon, which is nothing less than to pay more honour to the Devil than to God. For devils never appear more frequently in the mouths of medieval moralists than when the wickedness of dancing is discussed. They are the authors and founders of the whole business; they are seen upon the shoulders of dancers; they draw lightning down upon a church the day after dancing has taken place in the churchyard, burn the very vestments of the altar, and, put to flight by the sign of the cross, depart in anger, leaving the marks

---

[1] Bromyard, L. vi. 8, 10, A. xxiii. 2; Cantimpré II. xlix. 3–6.
[2] Cantimpré II. xlix. 4.
[3] *Max. Bib. Pat.* xxv. 559.
[4] II. xlix. 4. See also a condemnation of hunting in id. §§ 16, 17.
[5] Id. § 8. See also Bromyard, D. xi. 23, L. vi. 1.

of their teeth upon the church-yard wall.[1] This last story is told
at considerable length, and must have been, then as now, recog-
nisable as but the dramatisation of a violent thunderstorm.
Those who actually experienced the storm, burdened with
guilty consciences, may well have believed they saw evil spirits,
but it would be very interesting to know what was the attitude
of congregations to whom the incident was repeated for a moral
purpose. It is difficult to believe that this was a very successful
exemplum.[2] Another thunderstorm story presents a good moral
against the musicians who play for dancers, and a pleasant little
Flemish exterior at the same time. For the feast of the dedica-
tion of a church in a very populous town upon the borders of
Flanders and Brabant, there appeared

a certain flute-player, who by his antics and gestures urged on the
dancing youths and maidens to obscene and vulgar songs. About
vespers the sky became overcast, and everybody went home. The
flute-player alone, not having had enough of the sport, remained by
himself in the street, dancing and playing and making vulgar noises.
Two shepherd boys, seeing that thunder and lightning were approach-
ing, took refuge in the bushes nearby, and as they watched, the lightning struck the flute-player, killed him, and tore off his arm. [He
was buried in holy ground, in spite of his justly-earned punishment,
but devils carried the body away during the night.][3]

The evils of dancing and similar fleshly pleasures were only
increased when they were indulged in upon feast-days, when all
should be in Church at prayer in honour of the saint or the
point in the Church's year then being celebrated. But instead,
most people, if they remember these days at all, use them only
as an opportunity for idleness and play. Gay clothes are worn,
and the time is given up to amusement. Those who find it in
their interest, continue to transact their ordinary business, and
some fairs are even deliberately held at such times because of
the greater number of buyers who may be expected. The real
root of this problem lay in the excessive number of the feasts.
There were so many that the village populations could not remember them, and very often the first they knew was the sound

---

[1] *Anecdotes*, p. 398, cf. id. 397, 399, 161; Bromyard, C. xv. 9; Cantimpré
II. xlix. 12, 14.
[2] Cf. the remark quoted below, p. 126.
[3] Cantimpré II. lvii. 4.

of the church bells.[1] Moreover, they were also sufficiently
numerous (about fifty a year) to form a serious interruption of
the year's work, if all were observed; so that both the town
artisan, intent on profit, and the agricultural worker, with a
weather-wise eye turned on the probability of his standing corn
being ruined by rain before the day was out, were prompted by
their own interests to disregard these enforced holidays whenever possible. It is in consequence very interesting to find
Humbert de Romans recognising this, and proposing a reduc-
tion in the number at the Council of Lyons in 1274.[2]

Medieval puritanism finds its strongest expression in the
repeated attacks on feminine fashions and ornaments. The note
most frequently sounded is that of decorating the "wretched
and decaying house of the body" while leaving the welfare of
the soul uncared for.[3] Thus dress, washing, bathing and the use
of mirrors and paint, are all condemned on this ground, and
men are recommended to remove these causes of sin from their
wives and daughters.[4] For damnation inevitably follows such
frivolities, whether they are used with sinful intent or not:[5]
Étienne de Bourbon has a story of a countess who, though
chaste, abstinent and merciful, was damned for her love of
finery.[6] Most significant here is that entire lack of comprehension of the real facts at issue which has already been noticed. It
is obvious that pretty clothes worn with the deliberate intention
of attracting may lead to sin, but it is very difficult to see exactly
what, unless it was simply the weight of orthodox doctrine, could
lead so intelligent a man as Bromyard, for instance, to write a
passage like the following:

Some women excuse themselves, saying that they dress themselves
up to please their husbands, so that the latter shall not see other [i.e.
better-dressed] women and so despise them. Yet the contrary of this
appears to be true, because they do not put on fine clothes at home

[1] *Anecdotes*, p. 273, cf. Lecoy, *La chaire*, p. 424.
[2] *Op. tripart.* III cap. 1 (Brown, p. 223). Other references in this paragraph: St Cher vi. 146 col. 4; Bromyard, F. iii. 6, 8; cf. Cantimpré II. liii. 9
(wickedness of working on the vigils of saints' days).
[3] Bromyard, O. vii. 3.
[4] Id. P. xiii. 7, L. vii. 45.
[5] Id. L. vii. 39.
[6] *Anecdotes*, p. 27.

in their husbands' presence, but when they are going outdoors into the public eye, and often when their husbands are not present.[1]

As a reason for condemnation, this appears to-day to touch almost the depths of absurdity, so many overwhelming psychological and practical grounds are there to explain the wearing of old clothes when working in the home and new ones outside. Moreover we know enough of social history in the Middle Ages to be able confidently to assert that human nature has not changed enough to invalidate these explanations. There remains then the mystery of such an attitude. Complete condemnation is quite understandable on doctrinal grounds; what is far more difficult is to see why a friar, well educated and experienced in the ways of the world, did not realise that the argument with which he justified his condemnation was absurd, and further, that he might have had a much greater success if he had paid more attention to human nature. In cases like this, the Mendicant Orders, in spite of their greater contact with daily life, showed no advance upon the outlook of a thousand years of monasticism.

One possible explanation is the conventional medieval contempt for women, which regarded them practically as a lower order of creation. Dominated by the celibate clerical outlook, the Church always possessed a narrow masculine point of view, and far from granting any kind of equality to women, regarded them alternately as objects of scorn and derision or as so many living temptations always trying to draw men down to perdition.[2] Satire was perhaps the best weapon against the exaggeratedly tall head-dresses and trains that were frequently in fashion, or against garrulity (St Cher quotes the pithy remark of Chrysostom: "quia nimia loquax est hoc genus"), but the attitude was fraught with danger when pursued to the extent which was usual.[3]

It is difficult to see, for instance, that to repeat that women

---

[1] Bromyard, O. vii. 10, cf. *Anecdotes*, p. 236. See further references to feminine adornment in St Cher ii. 169 col. 2; iii. 188 col. 1; vi. 175 col. 1.

[2] Adverse views of women: Bromyard, A. xxvii. 10, C. ii. 7, L. vii. 43, M. xiii. 10, R. v. 15 (note that here, as so often, the usual adjective coupled with *mulier* is *fatua*); St Cher iii. 40 col. 3, 223 col. 1; vii. 34 col. 1, 101 col. 4, 177 col. 1; *Anecdotes*, pp. 202, 207–9, 228, 230, 390.

[3] Head-dresses, St Cher vii. 211 col. 3; *Anecdotes*, p. 233. Garrulity, St Cher id. and iii. 223 col. 2, cf. *Anecdotes*, p. 231 (painting).

were so dangerous that the wise man would avoid them altogether could have any good effect upon a lay congregation. It
was suitable enough for clerics, and—granted the desirability of
the monastic life and the unpolished state of medieval society—
quite possibly was very good advice; but must have appeared
manifestly absurd to an assembly of husbands and fathers.
Grossly unreasonable too is the constant dwelling upon the
crimes of Eve, Jezebel, Bathsheba and other notorious women
of the Old Testament, and upon those sections of the New
which enjoin subjection to their husbands as part of the duty of
women.[1] The uniformly dark picture is only very occasionally
relieved by a story like that of the abbess who secured the
settlement of her case in a court of law, after several unsuccessful
attempts, by bringing her prettiest nuns with her to influence
the judge;[2] or when Bromyard sums up his teaching by making
puns in complicated leonine hexameters—

> Emineas cum femineas discernis ideas;
> Ne sedeas, sed eas, ne pereas per eas.[3]

Such opinions upon women are, however, a clerical commonplace throughout the medieval centuries; and it is more interesting to glance for a moment at two passages which show, the one
how far this scorn of women and distrust of dress could go, the
other a more liberal outlook than usual. Hugh de St Cher, in
the course of a long passage on the subject, asks to what extent
it is permissible for women to wear ornaments.[4] He suggests
social class and the custom of the country as possible justifica-
tions, only to dismiss both; they are not *fines debiti*, adequate
ends to justify a transgression of the Church's law. In order to
illustrate what he means by a *finis debitus*, he quotes with approval the story of a woman who by this means won back the
affections of her husband and so prevented him from committing
adultery, all other means having proved unsuccessful. The sole
justification here was that it was the only means to the end.

And I say, *finis necessarius*, because if a woman uses ornaments,
hoping by this means to draw her husband back from adultery, when
she could have restrained him in other ways, it is not a *finis necessarius*,
and does not excuse her.

---

[1] Especially I Tim. ii. 9–15, I Pet. iii. 1–6.
[2] Bromyard, I. ix. 10.   [3] Id. L. vii. 41.   [4] vii. 331 cols. 2–4.

This seems most strangely immoral, involving a compromise
with the forces of evil in a particularly questionable way; but it
can perhaps be logically justified on the basis of its own assump-
tions.

As in so many cases, Humbert de Romans is more inclined to
be pacific and to see all the good he can. Like all the others, he
condemns wanton ostentation, but in shorter and more moderate
terms, and prefixes this by a materially different attitude towards
the position of women in society. Woman possesses many privileges; for instance, she was created to be a help meet for man, not
to be his servant: witness the fact that Eve was created from
Adam's rib, not from his foot, as might well have been the case.
He then goes on to point to the example of the Virgin, and
recommends its excellence.[1]

The friar attempted to drive home his teaching upon these
and countless other subjects by three methods in particular,
beyond his own example and repeated exhortations: the fear of
death, the fear of the Devil, and the fear of Hell. None of these
was new or peculiar to the Mendicant Orders, but all were
characteristic of them, and in the first at any rate they had a
considerable influence in causing the gradual increase in the
morbidity and crudeness of the images under which death was
portrayed, which reached its climax in the cult of the *macabre* in
the fifteenth century, seen at its best in the poems of Villon and
in the paintings of the *Totentanz* (Dance of Death).[2] Fear was
the main essence of all this, and it is fairly plain that the intention
was that if people could not be brought to love good for its own
sake they should at least be made to shun evil for fear of the
consequences. Hence such stories as that of the German knight
who, for his sins, was "translated" like Bottom, and acquired
the head of a demon, so that his wife screamed out in terror at
sight of him, and, when he walked down the village street to
confession, the cattle ran lowing into the fields and the priest
bolted himself into the church for fear.[3] From this come also
the repeated admonitions to remember that death is never far

---

[1] *Max. Bib. Pat.* xxv. 503. Contrary view of the Creation in St Cher ii.
211 col. 3, Bromyard, C. ii. 2.
[2] See Huizinga, *Waning of the Middle Ages*, pp. 124–35.
[3] Cantimpré II. xxx. 39.

away and that when it comes it will mean a rude awakening for many who have slept in their sins. "Memento mori" is the constant tone of such preaching, and the way in which there began the crystallisation into the image of the decay of fleshly charms with advancing age, and the ghastly skeleton figure of death, that later became so common, is already obvious in one story related by Thomas of Cantimpré.[1]

After death came the Last Judgment, when the Devil would carry off many to eternal torment, but even in the meantime his powers on earth were great. Practically all the pulpit attacks upon the vices of mankind ended with the stated or implied conclusion, "If you do not reform, you will be damned," as is plain from the frequent mentions of the Devil and the success with which he works, made in the course of the immediately foregoing pages. In addition to this Cantimpré, for instance, devotes several complete sections[2] of his work to describing demonological visitations, and to explaining them as sent to test the constancy of the victim's belief. So strong are the powers of evil that they mix in the very Church processions,[3] and some people even burn propitiatory candles in their honour in the same way that they do to God and the saints.[4] All the trials and troubles of this world are in reality due to "una generalis daemonis tentatio et seductio".[5]

In addition to all this, the pains of Hell and the easy way that leads thither are never very far away from the speaker's thoughts. God needs it as an essential attribute of his royal dignity, just

---

[1] II. xxx. 31. A priest happened one day to see a beautiful girl, and, though she shortly afterwards died, was haunted in dreams by her image for three years. At last he could stand it no longer; "seeing therefore that the devil did not cease to plague him, he went secretly at night, opened the grave of the dead woman and held his face so long in the filth of the putrefying body that he was almost suffocated by the stench, and fell down as if dead. This so profited the holy man that he never afterwards felt any temptation of the flesh".—Bromyard's section on *Mors* (M. xi) is one of his longest, running to 132 closely printed columns. See esp. M. xi. 30, also St Cher vii. 127 col. 3, 154 col. 4, 211 col. 1, 242 col. 3, and *Anecdotes*, pp. 58, 65, 222.

[2] II. lv, lvi, lvii. The last-named contains an attempt to explain the origin and purpose of the demons' powers (§ 62).

[3] Bromyard, C. xv. 5.

[4] Id. A. xx. 9.

[5] Id. M. ix. 48. See also the interesting discussion of the nature of the Devil's temptations in the next two paragraphs. By these means "quasi totum mundum deciperet" (§ 50).

as much as an earthly sovereign needs a prison in which to shut up criminals.[1] Its punishments are enumerated—heat and cold, hunger, thirst and terror[2]—and the arguments of those who try to convince themselves of its unreality are exposed.[3] The wicked will discover the reality of it quickly enough when they come to die, and will find a welcome awaiting them in the infernal regions, where there is "a horse in the stable ready for every rider".[4] Actual statistical estimates of the chances of damnation show how real this fear was, and give a pale and shadowy idea how strong was the effect which a powerful speaker might have on a rude and inexperienced country audience. The most unfavourable occurs in a story of Cantimpré's.[5] In 1248 a certain cleric was appointed to preach before an episcopal synod, and when he was unable to compose a sermon, a demon appeared to him and suggested the following:

The princes of the infernal shades salute the princes of the Church. We gladly return thanks to them, because, with themselves, their subjects are handed over to us, and through their negligence almost the whole world (*totus pariter fere mundus*) falls into our hands.

Bromyard on one occasion quotes with approval a saying (supposed, according to him, to come from St Bernard) that only one in four should be saved,[6] and on another relates a story that on the day St Thomas of Canterbury died, there died altogether three thousand and thirty-three persons, of whom three thousand went to Hell, thirty to Purgatory and three to Heaven.[7] Humbert de Romans again gives the most moderate opinion. He comments (Luke xvii. 34) "There shall be two men in one bed; the one shall be taken, the other left," interprets it as meaning that only half of mankind will be saved, and is shocked at this appalling possibility, which he calls a "terrible saying" (*terribile verbum*).[8] St Cher says nothing definite upon the same text, but appears to accept the equal division without comment.[9]

[1] Bromyard, P. viii. 8.   [2] St Cher iii. 121 col. 2, cf. *Anecdotes*, p. 22.
[3] Bromyard, A. xxvi. 7, D. i. 16 sq.
[4] Id. A. viii. 6.   [5] I. xx. 8.   [6] M. xiii. 17.
[7] M. xi. 36. For a close parallel (probably the origin) to this story, and many further illustrations of the whole subject, see Coulton, *Five Centuries*, i. Appendix 2, esp. pp. 445–451.
[8] Humbert i. 127.
[9] St Cher vi. 237 col. 3. Aquinas (*Sum. Theol.* 1a, Q. xxiii. art. 3) takes it for granted that the damned will outnumber the blessed.

Here as elsewhere, however, it is questionable whether the intended effect was secured. Certainly the result was a very unspiritual attitude: by the fifteenth century the thought of death had become simply that of the physical death of the body and the ensuing corruption; the hoped-for life of the soul after death fell more and more into the background. In the same way continued horrors palled and lost their force as a means of turning people from evil. On hearing a preacher hold forth upon the torments of Hell, many say:

We believe what God tells us; but there is no need to put faith in the stories and *exempla* of other preachers, because they relate such dreadful things to frighten sinners, or for other reasons.[1]

Before concluding this study, there is one more means of conversion, and a very illegitimate one, which deserves mention. It comes to particularly strong expression in Bromyard, and is apparently again linked with the all-pervasive and too often harmful literalness of the medieval outlook. The whole of the sixth chapter of St Matthew's Gospel is, quite naturally, a very frequent source of quotation; but verse 33 is specially often cited: "Seek ye first the kingdom of God, and his righteousness; and all these things shall be added unto you." A rigid interpretation is easily able to show that this means that the virtuous shall receive rewards for their virtue during this life: St Cher, for example, comments the last words very briefly: *scilicet temporalia*.[2] With comparative frequency we find it stated that the just shall receive earthly goods in return for their uprightness, as well as a crown of glory in Heaven;[3] that the decline of religion is proved by the decrease in the endowments and gifts made to monasteries in "these modern times";[4] even on one occasion there is the clear statement: "this we see by experience, that those who rise in the middle of the night or early in the morning [i.e. to attend services] and live frugally, live longer and are better-looking (*pulchriores*) than others".[5] But so literal an interpretation of the Bible very frequently leads to contradictions, of which Bromyard was apparently not aware—and indeed in so enormous a book he may well be excused for this. The repeated "Verily I say unto you, They have their reward" of verse 5, etc.

[1] Bromyard, D. i. 14.   [2] St Cher iv. 261 col. 4.
[3] Bromyard, R. v. 22–3, P. iii. 9.   [4] Id. R. v. 38.   [5] Id. A. vii. 14.

of the same chapter, could well be brought to mean the exact contrary. So we read that it is "causa admirationis" that good often happens to the wicked on earth;[1] or again,

Just as it is the best sign of salvation when a man lives well and things go badly with him, so it is the best sign of damnation when he lives wickedly and good happens to him.[2]

This is perhaps a more acceptable doctrine, or at least does not do so much violence to the modern understanding of Christianity. But consistency is too much to expect, and in our Dominican sources we see evil clergy brought to ruin and loss of their benefices because of their sins, usurers and oppressive nobility punished by sudden strokes of bad fortune and either by an entire absence of heirs or by having sons who are either vicious or weak-minded.[3] Looked at from such a distance of time, these cases are most interesting as an example of the strange uses to which Scripture can be put, and of the avidity with which, even in the fourteenth century, the friars used their Bible and brought all their school-trained reasoning powers to bear on all kinds of texts, in their search for yet new ways of keeping their congregations within the narrow path of virtue.

[1] Bromyard, M. xi. 17.
[2] Id. D. xi. 33.
[3] Id. L. vii. 33, N. iii. 14, V. xii. 21, cf. also D. xi. 26.

CHAPTER VIII

THE DOMINICAN ORDER IN ITS RELATIONS WITH THE SURROUNDING WORLD

IN spite of the vast amount of literature devoted to preaching, it is impossible to estimate the extent of the success which the Dominican Order achieved. Though it is clear that thousands of sermons were preached and that thousands of men, many of them thoroughly earnest, spent their whole lives in the work of conversion, there is no tangible memorial of the results of their preaching. For some years after the Bull of foundation, popular interest in religion was greater than ever before, and the two Orders of friars gained their success by playing upon an enthusiasm which they were not solely responsible for creating. If the number of recruits they gained to their own ranks may be taken as an indication, then the total gain from their preaching was great; but there is no means of going further and making even the roughest conjecture of the numbers they brought to a real belief in Christian truth by their activities.

One possible indication of the effect the friars had is to be gleaned from their conflicts with rivals within the Church. If the opposition of the seculars mainly proceeded from the loss of money which the friars' success in attracting burials and gifts entailed, yet it was also due to a deep-rooted feeling that they were being "shown up" in some way. The second Encyclical of 1255[1] gives us an idea how greatly the parish churches suffered from the attractiveness of their rivals. Tact is enjoined in large quantities. It is better not to fall out with the Mammon of the world; even though you may have privileges entitling you to do this or that, the sensible course is to apply for the bishop's licence as well.[2] Above all, avoid arranging a sermon on the day he is going to preach; it can only have bad results for you if he speaks to empty aisles while the crowd surges round your pulpit! Such is the tenor of the letter, and all the evidence goes

---

[1] *Litt. Encyc.* p. 21, cf. ALKG. i. 224.
[2] Cf. similar commands in the consts. of 1228—ALKG. i. 224.

to show that it is a true picture of conditions at the time at which it was written. The age of the Alleluia was quite willing to follow the Church, if the Church would only lead, and as a result of the friars' efforts a lead was given for the space of two generations. It may not be without significance that the enthusiasms of the later thirteenth century fall into the errors of exaggeration rather than of heresy.

But it may be doubted if the success gained was as real as it was apparent. There is a vast difference between averting a threatened revolution and making it impossible for that revolution ever to occur in the future. Since the Middle Ages are no longer regarded as the Ages of Faith, it would be misleading to imply too great a success in any branch of medieval ecclesiastical life. The heretical areas of Southern France are no doubt an exceedingly bad example to take, because bigotry complicates the issue beyond disentanglement; but only here is there even a chance of estimating the growth of the faith. It is legitimate to doubt whether preaching pure and simple had any really perceptible effect in Languedoc. Dominic and de Montfort both failed utterly to shake the heretics' resistance, and it was only after long years of war had given place to the longer years of the Inquisition's tyranny that Bernard Gui in 1320 was able to regard the work as finished. Final success is unquestionable, but that success was gained by illegitimate means. Compulsion never has been and never can be an adequate substitute for conversion, because no law, however brutal, can affect the inner places of the mind.

Of the Inquisition itself little need be said. It was neither founded by nor solely confided to the Dominicans. On at least one occasion, in 1243, a number of the faint-hearted wished to resign its burdensome honours—though in view of the previous year's massacre at Avignonnet their discretion is thoroughly understandable.[1] Nor was the Inquisition ever regarded with full favour by the Dominican authorities—it interfered with the more important work of preaching and was listed under the head of *impedimenta*.[2] It had the immediate effect that was intended, at the expense of a vast amount of cruelty both mental and physical. The effect was, however, hardly worth the having. It

---

[1] Mortier i. 356.　　　　　　　[2] Humbert ii. 36.

was a complete negation of the milder and more reasonable purpose for which the Dominican Order was founded, when that Order was given charge of an institution which existed for the purpose of using violent methods. The sons of Dominic sold their birthright when they became Inquisitors, and sacrificed an ultimate success which was just within the bounds of possibility and of their own powers, for the specious attractions of present gain. Neither they nor the Pope should perhaps bear too heavy blame for creating the Inquisition. Toleration was a principle unknown outside Languedoc (even if it was really known inside), and was suspect as being equivalent to heresy just because it was a Languedocian ideal. In attempting to apply the methods of the police-state all parties were acting in what they considered the best interests of religion. They could plead that gentler methods had been tried without success, and can hardly be expected to have realised that in using force they were admitting their own defeat.

The greatest praise the Dominicans can truly claim is that they helped to bring back the Church of their time to a sense of its duty. This is, quite clearly, to regard them merely as another monastic reform, and so far as this view is concerned they need have possessed no special characteristics distinguishing them from earlier reforms, save those of popularity and ubiquity. It was these qualities which enabled them to shame their contemporaries into further efforts, and it is not without significance that great reforming bishops like Odo Rigaldi and Robert Grosseteste did their work after the two Orders had come into existence. In view of the mass of evidence which can be quoted for the uniformly bad state of the medieval Church, it is risky to attempt to show that any great improvement actually came about. Reference shall be limited to the description of Alsace which has already been quoted.[1] Jaffé[2] dates the description as about 1300; it is noteworthy that a writer of that time—when the Dominicans were already on the decline, as the rest of the Colmar Annals, with their inordinate interest in stupid "miracles" or natural portents, show only too clearly—believed, contrary to the overwhelmingly general custom of the whole Middle Ages, that his own time was better than an

---

[1] MGH. xvii. 232; see above, p. 10.   [2] Ib. p. 187.

earlier century. If we accept his censures on the priesthood of
1200 on the ground that he seems to have studied contemporary
documents and not to have invented facts, then we must also
accept his unspoken implication that an improvement has taken
place. Within narrow restrictions of time and space a little change
for the better is visible in some corners of the ecclesiastical
world; and though the Order of Preachers has no claim to a
monopoly of responsibility for this, it may well claim a share in
it on two grounds: that it acted as an irritant, making others
consider whether they had not better mend their ways; and that
it gave its best men to the service of the Church it was created to
defend.

The number of Dominicans who were raised to the episcopacy
is even more striking than the number of their teachers. This is
plain testimony from a succession of Popes to the excellence of
their life and the ability which they were expected to show, and
suggests a more definite ground for assessing the influence of
the Order on the Church. For it may reasonably be assumed
that at least until well past the middle of the century the great
majority of Dominicans were earnest and upright men, and
therefore that the new bishops would be likely to show the
general characteristics. Relaxation had set in before thirty years
from the foundation, but it did not attain vast proportions for
another thirty years. In any case, a Dominican might hold
views on the possession of money which passed as lax in his
Order, and yet appear to be the embodiment of apostolic poverty
in comparison with his brother-bishops. The mere appointment
as bishop was, however, regarded by the disciplinarians as in
itself a sign of decay, and it is in consequence possible to regard
the matter in one of two ways, corresponding to the acceptance
or rejection of this point of view. It can be taken as an evidence
of a decline, or as a justified compliment from Rome which was
well-earned by the good lives of those appointed.

St Dominic himself had refused two or perhaps three bishoprics, but at least one of his followers had been elected and had
accepted by 1232—Raymond de Felga succeeded Foulques of
Toulouse in that year.[1] In consequence the next Chapter pro-

---

[1] Dominic's refusal, Mamachi, *App*. 117, Echard i. 35. Raymond, Mortier
i. 198. John the Teutonic was created bishop of Bosnia, 1233—ib. i. 295.

tested, and forbade any brother, under pain of *ipso facto* excommunication, to accept such an appointment without special licence of the Pope, the Master or the General Chapter. But prohibition was of little avail, least of all a prohibition which could be got over by application to the Pope, who was more interested than anyone else in making hosts of exceptions to the rule. Gregory IX made thirty-one such appointments during his reign,[1] and after his death Humbert de Romans was even put forward by a minority as his successor. Innocent IV in the space of eleven years, the last six months of which were spent in conflict with the Dominicans, chose thirty-five bishops, nine archbishops, a patriarch and a cardinal from among them; Alexander IV followed with twenty-six bishops, two archbishops and a patriarch; while it is estimated that, by about 1320, there had been 450 Dominicans among the dignitaries of the Church, and within this number are included two Popes and a dozen cardinals.

The best and strictest Dominicans objected to this tendency, and the *Acta*[2] show their attempts to stop it. Their reasons were simple and of three kinds. There was the well-established controversy which laid the eventual salvation of a bishop open to doubt; relaxation must unavoidably follow upon the state which even an ascetic bishop must keep (hence the commands that brothers who are bishops should conform to the constitutions "in vilitate vestium", e.g. 1247, 1252); finally, the necessity of providing each bishop with at least one *socius* was an unreasonable drain on personnel. This last soon became a severe problem. With Dominicans as bishops, inquisitors, ambassadors, royal counsellors and confessors, and in a host of other external appointments, all of which had to be duplicated in order to maintain the rule about *socii*, and with all these positions simultaneously demanding the best men possible, the man-power of the Order felt the strain; and it may be wondered whether preaching did not suffer in consequence. Examples of these views are found, for instance, in the Chronicle of Humbert, where it is said of the mastership of John the Teutonic: "under

---

[1] These figures are taken from Mortier i. 390, 646, and Mandonnet, *S. Dominique*, 101. Cf. lists at end of each Papal reign in *Bull. Ord. Praed.*
[2] See *Acta* 1233, 1247, 1252-4-5.

him also the Lord Hugo was made a cardinal and many brothers in divers places were raised to the episcopacy, to his great displeasure, and to the displeasure of those brothers who truly loved the Order ".[1] Or again, Thomas de Lentino, archbishop of Cosenza, 1267–73, is found asking the Milan Chapter of 1270 for their prayers, and referring in his letter to "praelatio mea, inquietatio potius ".[2] John's successor as Master-general is just as convinced of the undesirability of the episcopate and points an accusing finger at those who seek it;[3] there are many, he says, chiefly in rich churches, who think they are called by the Lord because they are canonically elected. But he, and Aquinas with him, are beginning to take a broader view of this as of almost every other subject. In spite of the well-known letter to Albertus Magnus ("I would rather see you dead than a bishop"), he can see three reasons why a friar may accept the honour: Divine vocation, charity to one's neighbour, and obedience;[4] the last being the most stressed. The advantages to the people were so apparent if they received a bishop who made more than a pretence of doing his duty, that by the mid-century those who spoke with the voice of authority were beginning to justify relaxation on this point. Quite in accordance with the Dominican spirit moreover; the friar exists more to save the souls of others than his own, and if he can best serve them by endangering himself, then the risk is justifiable. Such at least is a perfectly sound theoretical defence of the change; it was in this spirit, no doubt, anyhow during the thirteenth century, that many newly-elected bishops faced their duties.

The widespread influence of the Dominicans upon the secular world proceeded from the same causes—their learning, skill and reliability. It is in reality as little surprising that diplomatists should be found among them as it is that they should have produced scholars and bishops. The Order of Preachers was very much "imperium in imperio", and, working so much on its own, subject only to the Pope, it rapidly acquired a knowledge of affairs unrivalled in its time. This can be traced back to the time of its origins, to the abrogation of *stabilitas loci*. Wandering

---

[1] *Chron. Humberti*, in Mamachi, *App.* 305.
[2] Finke, p. 71.   [3] Humbert i. 544.
[4] Ib. Cf. *Sum. Theol.* 2a, 2ae, Q's 182, 184–5.

preachers were bound to know far more of the world than monks, indeed it was their duty to know their world as well as might be. Their travels brought them into contact with all sorts and conditions of men, and their travels were wider than anybody else's. Preachers-general, inquisitors, priors-provincial, and diffinitors of the General Chapter, to say nothing of the Master-general and his *socii*, saw a great deal of Europe. During the thirteenth century the annual assembly was held in towns as widely separated as London, Barcelona and Budapest. Moreover, provincials and diffinitors at least were constantly changing, so that this experience was spread fairly evenly over a large number of men. Their importance as the hierarchs of a powerful and well-organised body whose strength and influence were not to be despised, and also as in a special sense the emissaries of the Pope, made them welcome everywhere and especially at royal and baronial courts. Salimbene is the most perfect example of how far worldly wisdom could go in a thirteenth-century friar, but many Dominicans could rival his knowledge of men, if not his attractively garrulous method of recording it. It is hardly surprising, then, to find members of the Order occupying all kinds of secular and semi-ecclesiastical posts, and a few of the more obvious examples will show the extent of the political influence they wielded.

Apart from the more or less legendary friendship with de Montfort, little can be said of Dominic in this respect; his time was fully occupied with preaching and with journeys to Rome to obtain privileges for the Order. Stephen of Spain[1] does indeed record that in his lifetime the brothers made peace in Lombardy and the Marches, where nearly all the cities offered them their statutes and plenary power of revision. But it seems not unlikely that he was actually thinking of what was going on at the time when he gave his testimony—1233, the Alleluia year. Jordan of Saxony is found on apparently friendly terms with Frederick II, whose friendship John the Teutonic also enjoyed both before and after his profession.[2] Diplomatic activity in Germany was indeed not uncommon. Many troubles occurred through the onerous duty of publishing the various excommunications of Frederick being confided to Dominicans, and on one

[1] Mamachi, *App*. 128.   [2] *Vit. Frat.* iii. c. 31.

occasion (1241) Frederick is found complaining to the Chapter that friars are concerning themselves with the quarrel of Pope and Emperor.[1] Jordan is better known for his friendship with Blanche of Castile and her young son Louis, who kept the same Dominican confessor for twenty-one years when he became king. It is not improbable[2] that this friendship enabled Jordan's influence to be used in healing the breach with the University of Paris in 1229. Raymond of Peñaforte had been a political figure of note before he joined the Order, but his assumption of the habit did not cause him to give up these activities. He was an adviser of the young king Jayme of Aragon from 1219, and sat, for instance, in the Cortes of Monzon which arranged for the conquest of Valencia in 1236. His companions on this occasion were Michel de Fabra and Berengar de Castelbisal,[3] who had earlier taken a leading part in the capture of Majorca. Spain did not lose touch with the Dominicans after Raymond's withdrawal from active affairs, and Alfonso is found in friendly communication with the Chapter of 1264.[4]

The officials of the Order were not alone in these activities. Brother Guala assisted in the negotiation for the treaty of San Germano,[5] and the peace-making career of that strange character, Giovanni Schio da Vicenza, is well known. He was distrusted by Gregory IX on account of rumours that he was considering making himself Pope, but carried out the valuable work of reconstructing the crumbling Lombard League. He was the chief apostle of the frenzied pacifism of 1233, and did much good in reconciling opposing factions in the North Italian towns. He was too violent for the people of Verona, however, when they made him Podestà, as he signalised his arrival in power by burning sixty heretics—men, women and children. The same city produced Peter, who was so energetic in repressing heresy and riots in Florence that a successful plot was made against his life.

Work such as this was very likely to lead to relaxation, as the friars occupied in it were almost entirely freed from the ordinary

---

[1] Cf. *Acta* 1246, 1247 (provision made for refugee friars from Lombardy, Tuscany and Germany), 1250.

[2] Jord. Sax. p. 90, cf. Mortier i. 244.   [3] Danzas, pp. 152, 258 sq., 290.

[4] Finke, p. 58 (cf. *Acta* 1291), cf. pp. 99–102 (Ottokar of Bohemia protects a provincial Chapter from violence, likely by reason of local disturbances).

[5] Mortier i. 207. See special Bulls for his protection in BOP. i. 21, 26, 30.

restraints of discipline. There are frequent condemnations of
visiting the courts of kings and princes in the *Acta*,[1] beginning
in 1239. On many occasions special reference is made to the use
of carriages and servants, which are strictly forbidden. A further
result was likely to be the interference of secular persons in the
government of the Order, a tendency which particularly enraged
Humbert de Romans. Thus the Scottish brethren all received
thirteen days' bread and water and thirteen disciplines in 1261
for attempting to gain their objects (unspecified) by persuading
the King to write to the Pope and the Chapter-general. A
similar prohibition is repeated ten years later, but in 1275
previous commands are reversed by an edict which draws
attention to the benefits accruing from the favour of princes and
prelates, and warns the friars to take diligent care lest they offend
the great; all who presume to do this shall be severely[2] punished.

The relations of the two Orders of friars with the secular
clergy are well known. In spite of continual efforts by Chapters
and Masters to smooth over difficulties as they arose, and to
prevent their subordinates from giving needless offence, these
relations were almost uniformly bad. There are three main
causes of this unfortunate state of affairs, of which two could not,
in the nature of the case, well have been avoided. St Francis
found it necessary to go to great lengths to make even his early
followers give that reverence to priests which he considered was
their due, and had to affirm that no matter how evil the life of a
priest might be, yet the hands that performed the mysteries of
the altar were holy, and worthy to be kissed by every true
Christian. A letter[3] of John the Teutonic in 1246 is to the same
effect. Honour must be given to priests, "quos, etsi desunt
merita, gradus tamen officii efficit reverendos". An organisation
which was itself composed of priests, however, was bound to
find this problem still more acute. In the second place, it was
plain for all to see that the Dominicans were more learned than

---

[1] *Acta* 1239, 1245, 1261, 1271, 1275 (Reversal). For carriages, etc. see
below.

[2] *Gravius*—a technical term referring to a particular class of offences, cf.
Consts. of 1228, ALKG. i. 208.—Further indications of this sort of activity
will be found in Jordan, *Die Briefe* (ed. Altaner), p. 36, Cantimpré i. xx. 10,
ii. lvii. 65, and Walz, *Compendium*, p. 187.

[3] *Litt. Encyc.* p. 8. St Francis' views, *Spec.* c. 23.

the secular clergy, and both parties were very sensitive to the difference between them in this respect. Scholarship and faith are not interchangeable terms, but it is very difficult to find a good debating reply to the argument which says that both are good, but that a combination of the two is better. Humbert and Aquinas, as we have already seen, are very prone to use this line of reasoning; it can therefore be readily imagined that the rank and file, restrained by little sense of responsibility, gave constant offence both to the worthy and the unworthy among the parish clergy by an indecent emphasis upon their own pre-eminent ability in theology. Here again repression was attempted from headquarters—the same letter may be again quoted—but with little effect.

To these causes of friction may be added an overwhelming ambition and the unthinking enthusiasm of reform on one side, and the stolidity of a conservative vested interest on the other. These alone would have made quite enough trouble; when the Dominicans gained privilege after privilege from Rome, freeing them from all obligation to the seculars in whose parishes and dioceses they were "squatting" (to use a medical analogy which affords a good illustration), confusion was confounded. Papal licences of every kind and for every conceivable purpose had been sought from the earliest days. The purpose was good, and even reasonable—only by securing freedom from the narrow and selfish restriction which bishops and clergy would impose, could the work of conversion be properly carried out. It was not until the end of the first half-century that it was realised that these privileges could become a doubtful benefit. Humbert's advice to his sons that, notwithstanding their legal right to do so, it is better not to preach without the bishop's leave, shows a dawning recognition that legal logic cannot solve all human relationships.

The journey to Rome in 1215 marks the beginning of an unending series of appeals to Caesar. It was followed quickly by the authorisation of 22 December 1216. From this time the founder spent most of his time near the chair of Peter, and avowedly called for help at every turn. "L'ordre des prêcheurs est autant l'œuvre de la papauté que celle de Dominique."[1]

[1] Mortier i. 94.

When the Spanish prelates, for instance, put difficulties in the way of the brothers in their country,[1] Dominic demanded and received a special Bull which should act as their passport and translate all opposition into a deliberate defiance of Rome. The best illustration of this policy is given by events which followed shortly. During his sojourn in Paris, Dominic found that the convent was poor and did not possess the right to public celebration of Mass. He promised Matthew of France to talk to the Pope about it. In December 1219 he met Honorius at Viterbo, and got his Bull, despite the opposition of Philippe de Grève, Chancellor of Notre-Dame, who feared lest his Chapter's revenues from the church of St Benoît, a close neighbour of St Jacques, might suffer in consequence.[2] No clearer example could be desired of the nature of and reasons for clerical jealousy, and of the coincidence of Mendicant demands with the assertion of Papal supremacy.

Later Masters-general continued upon the lines already laid down, and were in constant contact with Rome. "Curia romana visitanda est a magistro tam pro ipsius reverentia quam pro ordinis utilitate, temporibus opportunis....indulgentias et concessiones, etiam verbo solo utiles ordini quas poterit impetrare."[3] By 1261, with the publication of *Virtute conspicuos* by Alexander IV,[4] independence of everyone save the Pope was finally and completely attained. Lesser men than the Master also appealed with frequency to the seat of authority. Right from 1228 the Chapters had continually to prohibit journeys to Rome,[5] and in 1256 one Brother Trojan appears as permanent procurator at the Curia. His memorandum is appended to the *Acta* for 1257, and in it he complains that he is overburdened with debt, because friars ask him to expedite their business, and either send no money or send it late. In subsequent years his successors, like the diffinitors of the Chapter-General, inform the Order that no action can be expected when illegible communications are sent;

---

[1] Laurent 115, BOP. i. 8. For similar examples of Papal protection, cf. Laurent 123, 128, 130, 143, 144, 145, 147, 149, 153; and BOP. i. 5, 7, 11, 14, 15, 19, etc.
[2] Ib. 105–110. Laurent 121.
[3] Humbert ii. 186.
[4] BOP. i. 405. This is the so-called "Mare magnum".
[5] ALKG. i. 226.

it is not unreasonable to suggest that this indicates the receipt of letters from humble brethren in out-of-the-way convents where skill in penmanship was not high. The appearance of the procurator at this time is probably due to the crisis of 1254, when St Amour as procurator of the University of Paris had very nearly won the case for his side by his skilful advocacy, and the unofficial Dominican representative, Hugh de St Cher, had not been listened to. If careful preparation and the appointment of a special and permanent officer can do anything, a repetition of this disaster is not to be allowed.[1]

Clerical opposition developed *pari passu* with the increase in Dominican privileges. Their work, their honour and their money were constantly taken from the priesthood by an Order which theoretically existed simply to assist them in executing a duty which was beyond their powers. Small wonder that it is comparatively uncommon to come across examples of friendship between the two. In Finke's collection of letters, for instance, for one example of good relations (p. 69) there are five of friction (pp. 70, 90, 112, 154, 161). The first of these concerns trouble with the Teutonic Order; it is fair to oppose to this the voluntary submission by the Carthusians of their disagreements to a commission of Dominicans under Humbert's presidency.[2]

---

[1] One side of the procurator's duties is given by Humbert (ii. 187): "Cui enim committenda est potestas super apostatas ordinis et super fratres ad curiam inordinate venientes et etiam super illos qui ordinate veniunt, ut cum consilio suo procedant, et circa alia quaedam, prout visum fuerit expedire." The advice of one living at the Papal curia would naturally be of great assistance to friars who did not know the complicated procedure by which business was done at Rome. The main duty of the procurator would, however, probably be regular attendance in the *Audientia publica* and, when necessary, in the *Audientia litterarum contradictarum*. In the first, all those letters which had not to be seen by the Pope personally were read aloud, and it was open to anyone to protest at their contents; on protest being made, the matter was referred to the *Aud. litt. contradict.*, where the letter complained of might be destroyed, or an additional letter issued expressly exempting from the terms of the first letter the person who felt himself injured by it. The *Aud. pub.* and the *Aud. litt. contradict.* appear from Innocent III's reign onwards; from the later 1230's the vast increase in Papal business was forcing temporal and spiritual princes and the monastic Orders to keep permanent procurators at the curia to watch over their interests in this way.— See R. von Heckel, *Das Aufkommen der ständigen Prokuratoren an d. päpstl. Kurie im xiii. Jhdt.* in *Miscellanea Ehrle* (1924), ii. 290–321.—Masetti i. 268–70 has managed to construct a provisional list of procurators for the thirteenth century, with the help of documents of the Roman province.

[2] Berthier, *Le B. Humbert de Romans*, p. 57.

A solution was reached which has remained permanent to this day.

The difficulties caused by such enmity and the means used to combat it are best illustrated in the involved affair which occupied the first two years of Humbert's Generalate. To the existing trouble, caused by Gerard of Borgo San Donnino's *Introductorius*, was added Innocent IV's sudden revocation of Dominican privileges and the entry of the Seculars into the arena in May 1254; as a result the Preachers were drawn forcibly into a conflict which had hitherto been mainly the concern of the Minors. However, *Etsi animarum*[1] was speedily followed by the paralysis and death of Innocent, which gave an appearance of truth to the suggestion that Divine vengeance had overtaken an evil-doer, and within a month *Nec insolitum*[2] had re-established the original conditions. This return to peace with the friars' victory was most probably due to the previous personal acquaintance of Humbert and Alexander. The policy of dependence on Rome brought a rich reward. The whole affair produced two good sayings: the famous "Cavete a letaniis fratrum praedicatorum quia mirabilia faciunt", and the equally delightful but less well-known remark of the Chapter of Toulouse: "Fratres possunt amodo cessare a septem psalmis et letania dicendis in epdomada."[3]

The reason for these continued bad relations appears from even the most cursory glance at the way Dominican literature regarded the priesthood; and it may reasonably be assumed that the sentiments that there appear formed the subject of the sermon when a friar with the courage of his convictions was called upon to address a clerical audience. A fair specimen of such a sermon is given by the following passage, one of the few which state expressly that they were meant for this purpose:[4]

Item, this may be the theme at an election. [Presumably of a bishop. St Cher is commenting St John xv. 16: "Ye have not chosen me, but I have chosen you."] The candidate is chosen by common consent, and ordained by confirmation. And note that some are not

[1] 21 Nov. 1254 (Denifle, *Chart. Univ. Paris.* i. 267–70).—This Bull revoked all the friars' privileges.
[2] BOP. i. 267.
[3] *Acta* 1258. The brothers had recently been commanded to say these psalms and litanies for a speedy and peaceful settlement of the dispute.
[4] St Cher vi. 377 col. 3.

chosen by the Lord, but by themselves, for they violently intrude and force themselves into a prelacy.... Others are chosen by the devil, like those who are elected out of jealousy, that another may be turned out.... Others are chosen by the flesh, because they are nephews or relations.... Others are chosen by the world.... *Item*, many say: This man will preserve the rights of our church and successfully prosecute our business, he will go out to seek the asses [a reference to the choice of Saul as king (I Sam. ix, x) which was quoted immediately above] not souls, and will defend our property, because he is powerful, or noble, or a great pleader (*magnus placitator*)....

This is very mild, however, in comparison with what the same writer can say on other occasions; on Ezekiel xxii. 2 ("Now, thou son of man, wilt thou judge...the bloody city?"), for instance, he comments:[1]

The bloody city is the world, which is full of sin.... Or the Church may be called the bloody city, because to-day it is founded in the blood of nephews [here, as often, the scornful diminutive *nepotuli* is used] and is stained by carnal love...because bad prelates make their relatives into bad canons, just as bad canons make a bad priest. Sufficient is said about this matter above [referring to v. 56 col. 2, which contains a long tirade against nepotism and immorality; when a man is promoted "then a great affection is born, and many relations are raised up to him"].

Satirical attacks on nepotism are by no means uncommon; apart from the often-repeated story of the child whom his uncle, the bishop, had created archdeacon, but would not trust with a basket of pears,[2] Étienne de Bourbon has this pleasant image:

...Some, when they come to the Chapter, come like a hen with a brood of chickens, because their nephews run after them like chickens and call after them, following their voices and their wishes, wherever they turn.[3]

The way the state of the Church was constantly in the minds of these writers appears from a rather surprising remark of St Cher's. He comments various aspects of St John xiii. 1–3, and then goes completely off at a tangent with the next verse, to

[1] St Cher v. 80 col. 4.
[2] *Anecdotes*, pp. 353, 383, 421.
[3] Ib. p. 383, cf. St Cher ii. 29 col. 1.—"In the time of the apostles, flesh and blood could not possess the kingdom of God, but in this miserable age scarcely anyone possesses the kingdom of God, that is, the Church, except the flesh and blood of prelates."

write what has nothing to do either with the text, in any imaginable interpretation, or with what he has just been saying.

He riseth from supper—this is against priests, who do not want to
rise from table when they have to hear the confessions of the sick or to
offer them the viaticum.[1]

For the rank and file of the clergy come off no better than their
superiors at the friars' hands. "From the least up to the greatest
they all study greed, falling into theft and rapine, and thus
surpassing the bounds of avarice."[2] There are so many in Hell
that a wandering spirit from those regions is surprised to find any
remaining on earth;[3] they enter the Church to benefit themselves
alone;[4] they will be incapable of giving satisfactory answers to
the questions that will be put to them on the Day of Judgment;[5]
they celebrate infrequently—"scarcely four times a year, and
even some (which is worse) not once in ten years";[6] they give a
bad example;[7] they are confirmed pluralists.[8] Even the gentle
Humbert de Romans accuses them of ignorance, of bad example
and of concerning themselves too much in secular matters,[9] and
makes several specific proposals for remedying this disastrous
state of affairs. Greater care should be taken in choosing
bishops: the Curia is "basely deceived" by the commonly
accepted principle that a man should be assumed good unless
anything definite is known against him. He would also like to
see the procedure for deposing an unsatisfactory prelate made
shorter and more simple.[10] All this, which is but the scantiest
selection from material which would fill many pages, combined
with the actual interference of the ecclesiastical authorities with
the business of preaching,[11] makes it merely a matter for wonder

---

[1] St Cher vi. 365 col. 2.   [2] Id. vii. 36 col. 3.
[3] Bromyard, L. vii. 18.   [4] Id. O. vi. 9.   [5] Id. § 13.
[6] Id. § 26.   [7] Id. §§ 65, 78, R. v. 5, etc.
[8] St Cher v. 375 col. 4.   [9] *Max. Bib. Pat.* xxv. 484.
[10] *Op. trip.* III cap. 4 (Brown, p. 225). Since this does not seem a suitable
place for going at length into the Dominicans' views upon the clergy, I
content myself with the following references: Bromyard's attitude is examined
in extenso by Owst, *Pr. in Med. Eng.* p. 36 sq. (cf. 251), *Lit. and Pulpit*,
pp. 242–286. Étienne de Bourbon is well known, and in any case Lecoy's edn.
includes a good table of contents; Cantimpré's views are summarised by
Berger, pp. 47–51 (most of the refs. will be found in I. iii, iv, vi, xix and xx;
Dr Coulton has translated typical passages from St Cher in *Five Centuries*, ii.
527–31).
[11] St Cher iv. 227 col. 1.

that the conflict between vested interest and the progressive, enthusiastic party was not still more acute than we know it to have been.

Ambition and excessive rivalry contributed to friction with the Franciscans. The satirical will attributed to Frederick II contains this legacy: "Item relinquimus et legamus praedicatoribus et minoribus discordiam quam debent habere quamdiu ipsorum carnem et ossa spiritus vegetabit."[1] The efficacy of both Orders was impaired by their constant conflicts, and at the end of the first generation we find injunctions by the rulers calling for the maintenance of peace. The legend of the friendship of the two saints appears in the *Vitae Fratrum* and in the joint encyclical of 1255. There remains very little evidence of their alleged friendship,[2] but plenty showing that in early years their followers rendered each other mutual assistance. The first Franciscans to visit England lodged in the Dominican convent in London immediately after their arrival, and were well looked after. Jordan of Saxony is mentioned several times by Eccleston, always with the reverence due to a holy man. Most notable is the record of Aymo of Faversham's consultation of him when he first thought of joining the Franciscans.[3] Jordan approved, and incited him to carry out his intention, and there is no word of an attempt to persuade Aymo into the Dominican Order, which was at the time infinitely more suitable than the other to a man of his type. The only two references to the Franciscans in the *Acta* belong to primitive times, and both are friendly. Indeed the former (1234), if it ever came into operation, would have meant something like a series of local federations of the two Orders. Each is to elect a member of the other in every province, and these two, in place of the Minister-provincial and the Prior-provincial, are to correct all "excesses".[4]

There were too many obvious grounds for jealousy, however, to allow these idyllic conditions to last. Though a common danger drew the two together in 1255 and 1274, even to the issue of a joint letter by the two heads, nothing could prevent petty

[1] Gratien, *Histoire...de l'ordre des frères mineurs au xiiie siècle*, p. 591.
[2] See above, p. 43.
[3] Eccleston, ed. Little, p. 11 (London), p. 34 (Aymo).
[4] *Acta* 1234, 1236, cf. Humbert ii. 189.

irritation and minor feuds in the lower ranks. The tone of the letter of 1255 is worried; it appears to emanate from two sensible men who want to get on with more important matters, but are hampered by a world of fools who quarrel over stupid trifles. Mortier's "frères jumeaux" is all very well as an ideal, but it was hardly borne out in practice. Each wanted to attract the most wealthy and important converts, each drew its sustenance by means of the quest from the same people; and if one was favoured more than the other, trouble soon commenced. Two rather larger and very fruitful causes of dissension were slight differences in the nature of the privileges accorded to each, and the close juxtaposition of their convents in many towns. This last prevented the expansion of either on one side, and caused great resentment. The Minors of Strassburg, for instance, "enormiter excesserunt", say the Dominicans of the same town,[1] by building a church right up against the latter's house. So acrimonious did this particular question become that Popes were forced to make regulations fixing the minimum distance between convents. Finally it is clear that there were no lengths to which rivalry could not go, from the story that each Order was using the Inquisition against the other in Southern France in 1266.[2]

[1] Finke, p. 167.
[2] Lea, *Hist. Inq.* i. 300.

CHAPTER IX

SIGNS OF DECAY

To what extent did contact with the sordid things of daily life affect the Dominican sincerity of purpose? How far, and at approximately what date, was the primitive austerity seriously impaired? These two questions must be answered before an estimate of the Order's work can be made. The General Chapter Acts give the most helpful information towards this end, and the succeeding study is based mainly upon a comparative analysis of the evidence they afford,[1] classified under several heads—poverty, learning, morality and discipline. At least one of these subjects is mentioned in almost every year, so that the material is large in amount and at first sight amorphous in character. An attempt will be made, however, to show that a rough scheme can be superimposed upon the mass of entries, thus reducing them to some show of meaning. There appear to be two fairly well-determinable points at which the tone changes. In the early years new legislation is introduced, giving greater precision to the commands of the primitive constitutions; the spirit of the law remains the same, and it is only details that are added. There succeeds a period of about forty years during which there is little additional legislation, but an immense series of admonitions directed towards the better execution of the law; this is a static period, and discipline is the main interest. Then, shortly before the end of the century, signs of relaxation appear in earnest, and the law is modified from its first austerity; the ruling body is now legalising what appears to have been the frequent practice of the preceding period.

In the succeeding pages each of the four subjects mentioned will be examined in this light, and the position of the two dividing lines marked out as clearly as possible.

---

[1] For the thirteenth century alone. I have limited the following examination to the first volume of the *Acta* (1220–1303); after the latter date decay is generally admitted, and there is nothing much to be gained by pursuing the study further.

Poverty calls for first notice. It will be convenient to treat it under six heads:

(i) *Ornaments*.[1]—The Chapter of 1239 translated the "mediocres domos et humiles" of 1228 into greater detail by enacting that gold and silver should not be used except for chalices, and forbidding silk, precious stones, statues, paintings, and illuminations in books. One bell only was to be kept to sound the hours. The next year's assembly revoked the greater part of this legislation, except in so far as statues and bells were concerned. (Revocation was of course actually unnecessary; but although the approval of three successive Chapters was required by Jordan's constitutions for any change, the full implications of this had not at first been understood, and in the same year, 1240, a constitution was inchoated setting up the three stages.) In the same year it is ordained that "notabiles superfluitates" shall be removed from the choir, and none shall possess a private seal unless he be a preacher-general. A protest of a similar nature occurs in 1245: "Non fiant in ecclesiis nostris cum sculpturis prominentibus sepulture, et que facta sunt auferantur." Complaints of this kind appear at regular intervals, including a constitution[2] which was theoretically unnecessary, and must be regarded as a sign that the ornamentation it attempted to prevent was becoming common. To the constitution "de domibus concedendis" are to be added the words, "Nec fiant in domibus nostris superfluitates et curiositates notabiles in sculpturis et picturis et pavimentis et aliis similibus que paupertatem nostram deforment." This constitution may very likely be attributed to Humbert de Romans, within whose generalate it was passed. His views on ornaments are distinctly puritan.[3] He refers to illuminations in manuscripts as puerilities, and quotes with the strongest approval St Bernard's letter to William of St Thierry. Succeeding Chapters did their best to secure the enforcement of this rule until 1297, when the original measurements limiting

---

[1] Ornaments are mentioned in the *Acta* for the following years: 1239, 1240, 1241, 1245, 1250, 1252, 1260, 1261–2–3, 1265, 1273, 1276, 1290, 1297. This list, and others given below, are probably not exhaustive, though every effort has been made to avoid omissions. An admonition is to be understood where a single date (e.g. 1239) is given, a constitution where a multiple (e.g. 1261–2–3).

[2] *Acta* 1261–2–3.

[3] Humbert i. 448, 582.

the size of houses was abolished. This can mean nothing less than the permission of "opera sumptuosa",[1] and the legalisation of what had probably for long been the practice. The seriousness of the question earlier in the century, and the extent of relaxation which the 1297 concession implies, is best seen from the penances distributed broadcast by two of the strong disciplinary Chapters who took this matter up. In 1250 many priors, especially in the English province, suffer because they have built schools which are too large, or a second cloister. In 1261 the late prior of Barcelona and the present "building committee" are given thirteen days' fast and thirteen disciplines for having made their dormitory higher than is allowed. It is probably significant that these two Chapters were held in London and Barcelona respectively; it can hardly be unjust to suggest that only in those places where the Chapter met could a really thorough supervision be exercised.

(ii) *The quest.*—When he destroyed the charter of Odoric Galiciani in 1219, Dominic had demanded that the friars should live upon alms, which should be collected for the needs of one day only at a time. As early as 1239 this was modified so that as much wine and corn could be collected as was required for a year's subsistence—"*Nisi* ad presentis anni necessitatem";[2] clearly this was merely a partial concession and did not represent fully what was actually being done. The same provision was repeated next year, and then the quest practically disappears from the pages of the *Acta*. With the change to the use of money which was rapidly taking place there was no further need of regulation.

(iii) *Money.*[3]—The first mention of money is in 1234, when the friars are forbidden to drive hard bargains with each other

---

[1] E.g. Part of a new cloister erected at Toulouse about 1306 was built of marble.—Douais, *Études*, p. 39.

[2] It is difficult to understand how Lambermond (p. 24) can quote this as an example of poverty. The kind of attitude which did a lot to bring about the decline of mendicancy can be seen in the words Bromyard wrote over a century later: there are many friars who say "Volo vivere in pace in conventu et legere et cantare, nolo per mundum currere; multa taedia sunt ibi, et scrupulus conscientiae in confessionibus audiendis et hujusmodi, et verecundiae et labores in mendicando."—A. xxiv. 12.

[3] See *Acta* 1234, 1245, 1255, 1257, 1258, 1261–2–3, 1265, 1268, 1269, 1270, 1272, 1275, 1276, 1278, 1279, 1283, 1285, 1289, 1290, 1291, 1298.

over the sale of books ("Ne biblia fratri a fratre vendatur carius quam emerit, et idem de aliis scriptis servetur"). Various admonitions follow, ordering priors and visitors to see that the constitution about not carrying money on journeys is kept, while in 1261 we find the reforming Chapter of Barcelona acting on the defensive. Every brother who has received or used money must give an annual account of it to a superior officer, and rules are laid down governing the execution of this. Effort is now concentrated on securing the observance of this half-measure; since the use of money could not be got rid of, careful account should be kept that it was used in the right way. Thus more details are added in an admonition of 1270, and still more by the same means in 1276, though so minute are the sanctions imposed (e.g. a delay of more than three days between the receipt of money and application for a licence entails automatic forfeiture) that suspicion is aroused. In 1278 the same rules were repeated almost word for word, with an addition which made the whole thing practically a farce—"In hiis tamen casibus omnibus, prior provincialis vel conventualis ex causa legitima et rationabili, prout sibi videbitur, poterit dispensare, non obstante ordinacione alias de hoc facta." By putting it within the power of the conventual prior, to whom only the less important decisions belonged, the diffinitors showed that they did not regard the matter as of the most vital importance. The practical permission of loans in 1290 (forbidden "Nisi in aliqua pecunia modica") and the demand in 1291 that necessity *or* licence must be shown as an excuse for the use of money, show relaxation advancing further.

The question of money can be illustrated in other ways. The General Chapter was frequently concerned with debts,[1] wills[2] and gifts offered at confession,[3] and Humbert devotes considerable space to it. In the Exposition of St Augustine's Rule, which he may have begun while provincial of Tuscany (1240-3), he makes the usual point[4] that no one, not even the Pope, can dispense the vow of poverty, but adds that dispensation may be granted

---

[1] *Acta* 1236, 1244, 1248, 1249, 1274, 1293.
[2] *Acta* 1239, 1240, 1243, 1252, 1266, 1275.
[3] *Acta* 1261, 1263, 1278.
[4] Humbert i. 84.

for the *use* of a thing. Three conditions must be fulfilled: the use must be removable at a moment's notice, the possession must belong to another, and either utility or necessity must be served by the dispensation. He is clearly compromising with his conscience, and is not at all happy about it. There are many advantages to be gained by such dispensations, yet they must not be granted too easily; "tamen species mali remanet ibi". In the *De Officiis*, written after 1263, he discusses the duties of the *depositarii*,[1] and warns them against the fraud of some, who may attempt to deposit sacks of lead in place of silver. Ledgering systems are discussed, and the repository of ultimate responsibility decided. Again, one of the replies to Peckham's attack on the Dominicans was that they at least made no difficulty about receiving money, whereas the Franciscans saved the letter of their rule at the expense of its intention by the system of the "interpositae personae".

(iv) *Horses, carriages, servants*.[2]—Apart from the friars of the Toulousain, who, as we have already seen, had refused to accept apostolic poverty down to 1220, there is at least one mention of servants in the early sources. Jordan[3] refers to one Nicolaus Bush (de Bosco), an Englishman, who was ill and could not move "Nisi sustentaretur baculis vel servientibus". They were forbidden in 1233 and again in 1239, though at the later date the prohibition was expressly made dispensable, and then no further word is heard of them. Horses and carriages were condemned in 1239 and at intervals until 1291, when they are coupled with money in the regulation already noticed, that necessity or licence must be proved to make their use lawful.

---

[1] Id. ii. 279. This description seems to make it quite clear that Mrs Galbraith is in error when she speaks of "the *depositarius*, who kept a kind of left-luggage office" (*Const. Dom. Order*, p. 118).

[2] *Acta* 1233, 1239, 1240, 1245, 1250, 1255, 1258, 1264, 1269, 1273, 1276, 1289, 1290, 1291, 1298. It is interesting to note how much the use of horses seems to have been regarded as a sign of decline. There is only one prophet, writes Hugh de St Cher, who is recorded in the O.T. as having ridden, and he was devoured by a lion (I Kings xiii. 23–4); further, "Balaam equitavit, et ei mors eminebat" (Joshua xiii. 22). These quotations are from vi. 99 col. 3; cf. vi. 377 col. 4. Bromyard (P. iii. 26) attributes the decline of many houses to the friars' habit of riding, and says that in Apulia there are only five brothers where there once were forty "quia terra repleta est equis" (§ 27), cf. id. R. v. 58, V. iii. 11, and Cantimpré II. iii. 12, II. lvii. 55.

[3] Jord. Sax. p. 37.

(v) *Fasting, simplicity of food, meat, etc.*[1]—Injunctions on this subject are constantly repeated, and most Chapters are concerned with it. A sinister note is struck in 1255—"Dispensatio in jejuniis non fiat cum toto conventu"—and in the next two years: Chapters-General are not to be the occasion for notable super-fluities in food and drink, and novices are not to be allowed to give pittances. Yet we know that Aquinas gave one, so that there was nothing shameful or unusual about them. There is a moderate amount of relaxation in 1278, combined with a com-mand that certain statutory fasts are to be better kept, but there is no complete re-shaping of the whole rule before 1303.

(vi) *Silence at table.*—This occurs almost annually between 1240 and 1250, and towards the end of the century the idea suggests itself that an admonition directed towards its enforce-ment was conventionally inserted in the *Acta* every five years—it is mentioned in 1283, 1288, 1293, 1298, 1303. Certainly the Encyclical of 1283[2] (which is of course likely to exaggerate in the interests of discipline) complains that silence has almost dis-appeared.

Learning has already been fairly thoroughly treated, and it only remains to point out that whereas up to the *Ordinaciones* of 1259 the general rule is that when the subject is mentioned, new legislation regarding details is introduced, after this date an

---

[1] *Acta* 1234, 1236, 1239, 1249–50–1, 1252–4–5, 1255, 1256, 1269, 1273, 1278, 1280, 1283, 1294, 1297.

[2] *Litt. Encyc.* p. 126. The later history of poverty can be followed in detail in Walz, Mortier or Lambermond. Growing property and the consequent privileges in defence of it (e.g. BOP. i. 131, 315, 405), together with the deliberate action of Popes like Gregory X, Boniface VIII and Benedict XII, had led to such a decline in poverty that when the Master-general Hugh de Vaucemain (1333–41) put certain questions on the matter to the Dominican theologian Petrus de Palude, the latter could reply that possessions are not an infringement of the vow of poverty (because the monks are possessionate); though they do constitute a breach of the constitutions, this does not lead to a breach of our vows, because we have not sworn to keep the constitutions, but only to live according to them. Therefore all is well unless we are put under a special obedience concerning poverty. The re-establishment of strict poverty and of mendicancy was, of course, a main point in the reform of Raymond of Capua (Master-general 1380–99). It is worth noting that in his account of all this (*Compendium*, p. 47), Walz is inclined to lay chief blame for the decline upon the Popes, without sufficiently regarding the evidence set out in the text here.

ever-increasing attention is paid to the friars' slackness in study.[1] Hugh's letter of 1257[2] gives the cue, and this is followed up, for example, by the decree that those who are negligent shall be severely punished (1276), and by the order two years later that neither priors nor others are to absent themselves from the schools without due cause. There could be no legal relaxation under this head without an implicit denial of the Order's whole reason for existence, so, as might be expected, no second dividing line can be discovered here.

Suspicious familiarity with women is first met with shortly before the middle of the century. In 1242 the brothers are forbidden to visit religious women without good reason. "Mala familiaritas" was the subject of a constitution inchoated in 1262, but this never got further than approbation, and was re-written in 1264 with what appears to be a more severe penalty—denunciation to a conventual Chapter in place of suspension. An admonition of 1277 drew attention to the constitution about not allowing women into the cloister, and the entries for 1280 contain a similar command. In 1290 the brothers were warned not to enter the convents of women "nisi pro necessitate evidenti". It is possible that one may see here an attempt to restrain the mystically inclined, though it is probably too late for this; but at least it appears from Finke's collection[3] that this particular sort of misdoing was by no means uncommon. Finally, there is another prohibition upon entering a *clausura* of nuns in 1294, which by reason of its exceedingly weak sanction—no more than three days' bread and water—may perhaps be accounted a slackening of the previous strictness.

Most serious of all was the decay of discipline. Two letters already quoted several times give an exceedingly black picture, and are no doubt making the worst of the case in order to bring

---

[1] In the following list the years marked with an asterisk are those in which mention is made of slackness. It will be seen that this becomes frequent after about 1270.—*Acta* 1246, 1252*, 1258, 1259*, 1261, 1264, 1265, 1271, 1274*, 1276*, 1278* 1279*, 1283, 1287*, 1300*. Cf. also complaints of decline at the provincial Chapter of Périgueux, 1309, in Douais, *Org. des Études*, p. 28.

[2] Printed in Humbert, op. cit. ii. p. 507, note.

[3] E.g. pp. 118, 132, 133 (two letters), 137, 166.

the wicked and the idle to a sense of their responsibilities. Yet
we can by no means discount the whole of their tenor in this way;
had there been no decay, there would have been no need to draw
attention to it, by exaggeration or otherwise. In 1257 Hugh de
St Cher thought it worth while to write an entirely spontaneous
letter to the Chapter, putting forward his view of affairs, and it
agreed so well with the temper of the meeting that it was
ordered to be read at all provincial Chapters. Four years later
Humbert saw the Rule being broken on all sides:

apud multos nondum cessaverunt superbia in hedeficiis, notabilitas
in vestibus, curiositas in operibus, superfluitas in conviviis, notae
suspiciones in quibusdam familiaritatibus, discordia inter alios in
quibusdam agendis, quae mundum non mediocriter scandalizant.[1]

The original conception of discipline was strict. The rule was
binding under pain of penance, not of sin; the advantage of this
novel conception being that it made punishment automatic and
avoided the characteristic medieval error of translating everything into its highest terms without remembering that though a
complex fraction may express the same mathematical idea as a
simple one, it is more difficult to understand. The 1228 version
of the constitution makes, on the contrary, a clear distinction
between quarrelling with another friar, disputing unwarrantably
with a superior, and being incorrigible by any punishment what-
soever: that, namely, between *gravis*, *gravior* and *gravissima
culpa* respectively.[2] The paragraphs devoted to the first two
both occupy at least a page in print, and foresee most of the
events of convent life.

It was not long, however, before there appeared a nuisance
which was to be permanent. In 1240 prisons were ordered to be
made "ad compescendam insolentiam perversorum"—insub-
ordination, presumably, which was foreseen twelve years earlier.[3]
The nature of this trouble had been made more explicit in 1238.
"Damus licenciam captivandi apostatas et corrigendi inordinate
ambulantes. Volumus ut carceres fiant pro apostatis et fratribus
inquietis cohercendis." It is the old trouble of the *gyrovagi* who
were such a curse in the early Christian centuries, and is only
the well-known monastic accidie in another guise; some friars,

---

[1] *Litt. Encyc.* p. 58.   [2] ALKG. i. 207–12.   [3] Id. 211.

runs one complaint,[1] are unable to settle to anything, but wander incessantly between the garden and the kitchen, the guest-rooms and the locutorium. It is found among the Dominicans in many forms. We are reminded of one by Humbert's remark that some are affected by "levitas cordis, sicut accidit in goliardis".[2] There are others—as is shown by the penances frequently given to those who unlawfully come to the General Chapter, or by the prohibitions on unnecessary journeys to Rome.[3] "Combinaciones", which are condemned in 1289, demonstrate that Salimbene's delightful wanderings could be imitated in a less worthy manner by those who had become bored with convent life and its round of services. This was a particularly acute question towards the end of the century, when there were so many friars that useful work could not be found for all, and those who were less fit to be sent out preaching found time hang heavily on their hands. It is possible, though, that the 1289 order was called forth by repugnance at the habits of the ejected friars of Zofingen and Berne,[4] who had turned the vexation of the Order into a harmful liberty, and were wandering about like sheep without a shepherd.

A certain amount of trouble of this nature was perhaps only to be expected, and it must not accordingly be imputed to the friars for evil. Far more serious is the failure of the officers to retain control over their subordinates, even within the convents, and the discovery that many were slack in carrying out commands given them. The diffinitors of 1251 ordered that admonitions should be kept better, and in 1279 so far forgot the dignity of their office as to protest plaintively that it is no use making admonitions unless the brothers observe them; therefore let all priors punish those who transgress the admonitions of Chapters-general or -provincial. Next year it became necessary to assert that admonitions remained operative until revoked, but this met with disfavour, and was reversed in 1281, with a vague desire that they should nevertheless be observed, especially if they tended towards honesty or usefulness. Even this great concession to rebellion was of no avail, and discipline could not be

---

[1] Humbert i. 560. [2] Ib.
[3] *Acta* 1245, 1249, 1252, 1262, 1264, 1267, 1276, 1285, 1302, 1303.
[4] Finke, p. 127.

re-established upon a lower plane; in 1303 "by the negligence
of prelates...regular observances and the ordinances of Chapters
are far too notably neglected: let punishments be given to the
offenders ".

Other sources tell much the same tale. Lectors are not to use
general licences giving them power to remain out of choir, but
may only do so at the prior's command.[1] Provincial Ulrich of
Germany, visiting a convent between the years 1272–7, found
many infringements of the constitutions;[2] he ordered the erring
brothers to abide by the penances laid down at the Chapter:
"Nam de re potius quam de nomine curam gero." More serious
are several cases of forged licences which occur,[3] and Herman,
Ulrich's successor, found licences quoted against his disciplinary
vigour which were said to bear his seal, but which he could not
remember issuing. Obedience fails in many ways, says Humbert,[4]
through grumblings, refusals, discussions, excuses, etc., and
adds: "Alii sunt qui se tales exhibeant quod prelati non audent
eis imponere onus." Dispensations must not be excessively
used, and certain subjects are expressly reserved for certain high
officers.

La Flamma's chronicle is useful at this point. He is practically
worthless as a historian except where he repeats the words of
others, Theodoric of Apoldia as a rule. But he is very sure that
what is needed is greater discipline and austerity, and is not
above twisting the events of the primitive times to suit the case
he is advocating. Thus he reads back the annual account of
money, whose origin we have seen, to the time of Jordan, maintains that clothes had always been possessed in common, and
favours the most rigid form of obedience, excluding all private
opinion in the subordinate.[5] This last is clean contrary to two
much greater authorities than himself.

It would appear, then, that the conclusion suggested at the
head of this section is proven. By about 1250 relaxation is
assuming threatening proportions, and repeated steps are taken

---

[1] Humbert ii. 256.   [2] Finke, p. 83.
[3] Id. pp. 133, 137, cf. 94, 134, 151.   [4] Humbert i. 535.
[5] La Flamma, p. 38, 18, 101–2, cf. Humbert i. 7, 531 and Aquinas 2a, 2ae,
Q. 104.

to check it. But the labour of thirty years produces little or no
result, and the legislators themselves are affected before the end
of the century. All the serious modifications of existing rules
fall within the last twenty-five years.

Further colour is lent to this suggestion by a deeper inquiry
into one or two sentences from Humbert which have already
been used, for instance the chapter "Quod servis Dei large sunt
necessaria ministranda".[1] He points out that austerity lessens
activity and energy: the body must live in order that the spirit
may act. This suggests the thought that even so severe and well-
established a disciplinarian as he, could yet defend a moderate
amount of relaxation. It would be hopelessly incorrect, in view
of the strictness for which his rule is notable, to place too much
reliance on statements such as these, besides rendering foolish
our earlier use of him as one of the bases for an argument about
the poverty of Dominic. Nevertheless, the general impression
gained from his writings is that he is intensely conscious of being
at the head of a large organisation, with duties and responsibilities and a position to keep up. He is in many respects like his
contemporary, Bonaventura: a "conventual", but a good one.
Both just lack[2] that fire of enthusiasm which marks the first
generation; both ruled their Orders at the time of their greatest
glory, when their influence had spread everywhere, but had not
yet been seriously undermined by internal decay. Men such as
these, though stern disciplinarians, intent on maintaining primitive purity, might yet in some moods feel that there were other
ways of attaining the desired ends. If Humbert does seem on
occasion to be sapping the foundations upon which his building
rests, it is because two ideas meet in him. He and his Order
now hold a position of honour, and it ill becomes them not to
smooth over the crudeness and almost indecently single-minded
enthusiasm of the first friars with the polish of courtesy and
worldly-wisdom. Outwardly, nothing has changed; inwardly, as
we have seen, the forces of relaxation are gathering. The man
who ruled during this period of stillness is sometimes conscious

[1] Humbert i. 93, cf. i. 108, ii. 36.
[2] Cf. Id. 474. (The early friars were greater men than we. This may,
however, be entirely explicable by conventional medieval pessimism, except
that Humbert is less inclined to take a black view than most.)

that a tiny concession can do no harm, and may help a little to prevent a coming revolt. Yet this does not often occur. Duty and loyalty to his origins nearly always gain the day. Probably the strictest Chapter-General of the century, that of 1261, met under his presidency.

CHAPTER X

AUTHORITY AND THE CONSTITUTION

A NOTICEABLE feature of Dominican history is the growth of a tendency for all importance and a great deal of power to be concentrated in a comparatively small number of hands. To say this is not to forget that conventual and provincial priors were constantly "absolved" after a few years' service, reduced to the ranks, and only later, perhaps, re-elected to another charge. The tendency began with the preachers-general, who possessed privileges from the beginning which distinguished them from their humbler brothers. They were exempt from routine duties, could travel freely, owned a private seal (and so could maintain a free correspondence), and had great legislative power in the provincial Chapters. They formed the first aristocracy of the Order, and reigned unchallenged in importance until the gradual shift of emphasis from preaching to study raised up rivals to them in the Masters of Theology.[1] In their lesser way lectors were also marked off from the rest of the inhabitants of a house. They alone had the right to a private room when exercising their functions—not even the prior under whom they worked had this privilege. Similarly, Inquisitors were freed from disciplinary control, and could go to Rome and stay there irrespective of contrary commands by Chapters-General; though in their case the nature of their duties made them a scattered caste outside the Order rather than an aristocracy within. The dislike which the admission or education of "minus sufficientes" aroused has already been noticed. Similarly there was from the start an undue emphasis laid upon the value of great men.[2] The preacher too "debet habere aliquam praerogativam super alios...item non debet esse persona contemptibilis". Again, congregations are moved to hear the word

---

[1] Preachers' privileges, ALKG. i. 216, 223–4, cf. *Acta* 1256, 1286 (*frater*, not *magister* or *doctor*), and Humbert ii. 255, cf. St Cher ii. 303 col. 2.

[2] Humbert i. 472. Succeeding references are to ib. ii. 407, 445.

of God by the renown of the speaker, and will more readily listen to one who is great in authority or wisdom.

These instances tend to show the existence of an aristocracy of service or of learning, but there are also certain traces of the snobbery of birth to be found even in the first century of Dominicanism. This is, of course, a well-known factor in medieval ecclesiastical life,[1] and there is nothing particularly striking about finding it also in the Order of Preachers. It was nearly always easier for a nobleman to enter a monastery than for a man of lowly birth, and his chances of promotion to high office were infinitely greater. There were a number of cloisters to which entry was impossible for anyone under the rank of baron, and more than one cathedral chapter was for centuries under the control of a few noble families. Without looking far, we find that the Dominican Order admitted children to the noviciate under the statutory age of fifteen, if they were of good birth,[2] and that among the Dominican women, for instance, the majority of convents contained almost exclusively women of noble rank down to the seventeenth century.[3] Hugh de St Cher complains of the bad effects this introduction of class distinctions brought into the cloister, and refers to those

who wish to be called by the titles they had in the world, and dwell in their thoughts upon what they have left, often talking about it and glorying in their family and its deeds.[4]

If this aristocratic tendency is placed beside the decline of discipline and enthusiasm which was noticed earlier, the inquiry immediately occurs, Did the one attempt to remedy the other, and result in anything like authoritarian control?[5] The answer which has always been given is a firm negative. Democracy, it is said, was a leading characteristic of the Dominican Order, and the origins of the English Parliament have even been traced in

[1] See, for instance, Coulton, *Five Centuries*, iii. 323–335, summarising and adding to A. Schulte, *Der Adel und die deutsche Kirche im Mittelalter*, Stuttgart 1910.
[2] Evidence in Douais, *Org. des Études*, p. 13.
[3] Grundmann, p. 194.
[4] St Cher iv. 37 col. 2.
[5] The following account makes no attempt to describe the Constitution, except in so far as is necessary to bring out certain points in the argument. All further details may be found in G. R. Galbraith, *The Constitution of the Dominican Order*.

part to it.[1] Now it cannot be denied that there is a very strong democratic element in the governmental methods of the Dominicans. Every officer was appointed by, and responsible to, a committee composed of elected representatives of his subordinates or equals. The conventual prior was elected by the convent, was advised and limited in the exercise of his powers by the *consiliarii* of the convent, was confirmed and "absolved" by the provincial Chapter. *Mutatis mutandis*, the same is true of the provincial prior; while the Master-general was both elected by, and subject to, the General Chapter, which not only had power to depose him for inadequacy or heresy, but at its annual meeting could discuss his actions and impose penances upon him. Special regulations were made that the Master should cast himself at the diffinitors' feet, make his confession, hear any accusation against him, and then leave the room so that the discussion upon him should be the more free.

All this, and much more of a similar nature, is true. Yet it is admittedly very early to find so advanced a democracy actually functioning before the middle of the thirteenth century.[2] The doctrine of feudal limitation on the power of the ruler is only just beginning to have a really practical value—a great deal of our knowledge comes from men like Beaumanoir and Jean d'Ibelin, who were contemporaries of the early Dominicans. This is not enough, however, to create a body of democratic theory; it is a long time before the feudal council, in its new guise as the national parliament, recognises even in name the right of the people to take any share in government. Edward I quoted the Digest—"Quod omnes tangit ab omnibus approbetur"—in the summonses to his parliaments, but he meant very little by it. The Commons at Westminster were far more a new means of exercising kingly control than a check upon it. The Middle Ages did not, of course, formally recognise autocracy:

> Decet regem discere legem,
> Audiat rex, quod praecipit lex,
> Legem servare, hoc est regnare,[3]

---

[1] Barker, *The Dom. Order and Convocation.*
[2] But see M. V. Clarke, *Med. Representation and Consent.*
[3] Proverbs of Wippo, eleventh century, quoted in Carlyle, *Med. Polit. Theory*, iii. 128.

—but in an unsettled state of society it was a long time before practice and theory coincided. Justice and the law of God had a poor chance amid all the crudities of medieval life, where the best guarantee of peace and prosperity was the strength of the ruler.

Moreover, medieval theory granted a certain freedom of action to the ruler, even though this was circumscribed. His power was derived from God as well as from election by the people; to him alone belonged the right of promulgating new law, though he must take existing custom and good advice into account. Further, medieval limited monarchy is not modern constitutional monarchy: ultimately, the ruler's power is bounded by his own moral sense and the subjects' right of resistance, and the former might not always prove efficacious. Analogously, therefore—and remembering that analogy is not argument—we may suggest that a strong democratic element in the laws of the society which he governed does not in effect preclude the possibility of independent action by the Dominican Master-general.

Another influence must be taken into account, as it has a distinct bearing on the case. Particularly on the continent, the re-discovery of Roman law aided materially towards the increase of royal power.

> Caesar lex viva, stat regibus imperativa
> Legeque sub viva sunt omnia jura dativa.[1]

—so runs a lawyer's verse paraphrase of the ever-memorable tag from Ulpian. It is a conventionalism among Dominican historians that law is a paramount influence in the life of the founder. If this is so, then it is not impossible that this particular aspect of law, the absolutist, played some part either in the institutions he set up or in their working by later generations who also had some contact with the law. Raymond of Peñaforte's name at once comes to mind. This is not in itself, of course, even the shadow of a proof, but serves as a warning that it is disingenuous to admit legal influence without asking whether that influence was not partly in the direction of autocracy.

Perhaps within Dominic's lifetime, but certainly by 1228, an

---

[1] Baronius, *ad ann.* 1111, quoted in Danzas, 113.

almost complete scheme of government had been worked out. Thus even before Friars Preachers had begun to cause much stir in the world outside of Italy, machinery was created capable of dealing with any imaginable increase in their numbers. Very few essentials in the constitution of the Order have been modified since the time of Jordan of Saxony. This surprising attainment of maturity is due to the ability of the founder and to his intention of arranging everything so that as little time as possible would have to be spent away from study and preaching. He did not wish an evolution to be necessary, and was clear-sighted enough to be able to advance straight to his goal. It is a fair deduction from this and from the nature of the arrangements made either by him or by those who remembered him very well, that centralisation was a primary aim from the start. To use a modern phrase, the friars were "storm-troops", and their purpose would not be served if they were not directly subject to one headquarters, which could send them when and as it pleased to any area which had need of them. The separate and self-sufficient nature of the Benedictine monasteries was useless for this purpose, and in consequence the more highly-organised Premonstratensian Order was taken as a model. Granted the need for a constantly vigilant headquarters, it seems apparent that the permanent staff on duty there will have a great part to play in the direction of policy. Thus appears the first line of argument. The administrative functions of the officers, and especially of the Master, placed a great deal of power in their hands, the exercise of which was essential to progress and efficiency. They were constantly active, and, though never stationary in one place for any length of time, were always available for requests to be presented to them for administrative action. Thus there is a wide range of matters the decision of which rests with a particular officer, and he has power to issue licences to expedite his decision.

Necessarily, therefore, the personality of the officer made a great deal of difference to the way in which things were done. If he were efficient, for instance, in his visitatorial duties (to take the case of the Master or a prior-provincial) the convents or provinces would be kept up to the mark and the austerity of the rule maintained by stifling indiscipline or relaxation as soon as it appeared. If not, then regrettable habits might be formed or precedents established which would hamper the work of his more zealous successors. The personality of the officers also had scope in another direction, namely in turning the attention of the Chapters over which they presided into this or that direction as seemed to them most necessary. The influence the provincial prior exercised in this way could be great, for only he had been in touch with the business of the whole province since the last meeting of the Chapter twelve months earlier. Conventual priors and the elected representatives of each convent had been scattered far and wide, and only the preachers-general (who were ex-officio members of the Chapter) were bound to have more than a knowledge of local conditions. In the case of the Chapter-General this influence became stronger, because its composition varied from year to year. In spite of frequent "absolutions", a large proportion of the conventual priors assembling in any one year had also met at the provincial Chapter the year before, but the supreme body, composed of provincial priors in one year and elected diffinitors for the following two, was constantly changing. Continuity of policy could therefore only be preserved by the Master, as he alone knew why the previous Chapter had inchoated certain constitutions and issued certain admonitions.

That his influence was not all-powerful appears from the failure of certain constitutions to get beyond the first or second stage. Unless it is suggested that he changed his mind, it is clear that the only possible explanation is that the change in composition of the Chapter is reflected in the refusal to confirm or approve. Yet his influence must have been very real. Why, otherwise, are the two years of Raymond's mastership notable for the large number of minute and detailed regulations directed towards the enforcement of poverty, of which they saw the beginning?[1] So too, some of the zeal for poverty shown by succeeding Chapters is but the reflection of John's and Humbert's energy.

By its nature, most of this is beyond proof, because the *Acta*

---

[1] See *Acta* 1239, 1240. The *Chron. Humberti* says of Raymond: "...et apponens maximam curam, ut etiam in minimis rigor Ordinis servaretur"— ed. Reichert, p. 8, Mortier i. 280.

preserve only the decisions reached, not the discussions which preceded them. Administrative power, which can only be undertaken by full-time officials, has always had a tendency, however, to influence the law-making body to which those officials are responsible. An analogy will show this clearly. The Master-general had no power to alter the constitutions by himself: nor has the English Prime Minister. Yet the present Lord Chief Justice can complain that we are governed by a practical despotism of the Civil Service, which is composed of the executive subordinates of the Prime Minister and his colleagues; this service, says Lord Hewart, has been able to usurp power by virtue of the fact that it does the work.[1] Knowing the conditions under which administration will have to be carried out, it frames the laws in the interests of efficiency, even if that entails a considerable degree of autocracy and of interference with the subject, and is able to throw dust in the eyes of Parliament when it protests in the name of liberty. All this occurs under the eyes of a Parliament which sits about eight months in the year and in an age when communications are fully developed. Opposition parties, moreover, are only too happy to seize on any stick to beat the Government, no matter how slender it may be. How much more, then, is it likely to occur at a time when the last two conditions hardly apply and when the body to which the officials were responsible, the Chapter-General, sat for no more than a week in the year? Does it not appear that it would almost represent the facts if we called the Dominican constitution an autocracy working through democratic forms and with democratic checks which prevent the officials obtaining unbridled power, but no more? It is at any rate likely that this is nearer to comprising the whole truth than the usual statement that the constitution is completely democratic.

This view must now be justified by evidence. It must be repeated that in spite of many cases of apparently untrammelled authority on the part of superiors, each one of them was responsible to an elected body. The point is not to attack the reality of the responsibility, but the extent to which this acted as a limitation on the superiors' power. A text may be taken from a book which makes much of the democratic character of

---

[1] *The New Despotism*, London 1929.

the Dominican constitution, where it is stated that the democracy was "in its actual working compatible and connected with what we may call Caesarism".[1]

There is a conflict of opinion upon the extent of Dominic's own power. One witness at the canonisation, Fr Ventura,[2] says that at the first Chapter-General, the saint instituted diffinitors who were to have full powers "saving the respect due to his magistracy". Rudolf of Faenza,[3] on the contrary, asserts that the diffinitors have power "both over him (i.e. Dominic) and over the others". This question is probably not capable of a definite solution, but the abolition of the abbacy which was created in 1216, together with the representative nature of the diffinitors, may perhaps be taken to indicate a movement away from autocracy, as yet incomplete. Raymond and John both exercised their power to the full, and to a greater extent than Jordan had done. The former was a strict disciplinarian, and during his time as Papal penitentiary had acquired a reputation in Rome for severity. During his magistracy the *Acta* first begin to record penances given at the Chapters, and some of them are harsh. The same is true of John—he was a firm believer in poverty (*vide Acta* of 1241–52) and earned from his successor the title "Persecutor Malitiae". Of this successor we know enough already to admit his claim to disciplinary enthusiasm without further evidence.

The formula used on the admission of a novice was feudal in character, implying, that is to say, not the absolute rule of the superior, but a vague obligation to rule well. How real this obligation was depended normally upon the personality of the ruler. It is notable that no mention of obedience to the Chapters is made, but only to the Master: "I N. make profession and promise obedience to God and the Blessed Mary and to you N.,

[1] Barker, *Dominican Order and Convocation*, p. 17.
[2] Mamachi, *App.* 100. Ventura says that before 1220 Dominic "habebat plenam potestatem et dispensationem et ordinationem et correctionem totius O. F. P. post d. Papam" (based, for instance, on the control of irregularities given to D. personally by Honorius, Feb. 1220—Laurent, p. 125), and that in 1220 he caused diffinitors to be created who should have authority over all, himself included, "salva reverentia magistrali."
[3] Ib. 122, cf. Bull of Jan. 1221 (BOP. i. 12, Laurent 148)—no professed friar to leave the Order without licence of the "Prior Ordinis", i.e. the Master-general.

Master of the Order of Preachers, and to your successors...that I will be obedient to you and your successors until death."[1] Students were under the special control of the Master; on several occasions the sentence occurs at the end of the year's admonitions in the *Acta* "We commit to the Master the direction of the students".[2] The Chapter of 1254 handed over the revision of the Office to Humbert in a similar way, and in two later Chapters we find him issuing orders about the use of his version on his own authority, not the Chapter's—for instance, "The Master commands (*mandat magister*) that the brothers shall use the legend of St Dominic which is inserted in the lectionary, and that other new ones shall not be written".[3] In 1254, again, the Master ordered that *Acta* of provincial Chapters be sent to him, not to the General Chapter. In 1245 and on three other occasions[4] entries are made which show that authority not only of a strong but of an oppressive nature is being exercised. The first of these notices runs: "Caveant priores ne aliquem fratrem puniant vel notabiliter molestent pro eo quod eos in capitulo generali vel provinciali proclamaverit vel scripserit contra eos." Clearly a tendency of priors to revenge themselves for accusations made against them is objected to; clearly also, therefore, this tendency is noticeable, and while not wishing to deny the attempt to ensure the purity of democratic control, we must admit that this purity is in practice not always preserved.

A very strongly-held axiom was that none must preach unless sent, and this is constantly recurring.[5] Yet priors have power over all but preachers-general in this respect.[6] Administrative authority is here found in full command of the essential means of activity by which the Order carried out its purpose. A rather similar suggestion was made in 1260 with respect to the admission of lay-brothers, but was dropped next year. The supreme authority of the Master is seen at work in the various crises that arose over the Second Order. The increasing number of women's

[1] ALKG. i. 202–3.
[2] E.g. *Acta* 1264, 1276, 1277, cf. the separate lists of "moniciones magistri" at the end of some of the *Acta*, e.g. 1258.
[3] *Acta* 1260, cf. 1259.
[4] *Acta* 1263, 1272, 1280.
[5] See, for instance, St Cher vii. 114 col. 2, 138 col. 4, 223 col. 2, 224 col. 2 and above, Chap. IV.
[6] *Acta* 1234.

houses had alarmed the men, and it was decreed that no new houses should be received. The provincial of Lombardy interpreted this to mean giving up the existing houses, to the great terror of Diana d'Andalo and her convent of St Agnes. Jordan of Saxony, Master at the time, wrote a letter[1] to calm her fears, and in it this sentence occurs: "Definitores, qui de statu domus S. Agnetis parum cognoverant, quaedam ordinaverunt vobis non utile; quod, dum ego postmodum intellexi, videns quod non bene factum esset, penitus retractavi." He was actually, of course, only carrying out what the Chapter had intended, but evidently was conscious of exercising his authority with firmness, as appears again in his letter to the offending prior.[2] In the same way it was Humbert and Hugh de St Cher who were concerned in the revision of the nuns' constitutions, not the Chapter-General, though that body and the Master had equal powers over the acceptance of new houses. So again, the settlement reached in *Evangelicae Praedicationis* (26 September 1252)[3] was entirely due to John the Teutonic, who convinced the reluctant Pope that if he continued with his policy of forcible incorporation of women's houses, the First Order would be laid under an impossible burden.[4]

John's strength is seen again in connexion with the Inquisition. After Avignonnet he obtained powers[5] from the Pope authorising himself and the provincial priors to appoint, control and dismiss friars who were Inquisitors. This was only a temporary arrangement, since Inquisitors were normally subject to the Pope direct, and was intended to avert a repetition of the murders by removing unpopular men either to another district or from the exercise of their functions altogether. In so far as John was acting as a Papal delegate and not only as Master of the Order, this case lies partly outside our scope. John is also said to have refused to allow friars who became bishops to choose their own *socii*, but to have selected them himself. In addition, he obtained in 1252 a Papal privilege to the effect that none should accept a bishopric without the permission of his prior-

[1] Jord. Sax. p. 103 (ed. Altaner, p. 47). Grundmann, p. 242, from whose theme the question of authority is remote, also takes this as an example of personal power on Jordan's part.
[2] Ib. p. 105 (ed. Altaner, p. 49).
[3] BOP. i. 217.   [4] Mortier i. 354.   [5] Ib. 358.

provincial.[1] Here again, administrative necessity is putting power into the provincial's hands—speed in giving or withholding the permission was required, and so the Chapter-provincial is not given this power, for it only met once a year, and if its licence were necessary, bishoprics might have remained enforcedly vacant for practically that period.

The institution of the *circator* in 1254 must have contributed largely to the increase of authority. This is not the usual view, and short of evidence from several convents as to the way in which the office was exercised, the point cannot be resolved. But Sindolf, "the Abbot's privy whisperer" at St Gall, comes unpleasantly to mind,[2] and support is given to this interpretation by the words of the constitution which set up the office—"et insolencias quas viderit *prelato referre* et delinquentes in capitulo proclamare". Humbert only confirms the last few words ("et proclamare proclamandos in capitulo")[3] but it is hard to believe that the prior did not gain from the *circator* private information which he could put to oppressive use.

The censorship which was created in 1254 was an exceedingly powerful instrument, in whatever hands it might be, in view of the great literary output of the thirteenth-century Dominicans. Again, we find that this also was made over to the officers—no writing may be published until it has been examined by a committee appointed by the Master or the prior-provincial. Journeys to Rome show the same thing. There are constant prohibitions,[4] the only contingency which is legalised being the case of journeys undertaken on foot, in poverty and with the Master's permission.

Last among this class of evidence is the existence of a large series of acts for which licences could be obtained from either an officer or a Chapter. These cases have been used to show the Chapters' vigilance lest the priors should obtain too much power. But there is a plain alternative; each course is allowed and neither is urged at the expense of the other. Is it not equally possible

---

[1] Ib. 393–4.
[2] Ekkehard IV, *Casus S. Galli*, in MGH. *Script.* ii. 96 (translated in Coulton, *Life in the Middle Ages*, iv. 50–6).
[3] Humbert ii. 270.
[4] See *Acta* 1245, 1252, 1262, 1264, 1267, 1276, 1285, 1302, 1303, Master's licence, ib. 1264, 1276, 1285.

that, even supposing this was the intention, in practice it worked out in the contrary sense? Once more, a definite answer cannot be given, because any evidence that may be available has not been examined with an eye to this end, but it seems rash to assume that the operation of the alternative was entirely in one direction, particularly since, as has been shown, it is plain that at least from 1245 there were priors whose power had been used so autocratically that the General Chapter was forced to take action against them.

The scrutiny has been used most of all, however, to show the democratic character of Dominican government. Mrs Galbraith[1] says of its inception: "Hitherto the general chapter may be said to have ridden the executive officers on the snaffle alone. Henceforth the curb was added." The scrutiny was set up by the order of the General Chapter of 1273. It is repeated in four of the next five years, and the *Acta* of 1279 complain that it is not being used—"let the ordinance of the earlier chapter be observed"—and in the next year the diffinitors so far forgot their dignity as to say despairingly "hoc anno plenarie observetur". As the writer just quoted remarks elsewhere, the assemblies are obviously doing their best to keep the officers under control; but it is necessary to add that they were completely unable to do so. And in making this addition we have entirely altered the nature of the statement. If this stringent new regulation was necessary to enforce an old obligation, then the earlier checks on executive authority have become too weak. If in addition the new limitation is inoperative, by the admission of those most concerned to see it in working order, within eight years of its creation, the "curb" has manifestly been quite insufficient to do its work; to continue the metaphor, plainly the horse has bolted.

The conclusion, then, must be that it is incorrect to say that "the officers were the servants of the Order. This was the theory, and, in the thirteenth century at least, this was the practice".[2] It undoubtedly was the theory, but it has been shown that it was ceasing to be the practice by the middle of the century, and, before the end, had practically ceased. In fact, it is possible without dishonesty to make the history of authority agree roughly with the history of poverty or study. The approximate

---

[1] *Const. Dom. Order*, p. 188.   [2] Ib. 111.

dates 1250 and 1280 fit in with the scheme evolved in the previous chapter.

A different line of approach to the same problem offers itself in the shape of the views of various writers upon obedience. As we have seen, Galvagno de la Flamma, writing about 1330, is strongly in favour of rigid discipline, and is not above misrepresentation if it assists to achieve his end. In this he has both Aquinas and Humbert against him. Each lays great stress upon the distinction between the commands of God and the commands of man. It is right and proper to obey man, unless he commands something contrary to God, i.e. the inferior is free to use his conscience, and is at liberty to refuse obedience if he finds that submission will lead him into actions repugnant to that conscience. Aquinas is particularly enlightening: in resolving his doubts in the question "de obedientia"[1] he begins by pointing out that superiors are not over their subordinates in everything, but in certain fixed matters ("non...quantum ad omnia, sed quantum ad aliqua determinate"). He continues "et quantum ad illa medii sunt inter Deum et subditos". The superior is something more than the ordinary man. A little later he discusses various sorts of obedience. That which is limited to matters provided for in the Rule is necessary and sufficient for salvation. But there is another kind: "Si autem etiam in aliis obedire voluerint, hoc pertinebit ad cumulum perfectionis, dum tamen illa non sint contra Deum aut contra professionem regulae."

The ecclesiastical Middle Ages attached a very high importance to obedience—it is the last and greatest of the three regular vows. Being terrified of damnation and the pains of Hell, and uncertain of their own individual ability to earn a better fate, medieval churchmen were only too glad to shift the responsibility on to the shoulders of another.[2] Obedience was regarded almost as the one certainty in a shifting world, and was magnified into

---

[1] *Sum. Theol.* 2a, 2ae, Q. 104, art. 5 ad 2m.

[2] St Benedict's Rule had set the standard for the medieval view of obedience. E.g. the abbot's powers in controlling his inferiors are wide (cap. 2); "propter servitium sanctum quod professi sunt, seu propter metum Gehennae vel gloriam vitae aeternae, mox aliquid imperatum a maiore fuerit, ac si divinitus imperetur, moram pati nesciant in faciendo" (cap. 5); "ita oboediant fratres scientes per hanc oboedientiae viam se ituros ad Deum" (cap. 71). For the thirteenth century, see, for instance, two examples recorded by Cantimpré (I. xxii. 2 and II. lvii. 12) of fearful punishments being received for quite small breaches of obedience.

a sacred thing. Thus Humbert's advice to subject friars is "sitis sicut aurum ductile",[1] and he tells them that it is their duty to reveal everything to a superior when he commands it.

There are several passages in Humbert with a similar content.[2] The seculars, he points out, are our equals in everything but obedience and the rejection of the private will; it is in virtue of our superior excellence in these two respects that we shall take precedence of them in Heaven. Community life in a monastery is preferable to the life of a hermit, because those who are subject to a rule of this kind live not according to their own will, but according to the will of another. The superior may use hard words to his subjects in the interests of discipline. Even if he goes too far he is not bound to ask pardon—"Non enim omnis humilitas est virtuosa". "Enervatio auctoritatis in rectore inducit contemptum ipsius qui in honore debet esse inter subditos." There must be certainty whose duty it is to punish, or abuses will grow during a period of indecision, "as happens frequently in the chapters of secular clergy, in which many things remain without correction, because it is not known whose duty this is, whether the bishop's, or the dean's, or some other person's". The prelate must give a good example, but he must also be sharp in correcting evil:

Item isti sunt qui nunquam utuntur irascibili potentia in bonum, non irascentes contra delicta; sed omnia cum quadam stulta patientia, quasi insensibiles, sustinentes.... Item, isti sunt qui in excusationem suae ignaviae dicere solent quod religiosi subditi magis regendi sunt benignitate quam severitate, magis amore quam timore: quod licet interdum habent veritatem, non tamen semper.

Many evils follow on sloth in correction—indiscipline, blame and punishment to the prelate; blindness, repetition of the offence and final perdition to the delinquent; the infection of others, difficulty of correction owing to greater numbers of sinners, and rebellion against all good in the body corporate. (It is worth remarking that Mortier, *Hist. des Maîtres-gen*. i. 489, in using this passage, gives inaccurate references and only quotes certain sections of it which support his more gentle conception

---

[1] Humbert i. 4.
[2] References in this paragraph are to Humbert i. 5, 67, 516, 518, 539, 558–60, ii. 192.

of authority. The rule of a prelate is the rule of a father, he says, which is manifestly less than Humbert's meaning.) A final quotation shall be made from the account of the Master's power. This is more enigmatic and is open to widely differing constructions. "Licet autem magister habet plenam et generalem potestatem in ordine, tamen nunquam est ei utendum hujusmodi potestate ubi causa rationabilis non occurrerit." It is a little difficult to explain the first clause away, but until "reasonable cause" is defined almost any meaning can be put upon the sentence.

The chain of quotations may be completed by two contrary opinions upon the prelate's tenure of office. St Cher in 1257 dislikes annual mutation, and ascribes to it instability and a diminution in fruit of souls.[1] Humbert, at the Council of Lyons, pleaded for more easy dismissal of superiors.[2] Six cases of conscience which were debated in Paris at about the same time were similarly directed towards limiting the power of superiors, but all are concerned with extreme cases—e.g. Can the superior command the revelation of a secret?

With this evidence in mind, it seems safe to say that in spite of the superficial democratic theory, there was also a great deal of official authority, if not autocracy, both in theory and practice.[3] After all, centralisation and efficiency were the great needs, and even the modern world, with its much larger experience, finds that it is just these two things which are most difficult of attainment under a democratic system. Knowing the turbulence of

[1] St Cher, in Humbert ii. 507 n. Cf. Mortier i. 657, ii. 121.
[2] Humbert, *Op. trip.* III. cap. iv (Brown, p. 225).
[3] Practically the only modern writer whom I have noticed expressing views comparable to those in the text is von Loë, in QF. Heft i. pp. 1–2. (This is a short two-page introduction to his subject—Statistics of the province of Saxonia.) Summarising briefly the characteristics of the Order, he says: "Unter den geistlichen Korporationen der mittelalterlichen Gesellschaft gibt es wenige, die ein so einheitliches Bild zeigen, die eine so weise Zentralisation aller Kräfte in sich schliessen, wie der Dominikaner- oder Predigerorden.... Dazu [*sc.* to carry out the Order's purpose] war es unumgänglich notwendig, dass die ganze Fülle der administrativen Gewalt sich in einer Hand vereinigte. Diesem Bedürfnis entsprach die Verfassung des Predigerordens. Der Generalmeister der Predigerbrüder ist der absolute und unmittelbare Vorgesetzte.... Diesem stehen alle Kräfte zur Verfügung. Er ist in seiner Regierungstätigkeit durchaus unabhängig und an keine andere Behörde innerhalb des Ordens gebunden. Nur die Generalkapitel üben eine gewisse Kontrolle über seine Tätigkeit aus."

the Italian communes, the Dominicans of the thirteenth century may have felt the same. Further, the magnitude of Dominic's debt to Prémontré and the Hospitallers directly, and to Cîteaux at the first remove, has been demonstrated.[1] All these had autocratic constitutions, power was in the hands of the abbots. It is a little difficult to think that so much could be borrowed and yet so vital a part as this left out. A possible suggestion is that the representative element was inserted to preserve efficiency by ensuring criticism. No criticism is likely to be so much to the point as that of subordinates, provided intimidation does not stifle or influence it. It may be that the elective nature of the Chapters was intended to serve this purpose, while leaving a large amount of real power in the hands of the officers.

In conclusion, it has been said that Aymo of Faversham's adoption of a great part of the Dominican constitutions shows the triumph of democracy in the Franciscan Order over the absolutism of Elias. An equally probable interpretation, however, merely takes the Franciscan revolution as the introduction of order in place of chaos, and a definite in place of an indefinite localisation of responsibility. It was because there was no certainty as to the time at which Chapters were to assemble, and no machinery for bringing them together, save the Minister-general's command, that Elias was able to exercise his immense power. In any case, Elias' rule was an abuse; he was a tyrant, not a monarch or a benevolent despot. It is not fair to place him beside any one of the Dominican Masters-general of his time. Nor is it possible to apply to the Order of Preachers the description St Francis gave, in a letter to Elias himself, of the ideal Minister[2]—"... whoever does you harm, whether it be the friars or others, even though they beat you, all these things you ought to hold for grace.... And if a [brother] fall into any venial sin let him confess to his brother that is a priest, or if a priest is not near, to his brother until he may have a priest, and he shall absolve him canonically, as it is said [in the Rule]; and further these shall have no power of enjoining any other penance than this: 'Go, and sin no more'."

---

[1] Galbraith, op. cit. pp. 12–30.
[2] Ep. III, in *Opuscula S. Francisci*, ed. Quaracchi, pp. 108–10.

The decade 1270–80 saw the deaths not only of Aquinas and Humbert de Romans, but of several more prominent members of the first and second generations of Dominicanism.[1] All these men had either known St Dominic or his earliest disciples, and had spent their energies in doing the work he had begun. As the leadership passes to new men, so the first enthusiasm wanes, and the Preachers, like every other ecclesiastical reform in the Middle Ages, begin their long period of decline. The reign of John of Vercelli[2] saw unmistakable signs of it, in spite of the heroic efforts which the aged Master made to arrest its progress— even when eighty years old he was still traversing Europe on foot. Under Munio de Zamora[3] at the end of the century there occurs an obscure and sordid controversy, showing only too clearly that fruit of souls is no longer the primary interest.

This, then, is a convenient point at which to end a study of the early Dominicans. While its primitive austerity lasted, the Order held a position of the greatest moment, and was an immense power for good; but it was not superhuman, and no more than any of its predecessors was it immune from evil. In Bromyard's words,[4] "This Order of certain Religious became suddenly so excellently exalted and famous, by reason of its science and humility and other virtues, that by its wisdom it ruled the Pope and emperors and kings and well-nigh the whole world, so long as it kept its estate duly"; but "after it climbed upon horseback and affected vanities and unfitting superfluities, it fell down to the depths". For the first fifty years of its existence, however, it fulfilled nobly Jordan's definition of its vocation—"honeste vivere, discere et docere". During this period it produced many figures of the greatest note in every branch of life; one has only to turn over the pages of Echard's first volume to marvel that so many deservedly famous names can be found within a single

[1] Mortier ii. 167–8, gives a list: Aquinas died 1274, Raymond de Peñaforte 1275, Pierre de Tarantaise 1276, Paganus de Lecco 1277, Humbert de Romans 1277, Kilwardby 1279, Albertus Magnus 1280.
[2] 1264–83.
[3] Master-general 1285–91.
[4] Bromyard, P. iii. 32.

Order in so short a space of time. The thirteenth century represents the Middle Ages *par excellence*; most of the things Church and State had been striving after for hundreds of years reached their highest point then; the awful gap between intention and execution was never so nearly closed as in the lifetime of the Seraphic Doctor.

In distinction from most, the Dominican was a clerical Order. Dominic was an Augustinian canon at Osma before he ever ventured across the Pyrenees, and he gave his first followers the rule and the habit to which he had been accustomed. The canonical element remained, in spite of the adoption of a new form of dress under the influence of Reginald of Orleans, and of the substitution of "clericus" for "canonicus" in all the constitutions in 1249. Herein lies some of the Dominican originality. During its good period, the Order produced what the Middle Ages were always crying for—a class of priests who would do their duty as they ought, and bring the means of grace to all men in the hands of those they could respect. But unfortunately hopes were raised only to fall again. Before long the perennial question—Are the sacraments invalidated in the hands of an unclean priest?—which had formerly worked so much to the advantage of the Dominicans, now worked against them.

We have to admire, too, the high pitch of perfection which the organisation reached for a brief while. It was "l'esprit organisateur" not only of Humbert de Romans but of a succession of Masters-general that contributed very largely towards their success. Because of their continual contacts, Papal and Dominican organisation reacted upon each other, and while both were full of enthusiasm, good resulted. But the defeat of the Empire was the signal for the collapse of the Church. It dissipated its energy in the ever vainer quest of that unrealisable ideal, the New Jerusalem on earth which was to unite both in the service of God, just as the Dominicans at the same time were beginning to forsake the substance for the shadow. The best minds among the Preachers gave up the attempt to work the splendid machinery that had been handed down to them, and devoted their lives to mysticism, while the rest were sinking deeper into idleness. A self-regarding search after the Vision of the Spirit, or after riches and comforts, replaced that noble ambition of which

Humbert spoke[1] when he described the successful preacher in his glory; the souls he had saved for the Kingdom of Heaven should be the brightest jewels in his crown, and great should be his glory throughout eternity.

Dominic was not Francis, nor was he anything like him; there is no "holy foolishness" in the Spaniard. The history of poverty has already shown us the emptiness of comparisons between the two, and this is not the place to make them again in detail. The admirer of St Francis will be slow to admit it, but a great deal of the Poverello's attractiveness rests, unfortunately, upon an emotionalism which very easily becomes sentimental. This at least is true of the popular view of him. Actually, it would be sounder to say that it rests on St Francis' own character—wonderful, but by that fact inimitable—and on the Fioretti; in other words, upon a man and a book which never represented more than a minority in their Order. Dominic is truly typical of his foundation. By his learning and by his apostolate he was fitted to control the men he had called to follow him, quite apart from being an infinitely more practical nature. As a result, his purpose was more concise, if more narrow, and, by comparison only, less warmed by human affection. But to judge between the two is absurd; each approached the same problem in a radically different way, the one endowed with human, the other with superhuman virtues, and each had the natural qualities and defects. Of Dominic we can at least say this: that he showed his followers in no uncertain manner the path they should tread. Clear in his conceptions, he marked out a logical course, to which his Order adhered until it began to decline—

U' ben s' impingua, se non si vaneggia.[2]

So brightly-lit a way was never entirely darkened, in spite of everything. Bromyard and Raymond of Capua show that the fourteenth century was not without memories of the heroic years in Languedoc and Italy, and up to the edge of the Reformation Fra Angelico and Savonarola were still, in their different ways, witnessing to the faith that was in them.

[1] Humbert ii. 385–9.
[2] Dante, *Paradiso*, x. 96.

APPENDIX I

(see p. 42)

PROCUL A DOMO

THE fact that the land bought by St Dominic at Bologna in 1221 adjoined the convent raises an interesting problem with a close bearing on the general poverty question. Were possessions actually contiguous to a convent legal, others separated from it illegal? There is at first sight a good deal to be said for such a suggestion; there has never been any doubt that at all times the Order owned the land upon which its houses were built. It is pertinent to ask, however, whether any proof can be advanced that all the gifts or purchases of the Order were actually either intended or used as sites for buildings. Research of this kind has never, so far as I am aware, been undertaken, but any results that could be attained would help considerably in clearing up a point that seems to have been the source of much confusion. Such investigations should start from 1216, because possessions were then officially given up, and the nearer we get to origins the more likely we are to secure results.

The facts, so far as I have been able to ascertain them, are as follows: Certain writers have printed statements which take it for granted that contiguity with the convent spelt legality, separation illegality. While there is a certain amount of evidence leading one to this conclusion, I have been quite unable to find anything definite, and it is noteworthy that not one of the modern authors concerned gives a reference of any kind. It must be emphasised that the Constitutions of 1228, the earliest that we have, say nothing whatever about the existence of such a rule; nor do the Constitutions in Raymond's edition (ALKG. v. 530–564), or the *Acta capitulorum generalium*, give us any real help.

With this in mind, we may proceed to notice that Walz (*Compendium*, p. 21) writes that in spite of strict poverty, "possessionem rationabilem domus et ecclesiae conventualis, necnon et horti adiacentis vel vineae modicae in capitulo generali anno 1220 fratres admiserunt". One may legitimately ask what would be Father Walz's definition of "rationabilis" and "modicus", and point out that although he refers to the Constitutions of 1228 in the previous sentence, he supplies us with no footnote to this remark. Mortier i. 631 states: "Aucun couvent ne pouvait posséder de revenus fixes, de propriétés foncières, hors le terrain qui lui était adjacent", again giving no authority (see also i. 638). He refers to Palmer's collection of deeds relating to the London convent in *Analecta* 1897, p. 286. The gifts there listed seem to show such a rule in action: petition is made to enclose a lane, and a reasonable suggestion is that (since land on the other side had just been given) this was to preserve what may be called a *procul a domo* regulation, rather than sheer greed. Palmer's own commentary (*Reliquary* XVII. 436 sq.) includes a similar statement, again without authority. "The Friars Preachers, being mendicants, did not hold revenues or other possessions beyond the lands and buildings attached to the convents."

The origin of all these statements is probably to be found in Masetti, *Monumenta et Antiquitates* (pub. 1864). In vol. i. p. 78, he states that at the Chapter of 1220 all the possessions previously owned were surrendered "praeter domum et contiguum hortum". He then proceeds to insist that begging was the main source of revenue until well into the fourteenth century; and to defend the reasonableness of a small amount of possessions, the existence of which he proves from the *Acta* of provincial chapters of the Roman province in 1263 and 1282 (p. 81). Twice (pp. 81, 82) he actually quotes the phrase *procul a domo*, but without saying where he found it.—It would seem very unsafe, however, to generalise from two cases in Central Italy and one in England, and draw the deduction that there was an established rule that distant possessions were not allowed, particularly since, as stated, there is no sign of actual legislation to this effect.

My own reading has added the following:

1. Constitutions of 1228; "bote extra septa monasterii non portantur".—ALKG. i. 225.

2. Matthew of Paris, who accepted large gifts to the Paris convent, yet renounces one at La Ferté Alais in favour of the Cistercians in March 1220.—*Cart.* iii. 71.

3. "Inhibemus eciam districte ne fratres extra septa monasterii proprietatem domorum vel quamcumque possessionem ultra annum retineant ullo modo, sed alienare vel vendere teneantur." *Acta* i. 174 (1274).

Septa monasterii, however, is not a precise enough expression to build much suggestion upon (the fact that the house owned "precincts" does not prove that it had no other landed possessions), and in any case no. 3 appears to belong more properly to the history of personal, rather than corporate, property.

Finally, there would seem to have been far less need for a rule which would obviously lead to the creation of large enclosures round the house in an Order whose duty it was to mix with the world, than in a case such as that of the Clarisses (where this very question plays an important part) who were vowed to perpetual claustration.

178

APPENDIX II

(see p. 47)

ADDITIONAL EVIDENCE REGARDING POVERTY

It should be fairly plain that this chapter holds no intention of denying the very considerable sufferings the early friars went through in their devotion to poverty; but lest the evidence quoted in support of the argument in the text may seem to have been too heavily weighted on the opposite side, a few indications may be brought together here. Apart from the evidence in Gerard of Fracheto's *Vitae fratrum*, the quotations from Humbert de Romans scattered in the text *passim* will be found to express very clear and quite strict views on poverty, though not to the uttermost Franciscan limit. So, too, the evidence from the *Acta*, collected mainly in Chapter IX, shows the desire of the rulers of the Order to retain their holy poverty, if it also proves that they were unsuccessful from a time shortly after 1250 onwards. Strictness varied from place to place. One exceptionally good house, Cologne, practically avoided endowments of all kinds up to the end of the century (see QF. Heft 15: *Beiträge zur Geschichte des Kölner Dominikanerklosters im Mittelalter*, pp. 16–18). This was mainly due to the disciplinarian influence of Albertus Magnus. Thomas of Cantimpré (entered O. P. 1232, wrote 1258–61) relates an experience of his own, when he was unable to get sufficient by begging, but received divine consolation with the crusts he had succeeded in obtaining (*Bonum universale de apibus* II, x. 9). Other similar stories, (id. 10, 12; II. i. 21; II. lvii. 55). Étienne de Bourbon (O. P. 1223, wrote 1256–61) notes that excessive abstinence is a bad thing, and recounts that it got hold of some brothers in the early days of the Order: "Magister autem Jordanus, videns demonis fallaciam, monebat fratres contra indiscretam abstinenciam" (*Anecdotes*, pp. 164–165).

It may be noticed, however, that Dominican literature never speaks of poverty in quite the same way as Franciscan. I have, for instance, come across only one case of the use of the phrase so beloved of the Minors, *nudus nudum sequi*—in Hugh de St Cher vii. 354 col. 4. But even Hugh fails to take advantage of his opportunities, and makes no special comment on a text which cries for this interpretation (Matthew xix. 21, "Take up your cross and follow me") when he deals with it in vi. 64 col. 2.

APPENDIX III
(see p. 83)

SERMONS AND THE MASS

THE continual exaltation of preaching above all else raises the question of unsacerdotalism. Was preaching so emphasised that the importance of other elements in religion was denied or restricted? Neither Humbert nor Hugh de St Cher, for instance, goes so far as St Bernardino of Siena ("If of these two things you can only do one —either hear the Mass or hear the sermon—you should let the Mass go rather than the sermon": quoted by A. G. Little, *Studies in Eng. Francisc. History*, p. 133); yet both come to much the same conclusion in less definite terms. The first two of the three immediately following passages which may be quoted in support are, it must be admitted, slightly vitiated as evidence because of the semi-devotional character of the book from which they are taken. It may be that such a liberal construction as I propose to put upon them was not intended, and that the superlative nature of the eulogy is little but "common form". Nevertheless, if the words have any meaning at all, it is an unsacerdotal one, and surprisingly extreme. Without preaching, says Humbert, the fulness of the glory of the Heavenly kingdom would not be consummated, Hell would be more quickly filled, the world would be sterile, demons would flourish (and much more to the same effect), "...nec Ecclesia fundata esset, nec profecisset, nec staret". Again, a little later; Christ celebrated but one Mass on earth, the Last Supper; is not known to have heard confessions; administered few sacraments, and that rarely; and paid little attention to services. In fact, His life was spent in prayer and preaching, and the latter occupied by far the greater part of His time (*praedicationi imo...plus etiam quam orationi legitur impendisse totam vitam suam*) (Humbert ii, 397, 433). Hugh is a little less definite, and limits himself to condemning fasting which is performed for ostentation's sake, "which the Lord shall not hear" (St Cher iv. 139 col. 3). But he quotes and comments with sincerity and directness some of the more unpriestly Old Testament passages; e.g. Amos v. 23 ("Take thou away from me the noise of thy songs") and Isaiah lviii. 5 ("Is it such a fast that I have chosen?...is it to bow down his head as a bulrush, and to spread sackcloth and ashes under him?") (id.).

The insistence on one Mass is typical. All accounts agree in saying that Dominic never heard more than one a day (*Cart.* iii. 65; Mamachi, *App.* 99 ["fere singulis diebus celebravit missam"—Ventura's testimony at the canonisation], 295; Const. Orv. cap. 44, in Échard i. 35), and the same idea appears in the Constitutions of 1228— "Matutinas et missam simul audiant fratres nostri" (ALKG. i. 197). The significance of it is made more precise when we remember that a single daily Mass is characteristic of all monastic reforms. Dominic did neither more nor less than countless others in this respect. Here it must be noted that both tacitly and by implication Dominic is brought into line with the far more unsacerdotal Francis. Priest and layman are at one with their reforming ancestry upon the sacramental question.

A similar tendency is to be noticed in the Dominican Order with regard to Church services. In the interests of study, services are to be said "breviter et succincte" (ALKG. i. 197. Cf. the surprising comment in Humbert ii. 85—if services are too prolix, the friars will be so fatigued that they will be forced to go to the infirmary). It would seem that the balance was so heavily weighted against services that slackness crept in, for this seems the best explanation of the contrary command in the *Acta* for 1247: "fratres horas quas dicunt extra chorum, tractim dicant et distincte". Similarly, promotion to the priesthood was limited to those over twenty-five years of age.

It would seem that these instances outweigh to a considerable extent those that might be cited in the opposite sense—the essentially clerical and canonical nature of the Order, the devotion to the Virgin, the details of genuflections and ritual in the constitutions. The point is hard to decide; it is difficult, for instance, if we adopt the hypothesis that Dominic was definitely very unsacerdotal, to explain away the paragraphs taken up with these details last quoted. They are in that case out of place, and should have been omitted. Unsacerdotalism does not seem to have played a great part in the foundation of the Friars Preachers, yet it is a firm, if not leading, characteristic both of the founder and of some of the best among his followers at least as late as the sub-contemporary generation. The only explanations that can be advanced are that all reforms apparently take this line, and that a specific and intense emphasis on preaching logically supports what is otherwise a purely emotional rejection of sacramentalism. It is not likely that the founder had any very great influence in this respect, as the grant of portable altars occurs early (May 1221—BOP. i. 14) and anniversary Masses, obits and the like were soon sources of conflict with the secular clergy, who also made the more natural complaint that their parishioners attended Mass at the friars' churches because they were already within the walls to hear a sermon. All these things, in addition to the hearing of confessions, are mentioned very frequently in the General Chapter Acts, usually coupled with a condemnation both of their number and of the base profit-seeking purposes to which they are turned (see for instance, *Acta* 1261, 1263, 1278).

It may also be of interest to notice that there are only five references to *Missa* in the very extensive index to St Cher. None gives us any help in estimating the importance he attached to it; nor can anything definite be gathered from his commentaries on the accounts of the Last Supper in the three Synoptic Gospels—vi. 81 col. 2 sq., 116 col. 4 sq., 259 col. 4 sq. Cantimpré (ii. xl. 3) says it is meritorious to hear a Mass every day, if possible.

For the way in which the Mass was generally regarded during the Middle Ages, see Coulton, *Five Centuries* i. 100–137.

ABBREVIATIONS & AUTHORITIES

ABBREVIATIONS

AA. SS.   *Acta Sanctorum Bollandiana.*
ALKG.   *Archiv für Literatur- und Kirchengeschichte,* ed. Denifle and Ehrle.
BOP.   *Bullarium Ordinis Praedicatorum.*
EETS.   Early English Text Society.
MGH.   *Monumenta Germaniae Historica.*
PL.   Migne, *Patrologia Latina.*
QF.   *Quellen und Forschungen zur Geschichte des Dominikanerordens in Deutschland,* ed. Loë and Wilms.

AUTHORITIES

(i) Life of St Dominic

I include the following list of sources, arranged in chronological order of composition, in order to make clearer the argument of Chapters II and III. Several of the most frequently-quoted appear also in the general list. Their respective value for the historian has been roughly indicated in the text; fuller details may be found in Altaner, *Der hl. Dominikus.*

1232–3. Jordan of Saxony (in Échard, vol. i, and more recently ed. Berthier).

1235–41. Peter Ferrand (ed. Van Ortroy, in *Analecta Bollandiana,* vol. xxx).

1244–5. Constantine of Orvieto (in Échard i. 35 sq.).

1245–51. Bartholomew of Trent (in AA. SS. Aug. i. This work is of little value).

1250–5. Humbert de Romans.
    (Humbert's *Vita S. Dominici* is in Mamachi, *App.* 264 sq.; it may also, with difficulty, be reconstructed from the notes to Échard's edn. of Jordan. For his other works, see below.)

1256–61. Étienne de Bourbon, *Anecdotes* (q.v. below).
    (Contains a little, not very valuable, information about St Dominic.)

1260–2. Gerard de Fracheto, *Vitae Fratrum* (q.v. below).
    (Constructed from material collected by order of the General Chapters of 1255 and 1256; the first two parts principally concern St Dominic.)

1272–88. Sister Cecilia.
    (In Mamachi, *App.* 247 sq.; one chapter, missing in Mamachi, may be found in *Analecta* iv. 370).

(ii) GENERAL

Acta.—*Acta capitulorum generalium*, vol. i, 1220–1303. ed. B. M. Reichert. Rome–Stuttgart 1898 (= *Monumenta Ordinis Praedicatorum*, vol. iii).

Altaner, *Armutsgedanke.*—Altaner, B., *Der Armutsgedanke beim hl. Dominikus*, in *Theologie und Glaube*, xi. 404 sq. (1919).

Altaner, *Beziehungen.*—Altaner, B., *Die Beziehungen des hl. Dominikus zum hl. Franziskus von Assisi*, in *Franziskanische Studien*, 1922, p. 1 sq.

Altaner, *Briefe.*—Altaner, B., *Die Briefe Jordans von Sachsen* (= QF. Heft 20). Leipzig 1925.

Altaner, *Der hl. Dom.*—Altaner, B., *Der heilige Dominikus, Untersuchungen und Texte*, Breslau 1922.

Altaner, *Missionen.*—Altaner, B., *Die Dominikanermissionen des xiii. Jahrhunderts.* Habelschwerdt 1924.

Altaner, *Persönlichkeit.*—Altaner, B., *Zur Beurteilung der Persönlichkeit und der Entwicklung der Ordensidee des hl. Dominikus*, in *Zeitschrift für Kirchengeschichte*, XLVI. 396 sq. (1928).

Analecta.—*Analecta Ordinis Praedicatorum.* Various years.

Anecdotes.—*Anecdotes historiques...d'Étienne de Bourbon*, ed. Lecoy de la Marche. Paris 1877.

Barker, E., *The Dominican Order and Convocation.* London 1913.

Berger, E., *Thomae Cantipratensis Bonum Universale de Apibus quid illustrandis Saec. xiii moribus conferat.* Paris 1895.

Berthier, J. J., *Le bienheureux Humbert de Romans.* Lyon 1895.

Bromyard, J., *Summa Praedicantium.* Venice 1586.

Brown.—*Appendix ad fasciculum rerum expetendarum ab Orthuino Gratio editum*, ed. E. Brown. London 1690.

Bullarium Ordinis Praedicatorum, ed. A. Brémond. Rome 1729.

Burkitt, F. C. *The Religion of the Manichees.* Cambridge 1925.

Cantimpré.—*Thomae Cantipratani Bonum Universale de Apibus.* ed. Colvenerius. Douai 1627.

Cart.—*Cartulaire ou histoire diplomatique de S. Dominique*, 3 vols, ed. Balme and Lelaidier. Paris 1893–1901.

Chanson de la Croisade.—*La chanson de la croisade albigeoise*, ed. E. Martin-Chabot. Paris 1931.

Coulton, G. G., *Five Centuries of Religion*, vols. i, ii and iii. Cambridge 1923–36.

Cruel, R., *Geschichte der deutschen Predigt im Mittelalter.* Detmold 1879.

Danzas.—Danzas, A. *Études sur les temps primitifs de l'ordre de S. Dominique*, 2ᵉ série, tome 1ᵉʳ.—*Raymond de Peñaforte et son époque*. Paris 1885.

Denifle, H. *Die Entstehung der Universitäten des Mittelalters bis 1400*. Berlin 1885.

Douais, C. *Organisation des études dans l'ordre des frères prêcheurs au xiiiᵉ et au xivᵉ siècles*. Paris–Toulouse 1884.

Dufourcq, A. *Le christianisme et l'organisation féodale*, 1049–1294, 6th ed. Paris n. d. (? 1933) (= vol. vi of Dufourcq's series *L'avenir du christianisme*).

Échard.—Quétif, J. and Échard, J. *Scriptores Ordinis Praedicatorum*, 2 vols. Paris 1719–21.

Finke, H. *Ungedruckte Dominikanerbriefe des xiii. Jahrhunderts*. Paderborn 1891.

Galbraith, G. R. *The Constitution of the Dominican Order*. Manchester 1925.

Galvagno de la Flamma. *Cronica Ordinis Praedicatorum*, ed. Reichert. Rome–Stuttgart 1897.

Grabmann, M. *Die Bewertung der profanen Studien bei Thomas von Aquin*, in *Philosophisches Jahrbuch der Görres Gesellschaft*, xxxvii. 311 sq. (1924).

Grundmann, H. *Religiöse Bewegungen im Mittelalter*. Berlin 1935.

Humbert.—Humbert de Romans. *Opera de vita regulari*, ed. J. J. Berthier, 2 vols. Rome 1888.
    (An earlier edition of Humbert's works is to be found in the *Bibliotheca Maxima Veterum Patrum*, vol. xxv. Lyon 1677. The *De modo prompte cudendi sermones*, which was not reprinted by Berthier, is only to be found there.)

Jackson, A. W. V. *Researches in Manichaeism*. New York 1932.

Jarrett, Bede. *The English Dominicans*. London 1921.

Jarrett, Bede. *Life of St Dominic*. London 1924.

Jord. Sax.—*Jordanis de Saxonia opera ad res Ordinis Praedicatorum spectantia*, ed. J. J. Berthier. Fribourg 1891.

Lacordaire, H. D. *Vie de S. Dominique*. Paris 1852.

Lambermond, H. C. *Der Armutsgedanke des hl. Dominikus und seines Ordens*. Zwolle 1926.

Laurent, M.-H. *Monumenta historica S. P. N. Dominici*. Fasc. i. *Historia diplomatica S. Dominici* (= *Monumenta Ordinis Praedicatorum*, vol. xv). Paris 1933.

Lea, H. C. *History of the Inquisition of the Middle Ages*, 2 vols. New York 1908.

Lecoy de la Marche. *La chaire française au moyen-âge*, 2nd ed. Paris 1885.

Litt. Encyc.—Litterae encyclicae magistrorum generalium, ed. B. M. Reichert. Rome–Stuttgart 1900 (= *Monumenta Ordinis Praedicatorum*, vol. v).

Little, A. G. *Studies in English Franciscan History*. Manchester 1917.

Mamachi, T. M. *Annalium Ordinis Praedicatorum libri duo*. Rome 1756.
(There is a large and useful appendix of *Monumenta* at the end of this volume.)

Mandonnet, P. *Siger de Brabant et l'averroïsme latin au xiiie siècle*, 2nd ed. Louvain 1911.

Mandonnet, P. *S. Dominique: l'idée, l'homme, l'œuvre*. Ghent 1921.

Mandonnet, P. Article in *Catholic Encyclopaedia*, s.v. Preachers.

Masetti, T. *Monumenta et Antiquitates veteris disciplinae Ordinis Praedicatorum*, 2 vols. Rome 1864.

Michel, K. *Das Opus Tripartitum des Humbertus de Romanis*. Graz 1926.

Mortier, D. A. *Histoire des maîtres-généraux de l'ordre des prêcheurs*, 7 vols. Paris 1903 sq.

O'Connor, J. B. Article in *Catholic Encyclopaedia*, s.v. Dominic.

O'Leary, D. L. E. *Life and Times of St Dominic*. London 1912.

Owst, G. R. *Preaching in Medieval England*, 1350–1400. Cambridge 1926.

Owst, G. R. *Literature and Pulpit in Medieval England*. Cambridge 1933.

Renan, E. *Nouvelles études d'histoire religieuse*. Paris 1884.

Scheeben, H. C. *Der heilige Dominikus*. Freiburg i. B. 1927.

St Cher.—Hugonis de Sancto Charo opera omnia in universum vetus et novum testamentum, 7 vols. Venice 1600.

Vit. Frat.—Gerardi de Fracheto Vitae Fratrum Ordinis Praedicatorum, ed. B. M. Reichert. Rome–Stuttgart 1896 (= *Monumenta Ordinis Praedicatorum*, vol. i).
(There is an English translation, under the title *Lives of the Brethren of the Order of Preachers*, by P. Conway. London 1924.)

Walz, A. M. *Compendium historiae Ordinis Praedicatorum*. Rome 1930.

Welter, J. Th. *L'exemplum dans la littérature religieuse et didactique du moyen-âge*. Paris 1927.

Since writing, the following have been brought to my notice:

Heintke, F.—*Humbertus de Romanis*. Berlin 1934.

> (This is a very good general account, especially valuable on Humbert as the 'Apostle of the Golden Mean', and on the debated question of his election to the Papacy in 1241.)

Walz, A. M., Scheeben, H. C., and Laurent, M. H.—*Libellus de principiis Ordinis Praedicatorum. Acta canonisationis, legendae P. Ferrandi, C. Urbevetani, H. de Romanis.* Rome 1935. (= *Monumenta Ordinis Praedicatorum,* vol. xvi.)

> (Notices of this book have appeared, but I have so far found it impossible to obtain a copy. From the title, it should serve a very useful purpose in bringing together definitive editions of the greater part of the primitive material.)

INDEX

Abelard, Peter, 4; (condemned) 8; 58
Albertus Magnus, 62; (defends Aristotle) 66
Alleluia, The Great, 73, 84
Aquinas, 5; (and reason in theology) 8; (on poverty) 50–1; 55, 57, 60; (on purpose of study) 61; 63; (defends Aristotle) 66; 109; (on bishops) 133; (on obedience) 169
Aristotle, 8, 55, 62–4
Augustinianism, 8; (in theology) 63–5, 68; 95
Autocracy, (in Dominican Order) 159*sqq.*
Averroes, 67, 69
Avicenna, 67
Aymo of Faversham, 143, 172

Berengar of Tours, 58
Bishops, 131, 166
Boëthius, 67
Boëthius of Dacia, 69
Bonaventura, 64, 155
Bromyard, 29; (date of) 77, 78; and quoted *passim*

Cantimpré, Thomas of, 29, 77; and quoted *passim*
carriages and servants, 136, 149
Cathari, 3, 5; (not immoral) 6; (virtues of) 13; (preaching of) 14
Cecilia, Sister, (portrait of St Dominic) 19
censorship, 61, 167
Christina of Stommeln, 72, 74
circator, 167
Cluny, 3, 10
commerce, (growth of) 3; (results of this) 15; 103; (tricks of) 105; 116
communes, (growth of) 3; (movements in) 4
Constantine of Orvieto, 19, 47
constitutio, admonitio, (defined) 61 n.
Courçon, Robert de, 67, 69

dancing, 118, 119
death, (fear of) 89, 123–6
democracy, (in Dominican Order) 159*sq.*

Diana d'Andalo, 25, 50, 53, 73, 166
Diego d'Azévédo, Bp of Osma, 1201–7, (at Montpellier) 11, 36; (influences St Dominic) 21; (and poverty) 37; (returns to Spain) 38; 108
discipline, (decay of) 151–4
dress, 100, 120

Elias, 172
Eternal Gospel, 1, 61
Étienne de Bourbon, 20, 29, 77; and quoted *passim*
Etsi animarum, 140
Evangelicae Praedicationis, 166
Excuses, 99
exempla, 76, 88; (as pictures of social life) 90

Fanjeaux, 39, 42
Ferrand, Peter, 19, 46, 47
food, 28, 150
Foulques de Marseille, Bp of Toulouse, 1205–31, (appoints diocesan preachers) 22; 24, 39, 42
Franciscans, (poverty of) 43; (friction with O.P.) 143–4; (*interpositae personae*) 149
Fraticelli, 51

Galiciani, Odoric, 41
Gossip, 99

Hell, (fear of) 89, 123–6
Heresy, 5, 6, 7; (in Languedoc) 11, 16; (early) 15; *and see* Cathari, Waldensians
Hewart, Lord, 163
Hugh de St Cher, 12, 29, 54, 59, 60; (on philosophy) 64; 77, 171; and quoted *passim*
Humbert de Romans (and learning) 25, 58–9, 62; (and poverty) 46–50; 77, 78; (on preaching) 83; (and relaxation) 155; (revises Office) 165; (on obedience) 169–71; and quoted *passim*
Humiliati, 9

CAMBRIDGE: PRINTED BY WALTER LEWIS, M.A., AT THE UNIVERSITY PRESS